"Times Are Altered with Us"

The American History Series

"Times Are Altered with Us"

American Indians from First Contact
to the New Republic

Roger M. Carpenter

WILEY Blackwell

Registered Office
John Wiley & Sons, Ltd, The Atrium, Southern Gate, Chichester, West Sussex,
PO19 8SQ, UK

Editorial Offices
350 Main Street, Malden, MA 02148-5020, USA
9600 Garsington Road, Oxford, OX4 2DQ, UK
The Atrium, Southern Gate, Chichester, West Sussex, PO19 8SQ, UK

For details of our global editorial offices, for customer services, and for information
about how to apply for permission to reuse the copyright material in this book
please see our website at www.wiley.com/wiley-blackwell.

Library of Congress Cataloging-in-Publication Data applied for

Hardback ISBN: 9781118733257
Paperback ISBN: 9781118733240

A catalogue record for this book is available from the British Library.

Cover image: Detail from map of New England by John Ogilby and Arnoldus
Montanus, Novi Belgii, 1670. Reproduced by permission of Bert Twaalthoven
Collection of Antiquarian Maps of New Amsterdam, New York and New England,
Fordham University Library DRAFT.
Cover design by Simon Levy Associates.

Set in 10/12pt Meridien by SPi Publisher Services, Pondicherry, India
Printed and bound in Malaysia by Vivar Printing Sdn Bhd

1   2015

Contents

Contents

Contents

Contents

Contents

List of Illustrations

List of Maps

Introduction

In addition to standing on its own, whether as one of several core
readings or as supplementary (and hopefully engaging) reading for
a larger survey of United States or Native American history, this
book also will complement two other works about Native American
history originally published by Harlan Davidson in this American
History Series, now published by Wiley Blackwell. Philip Weeks'
"Farewell, My Nation": The American Indian and the United States in the
Nineteenth Century (third edition forthcoming) provides an overview
of Native Americans during the tumultuous nineteenth century,
while the second edition of Peter Iverson's and Wade Davies's *"We*
Are Still Here": American Indians since 1890 discusses the American
Indian experience in the twentieth and early twenty-first centuries,
and, as the title emphasizes, notes that American Indians did not
simply disappear with the closing of the frontier.

  "Times Are Altered with Us" takes its title from remarks made by an
Onondaga leader in the early phases of the American Revolution; yet
the ideas expressed in his comment can be applied to the native
experience in the first three decades of contact with Europeans.
"Times Are Altered with Us" begins with the settlement of the Americas
by the ancestors of Native Americans, and ends just about where
"Farewell, My Nation" picks up. The notion that native people settled
the Americas can be somewhat controversial, in that many Native

"Times Are Altered with Us": *American Indians from First Contact to the New Republic*,
First Edition. Roger M. Carpenter.
© 2015 John Wiley & Sons, Inc. Published 2015 by John Wiley & Sons, Inc.

Introduction

Americans assert that they have always occupied this continent; archaeologists and anthropologists, however, argue otherwise. Nevertheless, this work attempts to tell the story of the interactions between the original inhabitants of North America and European explorers, missionaries, and colonizers from Cristóbal Colón's land-fall on a Caribbean island in 1492 to the first years of the American Republic. In covering such a vast expanse of time, and the myriad experiences and interactions between Native Americans and Europeans, an author is forced by necessity to pick and choose what he or she believes to be the most important and consequential events.

It is difficult for anyone living today to appreciate the magnitude of change that contact between the *two* "old worlds" of Europe and the Americas ushered in. Two civilizations, wholly unaware of each other, began a process that would change the course of history. I am aware that the phrase "change the course of history" has become cliché: nearly every author of a work of history, or producer of a documentary that purports to portray the past, tends to use the term or a variation thereof. That said, in this case the phrase is an under-statement. The difficulty in appreciating the magnitude of how contact between Europe and the Americas changed the world lies in that its results are now part of the cultural milieu in which we find ourselves immersed; the consequences of contact affect each of us in our daily lives, right down to the food we eat. It is difficult to imag-ine, for example, present-day American culture without maize (corn). It is consumed by the cattle that are transformed into our fast-food hamburgers and it is present in our automobiles' gas tanks as an additive (ethanol). The potato, a plant native to South America, has also become the everyday. Taken to Europe, it fed the conti-nent's peasant populations over the last three centuries, and was re-exported to North America. Of course, it is also consumed as fries to complement our quarter-pounders, and perhaps more commonly, as chips.

In a very real and tragic sense, however, the largely unwitting importation of diseases from Europe and Africa did more than any other factor to change things for the peoples of the Americas. European missionaries and explorers would see the effects of these pathogens among native people first-hand, and they would describe mortality rates that range from 50 to 90 percent. It remains difficult, however, to assign an exact number as to how many native people died as result of diseases introduced by Europeans: this is because no one knows what the population of the Americas was at contact. While there is still disagreement among scholars, an estimate of 15 million people living north of the Rio Grande appears to be gaining acceptance. While it never will be possible for us to know with certainty how many people lived in the Americas in 1492, the late historian Francis Jennings did place the debate in its proper context. The numbers aside, Jennings noted, it was obvious that not long after the initial encounters North America had become a widowed land. The Pilgrims who landed in New England in 1620 certainly saw the effects of a disease epidemic: unharvested maize rotting in the fields, deteriorating wigwams, and, most tellingly, human remains lying above ground. Slightly more than a half-century later, the French explorer La Salle described the present-day American Southeast as a largely depopulated wilderness, yet more than a century before him, chroniclers of the De Soto expedition saw a very different landscape, taking note of its large villages and vast cornfields. In short, in the 130 years between the expeditions of De Soto and La Salle, the Indian population had declined and the landscape had been altered, not only because of De Soto's depredations, but because of the diseases his expedition had left in its wake.

Perhaps the greatest frustration for any scholar in writing Native American history is the elusiveness of the Native voice. Europeans wrote the vast majority of the historical sources for the first 300 years of contact and thereby seized control of the narrative. It is true that sources often contain remarks attributed to Native Americans, but we have to keep in mind that even then the Native voice is somewhat muted – since it must pass through cultural and linguistic filters. Indeed, some historians now assert that, at times, European translators present at treaty negotiations did not always keep a faithful record of what native people said. Historical accounts by missionaries are often tainted, not only by the difficulties in translation, but by the need of the authors to demonstrate to prospective readers that they were making headway in converting the "barbarians" of the Americas to whatever brand of Christianity they espoused.

In composing this book, I have attempted to use the terms "tribe," "nation," and "band" almost interchangeably, to try to avoid redundancy. I have also attempted to use the names of Indian nations that are most often familiar to readers. The tendency in academia – one with which I agree – is to attempt to use the names that native people called and in some cases still call themselves.

I have divided this book into a dozen chapters. Chapter 1 provides a capsule view of the Americas prior to contact between Indian peoples and Europeans. Among these key developments are the migration of the ancestors of Native Americans from Asia (which in itself is somewhat controversial), the development of maize agriculture, and the ongoing (and I believe irresolvable) disputes concerning pre-contact native populations.

Chapters 2, 3, and 4 deal with native contacts with the major European powers. Chapter 2 focuses primarily on Spanish exploration in North America, covering the wanderings of Alvar Núñez Cabeza de Vaca and subsequent expeditions led by Hernándo de Soto and Francisco Vasquez de Coronado. It also discusses the permanent Spanish settlements of New Mexico and the Pueblo Revolt of 1680. Chapter 3 examines contact between native people and the French, from Jacques Cartier's voyages in the 1530s, Samuel de Champlain's governance of New France, and the establishment of Louisiana at the very end of the seventeenth century. It also examines the missionary activities of the Jesuits. Drawing on their experience in Canada, the French (and the Jesuit order for that matter) took a different approach than did the Spanish toward native people in Louisiana. Chapters 4 and 5 both discuss relations between Native American peoples and English colonists. Chapter 4 treats relations between the English and native people in the Southeast, while Chapter 5 examines interactions between the two groups in New England.

Chapter 6 focuses mainly on the so-called Iroquois Wars, but it also discusses Dutch interactions with Native Americans. The Dutch receive relatively lighter coverage for several reasons – besides overall limitations of space. Chief among these is that the Dutch presence in the Americas, while important, was temporally limited; the colony of New Netherland barely existed for four decades. Second, while the Dutch constantly engaged in commercial interactions with Native Americans, their knowledge about them was extremely narrow. Indeed, Dutch traders at Fort Orange simply referred to all non-Mohawk Iroquoian speakers as Senecas, conflating the westernmost of the Iroquois Five Nations with all the others. But the most important portion of the chapter deals with the Iroquois and their wars against other native peoples that lasted until the end of the seventeenth century, and their positioning themselves as a force between the French and English for much of the eighteenth century.

Chapters 7, 8, and 9 discuss relations and conflict between native people and Europeans from the late seventeenth century to the years immediately preceding the American Revolution. Chapter 7 examines relations between native people and the Quaker colony of Pennsylvania, and the creation of what historian Richard White termed a "Middle Ground" in which American Indians and Europeans learned (sometimes reluctantly) to get along with one another through a series of creative understandings and misunderstandings. This chapter also discusses the eviction of the Lenni-Lenape people from their homes in eastern Pennsylvania and the movement of native populations – followed invariably by Europeans – into the Ohio country, and the transformation of that region into a scene of continual conflict. Chapter 8 dovetails with Chapter 7 in that it discusses native participation in the Imperial Wars between the 1690s and the 1760s. Chapter 9 provides a coda in that it discusses Pontiac's Rebellion as an outcome of the Imperial Wars. While there is some debate as to how much leadership Pontiac actually exerted over native people west of the Appalachians in 1763, the outcome of this brief conflict was important, and it represents one of the few times in which native people achieved a victory of sorts, even if it may not have been apparent at the time.

Chapter 10 deviates from the rest of the book in that it examines native contacts with Europeans in the Far West, ranging from Russians in the Bering Strait to the Spanish in southern California. It also deals with the creation of the horse and bison culture that had its beginnings in the seventeenth century and lasted until the last decades of the nineteenth. This chapter also discusses how a host of push and pull factors, such as the availability and adoption of the horse and the presence of millions of bison, fueled the migration of native peoples to the Great Plains, where the new arrivals created a new culture, and in doing so pushed other native groups off the plains and, in some cases, out of existence. Woodland peoples such as the Lakota and the Cheyenne moved from the eastern woodlands, while the Comanche split from their Shoshone brethren, moved south, and became the dominant force on the southern plains.

The final two chapters deal with Native American interactions with the New Republic. Chapter 11 lays out the choices with which native peoples were confronted during the American Revolution. The vast majority of them probably would have been content to remain neutral in what they viewed as an internal conflict among the English. But circumstances such as dependency on European goods, and the fear (not unfounded as it turned out) that the

Americans would take their lands if they won the war, led Indians to enter the conflict.

The last chapter looks at the formation of a nascent Indian policy by the US government, the initial phase of which simply called for native people to surrender their lands to the United States (which somehow assumed it had won Indian lands by right of conquest). A more realistic policy succeeded the first one and took two approaches. The first was an attempt to incorporate native people into the American nation, by making them more like Americans, meaning white Americans. The other called for war against any native peoples who would not follow this policy.

It is my hope that instructors of Native American History, at both the high school and college level, will see this book not only as a useful supplement, but in some cases even as one of several core texts. Much of what follows also is certainly applicable to courses in early and Colonial America, and it also could be used to give students a sense of the other side of the American frontier – the one that, as I point out in the first chapter, faced east. Instructors teaching the US survey course should also find it useful, since most big survey textbooks continue to give short shrift to the Native American experience, especially before the nineteenth century.

I do wish to explain here some of my choices of images placed in this work. As a student, I was fascinated by illustrations, but as I became increasingly interested in history, I found it somewhat dismaying to open a new book about Native American history or early America only to see the "same old" illustrations, images that had been repeatedly used in other works. Therefore, for this book I decided to seek out a number of images that seldom appear in other academic works, which led me to use what one might term neglected illustrations, such as cartouches, from seventeenth- and eighteenth-century maps. These images also serve another purpose: they give the reader insight as to how Europeans at the time viewed, and imagined, the Americas and its peoples. They also tell us much about how Europeans interpreted information they received from others about the Americas. For example, lacking a way to adequately describe a bison, European explorers used their cultural frame of reference, and called them "cows," perhaps adding that they had a shaggy appearance. Not surprisingly, European artists who read these reports, but never ventured to North America themselves, depicted bison as shaggy cattle. In any event, I think readers will appreciate illustrations that are somewhat unlike the ones they may have seen in other books about Native Americans during the first centuries of contact.

There are many people to thank for the completion of this book. I would like to express my gratitude to the anonymous readers who reviewed the manuscript and their suggestions that greatly improved the final product. I also wish to thank my colleagues in the history department at the University of Louisiana at Monroe. Terry Jones, Ralph Brown, Chris Blackburn, Monica Bontty, Jeff Anderson, and the late H.P. Jones have always made the department a collegial and pleasant place to work. Sean Chenoweth of the geography department helped me procure maps. At Wiley, Georgina Coleby and Lindsay Bourgeois provided cheerful and able assistance. Finally, I must also thank my friend and fellow University of California, San Diego graduate Andrew Davidson for giving me the opportunity to publish this work. I must also thank him for his unerring editor's eye. Andrew did not merely edit; he posed good hard questions about the content, and asked me to explain aspects of Native American culture and historical events in more detail. He also, like any good editor, did his best to make me stick to a timetable. The contributions of Andrew, my colleagues, and those anonymous readers who reviewed the manuscript, have made this a much improved work.

Roger Carpenter
Monroe, Louisiana

1

1492 and Before

Before Europeans

In 1492, Europeans believed that they had "discovered" a "new
world" when Italian explorer Cristóbal Colón (later anglicized into
Christopher Columbus), sailing under the Spanish flag, returned
from his first voyage. Native Americans would have dismissed both
notions, first by noting that they had long known of the two continents that would eventually be known as the Americas and,
therefore, they did not need to be discovered. They would have also
refuted the idea that their lands constituted "a new world." They
and their ancestors had lived here for several millennia; if anything,
Colón merely managed to connect two old worlds. Native Americans
claimed that they had always been here, and like peoples all over
the world, had their own explanations as to how the world began
and as to where their ancestors came from. On the eve of contact
with Europeans, over 500 different Native American communities,
bands, and tribes, who spoke approximately 350 different languages,
called North America home. With such a diversity of languages and
communities, it should not be surprising that native peoples also
had varying sets of beliefs concerning their origins. The creation
stories of Native Americans often reflected the environments in
which they lived.

"Times Are Altered with Us": American Indians from First Contact to the New Republic,
First Edition. Roger M. Carpenter.
© 2015 John Wiley & Sons, Inc. Published 2015 by John Wiley & Sons, Inc.

A common theme among native peoples of both the Northeastern and Southeastern Woodlands is the notion that at one time the earth consisted of nothing but water. The Iroquoian peoples of the Northeast, for example, believe they are descended from Aataentsic, a woman who fell from the sky into this world, which at the time consisted of nothing but one vast ocean. One day in the sky world, a tree fell down. Aataentsic looked through the hole, astonished to see a world composed entirely of water, miles below her own. As she gazed through the hole, she accidentally slipped and fell through it. Despite frantically clawing at the sides of the hole for something to hang on to, she plunged downward through space, toward the world made of water. Seeing her fall from the sky, the aquatic animals inhabiting the water world – the beaver, otter, and muskrat – decided they must do something to save her. They asked the geese for help, who caught Aataentsic and placed her on the back of an enormous turtle. Aataentsic began to weep, and the aquatic animals asked her what was wrong. She explained that she could not survive without land. The aquatic animals dived to the bottom of the ocean, found a bit of mud, and gave it to Aataentsic, who placed it on the back of the turtle and watched as it expanded and became Turtle Island, or as we call it, North America. Pregnant when she fell into this world, Aataentsic soon gave birth to a daughter, who years later bore male twins. Continually at odds with one another, the twins often fought each other in the womb. When it came time to be born, one of the twins entered the world in the usual way, encouraging his brother to follow him. But the other twin ignored his sibling's advice and introduced death into the world when he entered the world via his mother's armpit. The twin who had been born in the usual way set about the business of improving the world, creating edible plants and rivers that ran both ways, so that people would find travel easier. Lacking his brother's ability to create, the twin who killed his mother attempted to spoil his brother's work, adding thorns and briars to plants and changing the rivers so that they ran only one way. In short, one twin made everything that is good in the world, while his brother did all he could to make the world unpleasant. In one of the final conflicts between the two siblings, the malevolent twin locked all of the animals in an underground cave. Humankind, lacking a source of meat, suffered because of this. Discovering what his brother had done, the benevolent twin freed the animals, setting up an epic battle between the two. The good twin beat his evil brother, striking him repeatedly with a set of buck's antlers. The blood the evil twin shed as he fled from his brother transformed into flint, which Iroquois peoples used to make tools and weapons.

The Cherokee likewise believed that the earth at one time consisted wholly of water. In the beginning, all of the world's animals lived in a stone vault in the sky. As the animals reproduced, the vault became crowded. The animals sent a water beetle to search for another place to live. The beetle found this world, but could only skip along its watery surface. Diving underwater, the beetle found some mud and placed it on the surface, where it magically began to grow and became land. Eager to leave the stone sky vault, the animals waited impatiently as their sodden and muddy new world dried. Each day, the animals sent one of the birds to fly over the earth to examine closely whether or not it had dried enough so that they could live on its surface. One day the animals sent the vulture to scout the drying earth, but he flew too low and his large wings inadvertently carved into its smooth damp surface, creating the hills and valleys of the Cherokee country of northern Georgia, the western Carolinas, and Tennessee.

Peoples that lived in other regions, such as the Pacific Northwest, had creation stories that reflected their environment as well. A common creation story of the Pacific Northwest begins with a beach pea (an aquatic plant) that, much like other beach peas, washed up on shore. But unlike other beach peas, this one contained a man, who snapped into consciousness. In this first moment of awareness, he realized he was in a place that was dark, clammy, and cramped. Stretching his arms and legs, the man burst out of the beach pea and stood on the beach, blinking as his eyes adjusted to the sunlight. As he looked around, he saw only earth, sky, and ocean. After a while, the man saw something flying in the sky. The object drew closer, circled the man, and landed several feet from him. The object turned out to be the Raven, who stood gazing at the man for some time. The Raven finally spoke and asked the man "what are you?" The man replied that he did not know. The Raven then asked the man where he came from and the man gestured toward the shattered remains of the beach pea. The Raven expressed surprise, indicating that he created all the man saw, including the beach pea, but he did not expect the man to burst out of it. Raven asked the man how he felt and the man gestured toward his stomach, indicating he felt hungry. The Raven showed the man how to get food and created animals for him to hunt. In time, he realized the man felt lonely, and made him a mate.

Remarkably common throughout Native North America, the flooded world motif reflected a blend of traditional creation stories and the post-contact influence of Christian missionaries. Whereas the western religious tradition relies on an all-powerful being who creates all that exists, deities – or perhaps near deities – in the Native American spiritual convention are powerful, but usually not all-powerful – nor are all wise. In the Cheyenne creation story, a near-omnipotent being creates light, sky, air, water, and the creatures that live in water and sky. But he cannot create land until he secures help from birds who dive under water and find a little bit of mud which he uses to make earth. Native deities and powerful spiritual beings can also be fallible, and can sometimes be the subject of mirth in stories that emphasize their all too human failures and foibles. For example, Nanabush, the Great Hare of the Anishinabeg people, helped create the world, and could vanquish powerful enemies. Yet he also managed to be entertaining (or offensive depending on your perspective), such as when he amused himself after learning how to propel himself through the air with his own flatulence.

European explorers and missionaries often noted that the native peoples of the Americas lacked literacy, and concluded that this somehow deprived them of the ability to record the past, and that they therefore must lack history. But all peoples, logically speaking, have a past and preserve some knowledge of it in some fashion. Europeans did not seem to realize that while native peoples did not record events in writing, they developed their own ways of remembering their past. The peoples of the Great Plains recorded important events in winter counts, which consisted of pictographs painted on animal hides. Often begun by one person and continued by another, some of these winter counts recorded more than a century's worth of events. Peoples of the Northeastern Woodlands made belts or used strings of *sewan* (wampum) made from whelk shells that served as mnemonic devices. In the hands of individuals who knew what the strings and designs woven into the belts meant, the past could be preserved. Other native peoples used petroglyphs, carving their history into rock. Even today, in parts of the Southwest, the Great Plains, and western Canada, petroglyphs can still be seen (if not always wholly understood). But the most important element that enabled native peoples to preserve their past came through the development of strong oral traditions. In this manner, native peoples recorded histories, legends, and stories, repeating them and allowing them to be passed down to younger generations. While

11

many of these histories are still told, or were later preserved in writing by missionaries and scholars, many of these stories – and the histories that accompanied them – disappeared forever when Cristóbal Colón unwittingly initiated a 400-year campaign in October of 1492 that would see Europeans and their descendants invade the Americas.

Invasions of America

Americans often think of Cristóbal Colón as the "discoverer" of the Americas. The obvious problem with this formulation is that the Americas had already been discovered; both continents already hosted large populations of native peoples. But even the notion that Colón was the first European to set foot in the Americas is mistaken. Five centuries earlier, in approximately the year 1000, the Norse, reputedly led by Leif Ericson, explored Baffin Island and Labrador, and established a small colony at the northern tip of Newfoundland. According to Norse oral tradition, the colonists frequently traded and fought with the natives, whom they referred to as *Skraelings* ("ugly wretches"). Harassed and under sporadic attack by the natives, and far from their other colonies in Greenland, the Norse abandoned the "new-found land" after only a decade. For centuries thereafter, other Europeans and many Americans regarded the story of *Vinland*, as the Norse termed it, as a myth. That changed in the 1960s, when Canadian archaeologists unearthed the remains of a Norse settlement at L'Anse Aux Meadows in Newfoundland.

We do not know what Cristóbal Colón knew, or did not know, about prior Norse exploration to the west, when on the evening of October 12, 1492, he sighted a dim light on the horizon as his small fleet of three ships made their way west. The next day, Colón recorded the first contact between Europeans and the native peoples of what would become known as the Americas. Portraying the Taino people he met as children of nature, Colón described them as "simple-minded and handsomely-formed," and decided they knew nothing about war when one Indian – seeing steel implements for the first time – inadvertently cut himself when he handled a Spaniard's sword blade. Colón did not correct himself, even after noting that several Taino men evidently knew something about violence, since they bore the "marks of wounds on their bodies."

Implying that he could somehow understand the Taino language, Colón emphasized what he regarded as their submissiveness, noting they were "very docile" and "should be good servants." Having a messianic bent – Colón's first name meant "Christ Bearer" – he also thought the Indians "would easily be made Christians, as it appeared to me that they had no religion." While only initial impressions, Colón's notions about the New World's natives would dominate European thinking through the next 300 years and beyond, a period during which explorers, missionaries, and colonists embarked on the unsettling and resettling of the American continents. Subsequent European explorers made observations similar to Colón's.

Historian Daniel K. Richter conceptualized the native view of the invasion of their continent by Europeans as one in which they "faced east." Richter's formulation works as a reversal of the dominant narrative of American history that depicts Europeans and Americans as relentlessly pushing west and wresting control of the continent from native peoples – that is, when native peoples are even included as part of the narrative. As late as the mid-twentieth century, histories of the settlement of the Americas treated native peoples almost as bystanders in the process of European colonization. But the notion that the European invasion of the Americas came from the east misses a key point; the intrusion actually came from all sides. Algonquin peoples living along the Atlantic coast did indeed face east as Europeans landed on their shores, but the native peoples of the Florida peninsula and the Gulf Coast saw the European invasion surge at them not only from the east, but from the west and south as well. The native peoples in the Southwest saw Spaniards invade their homelands from the south while in the sixteenth century, California's native peoples faced west, and watched abortive Spanish and English invasions emerge from, then recede back into the surf of the Pacific. Two centuries later, the Spanish staged a successful overland invasion of the region from the south and would remain. The peoples of the Pacific Northwest – to some degree more fortunate since they were among the last to have contacts with Europeans – saw the invasion come at them from both the north and the south. Russian fur traders crossed the Bering Strait in the eighteenth century, gained a toehold in Alaska, and then moved south. Spanish traders, fearing Russian influence, moved northward from Alta California to counter them, only to later be displaced by the British.

Figure 1.1 A highly romanticized depiction of Cristóbal Colón's landing on Hispaniola. Native people greet him with what appear to be gold and gems. Spanish sailors erect a cross in the background, carrying out the first of numerous "ceremonies of possession" that Europeans would perform over the next two centuries. This illustration also highlights one of the key differences that Colón noted in his writings. He and his fellow Spaniards are fully clothed, while the Indians are almost naked. "El Almirante Christoval Colon descubre la Isla Española" by Pieter Balthazar Bouttats. Library of Congress Rare Book and Special Collections Division LC-USZ62-8390.

Rewriting "History"

European narratives often characterize contact with the Americas as a "discovery." Native peoples, however, knew better. They had lived here for centuries. Exactly how long ago their ancestors arrived in the Americas is a matter of some dispute. Since native peoples lacked writing, Europeans "helpfully" fabricated histories for them. Fascinated with this previously unknown continent and its peoples, Europeans concocted all sorts of fanciful theories as to the origins of Native Americans. One theory held that the ancestors of Native Americans escaped the lost continent of Atlantis. Some English colonists (and some nineteenth-century Americans as well) claimed they could hear traces of the Welsh language in native peoples' speech and argued that they must be the descendants of a lost western expedition led by a Welsh prince named Modoc in the twelfth century. One colonist went so far as to claim that he could speak Welsh and be perfectly understood by Indians. The most popular – and perhaps persistent – theory regarding the origins of native peoples drew on biblical texts, and argued that they must be descended from the 10 lost tribes of Israel. Scholars and missionaries claimed that many Amerindian languages contained a variety of Hebrew words. William Penn, the founder of the Pennsylvania colony, concurred with the 10 lost tribes of Israel theory, noting that "Their Eye is little and black, not unlike a straight-look't Jew." Penn also believed God imposed an extraordinary punishment on the 10 lost tribes by banishing them to America. Other Europeans, who had far more experience among native peoples, also argued for a supposed connection to the biblical Israelites. English trader James Adair, who spent four decades among the native peoples of the American Southeast, claimed in his 1775 book, *History of the American Indians*, that the languages, customs, and religious practices of Native Americans had many similarities to Jewish practices. As late as the 1860s, American missionaries still made the argument that native peoples had to be descended from the biblical lost tribes.

The Bering Strait Theory

Anthropologists and archaeologists, however, have other explanations as to the origins of native peoples. One of the earliest examples can be found in the *Natural and Moral History of the Indies* published in 1590 by Jesuit missionary and scholar José de Acosta. Acosta thought Native Americans resembled the peoples of Asia, and he speculated that their ancestors must have originated there. Acosta had no way of knowing about the existence of the Bering Strait (Vitus Bering, a Danish navigator in the employ of the Russians, would not discover it until the eighteenth century) but he imagined that somewhere far to the north, North America and Asia must be connected to each other. While Acosta's suppositions could hardly be called a theory – they are more along the lines of a wild guess – it is perhaps the earliest expression of what later became known as the Bering Strait theory, which is the most commonly accepted explanation among archaeologists and anthropologists for the presence of humans in the western hemisphere. A key support to this theory is that unlike Africa, Asia, and Europe, the remains of archaic humanoids have never been found in the Americas.

Employing archaeological evidence, scientists assert that approximately 20,000 to 30,000 years ago, during the latter part of the Ice Age, the ancestors of Native Americans migrated from Asia into North America. With a good portion of the world's ocean water locked up in ice, global sea levels dropped. Where the Bering Strait exists today, scientists believe Alaska and Siberia may have been connected by land. Even today, at their closest points, only 55 miles of water separate Alaska and Siberia, a fact that caused some consternation for both the United States and the Soviet Union during the twentieth-century's Cold War. Using this land bridge, as some have termed it, and perhaps later their own sea craft, Neolithic hunters followed large game animals such as mastodons and giant sloths, and unwittingly crossed into, and became the first human inhabitants of, North America. Over thousands of years, their ancestors coalesced into bands, tribes, communities, and nations – an estimated 500 in North America alone – that occupied all of the Americas, from the Arctic to the Straits of Magellan.

In all likelihood, the animals that populated North America did not initially fear the Neolithic hunters from Asia; they simply had no prior experience with human beings. In time, of course, they did learn to fear them. Ice Age North America supported an abundance of megafauna. At sites where Indian hunters butchered their kill, archaeologists have found the remains of mastodons and mammoths that weighed perhaps 10 tons. They have also found the remains of giant beavers, some of which reached a length of seven feet, and bison with horns that spanned six feet. Remains of other long extinct species, such as single-hump camels, giant capybaras, and tapirs that weighed in at perhaps a quarter ton have also been discovered. Wherever there are large herbivores, there also tend to be large carnivores. All of these animals had to be wary of the predatory creatures that also populated Ice Age America. The dire wolf, a distant relative of the modern grey wolf, could weigh in at close to 250 pounds, while short-faced bears reached 1,800 pounds. Several different species of large saber-toothed cats also preyed on Ice Age herbivores – and perhaps each other in times of scarcity.

Scholars have speculated that overhunting by the newly arrived humans may have played a big part in the extinction of many of North America's largest animal species, but one must also recognize that about 10,000 years ago the climate changed drastically, and in a fairly short period of time. As the glaciers receded and the climate warmed, many of the plant species that the giant herbivores relied on disappeared, which in turn contributed to the decline of the animals that preyed on them. While archaeological remains indicate that Paleo-Indians did kill lots of animals and were extremely efficient hunters, in all likelihood they cannot be blamed outright for the extinction of all of North America's megafauna. There simply were not that many humans in North America at the time, and they would have had to have been everywhere at once. As the large game animals disappeared, the human hunters adapted and sought smaller prey. They adapted to the swiftly changing environment, and learned to use the varied ecosystems of North America to their advantage.

Culture Areas

To make the study of North America's native peoples simpler, anthropologists generally divide the continent into culture regions that closely coincide with the environment of each area. While there may be some variation, the most common culture areas referenced are the Northeastern and Southeastern Woodlands (which are collectively referred to as the Eastern Woodlands), the Southwest, California, the Pacific Northwest Coast, the Great Plains, and the Great Basin. Even within a given culture area, however, there can be a great deal of environmental diversity. For example, the Northeastern Woodlands culture area extends as far north as the mouth of the St Lawrence

17

River and some formulations dip as far south as into what is now central Tennessee (depending on the map one is consulting). The Great Plains stretches from southern Alberta and Saskatchewan in the north and brushes up against the Rio Grande River in the south. Obviously, this means that a great deal of ecological diversity existed within each of these culture areas. The different areas do, however, share some defining traits. The dominant (and obvious) trait of the Great Plains, for example, is their flatness. Likewise, the Eastern Woodlands consisted of woods, rivers, and lakes. Yet it is obvious that a native person living in what is now Saskatchewan experienced a very different environment from that experienced by a native person living in what is now central Texas. Thanks to the environmental diversity of the Northeastern Woodlands region, a native person in northern Maine had to live differently from a native person in what is now Tennessee.

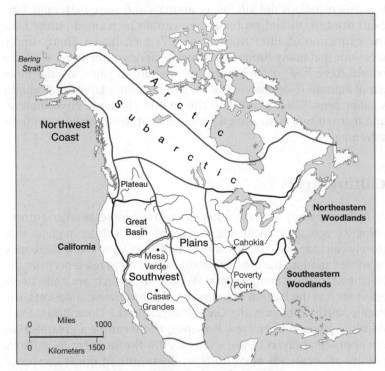

Map 1.1   Major geographic regions of North America

The Development of Maize

The development of New World agriculture may have been the most important occurrence in the pre-contact period. About 3,500 years ago, peoples in Central America began to experiment with teosinte grasses, which eventually led to the development of maize, the most important of the America's – one of the most important of the world's – food crops. Maize began to appear in the American Southwest and Midwest as early as 1500 BC, but most peoples shifted from hunting and gathering to agriculture only gradually, and some not at all. By about 600 BC, native peoples had developed strains of maize that thrived in the lands north of the Rio Grande. Planting mixed fields of maize, beans, and squash – what came to be known as the "three sisters" among peoples of the Eastern Woodlands – Native Americans developed a productive and remarkably efficient agricultural process. While maize tends to deplete nitrogen from the soil, the beans counter this by fixing nitrogen in place, thus preserving the nutrient for use by both the maize and the squash plants. The maize stalks become beanpoles, while the sprawling growth pattern of the squash and its large leaves shielded the soil from the sun, holding in moisture for the benefit of all three plants and also suppressing the growth of weeds.

Maize cultivation spread farther north over the ensuing centuries, and peoples in the Northeastern Woodlands developed strains that could ripen in as little as 120 days. Native peoples of the California and Northwest Pacific coast culture areas practiced little agriculture, primarily because they did not need to do so. In both regions, native peoples accessed the food resources of the sea, such as fish and marine mammals such as seals. In the Pacific Northwest, native peoples constructed giant canoes used in the hunting of whales. Both regions also yielded a bounty of natural plant foods, making the adoption of agriculture, with the exception of tobacco for ceremonial or religious purposes, unnecessary.

The Southwest

In the Southwest, the Hohokam people, ancestors of present-day Pima and Papago peoples, began constructing the first of what today we call "pueblos." (*Pueblo* is the Spanish word for town; the Spanish hung this moniker on the settled native peoples of the Southwest because they viewed them as more "civilized" than their nomadic neighbors, such as the Apaches and the Navajos). Living in a desert environment, the Hohokam constructed an extensive and elaborate irrigation network. Their success in irrigating their fields facilitated the building of their pueblos; the knowledge that they now had a permanent, reliable food source led to their constructing permanent housing. While irrigation made it possible for them to farm in the desert, the Hohokam may have unwittingly tapped water sources with a high saline content. In time, this would have made their fields infertile, which may have contributed to their disappearance in about the twelfth century.

The Anasazi (Navajo for "the old ones") constructed their first pueblos in the tenth century in Chaco Canyon, near what is now called the "Four Corners" (where the corners of the states of Arizona, Colorado, New Mexico, and Utah meet). These immense structures were the largest examples of apartment-style housing in North America until the construction of tenement housing in New York in the nineteenth century. Primarily agriculturists, the Anasazi had 200 villages in Chaco Canyon, all connected by roads. However, a shifting climate, which saw the land begin to become drier and made agriculture uncertain, contributed to the disappearance of the Anasazi by about 1100. The Anasazi left behind impressive testimony as to their architectural prowess, including Pueblo Bonito in New Mexico and the extensive cliff dwellings at Mesa Verde in southern Colorado, which are now part of the National Park system and a World Heritage site.

The Eastern Woodlands

The shift to agriculture also led to more stable and complex societies in the Eastern Woodlands. Over a period of about 4,000 years, these stable societies marshaled the labor of their members to construct large numbers of mounds throughout much of the Northeast, as well as the Southeast and its margins. They are collectively known as Mound Builders, a name that seems to suggest these peoples had a shared identity, which given the expanse of time and space would be incorrect. Mounds proliferated throughout eastern North America, ranging as far east as Virginia and as far west as the eastern fringe of present-day Oklahoma. The peoples who built the mounds seem to have had different purposes in mind. Nonetheless, all of them situated some of their most impressive collections of mounds at the confluence of major rivers, making the largest pre-Columbian communities the hubs of continent-wide trade networks.

Some of the oldest archaeological sites in North America are located in present-day northeastern Louisiana. Not recognized as a series of mounds until the 1980s, Watson's Break is the oldest collection of Indian mounds in North America, having been constructed perhaps a little more than 5,000 years ago. Located on private property, little archaeological work has been done there.

The other major site in northeastern Louisiana is Poverty Point, located to the east of Watson's Break. Close to the Mississippi River, Poverty Point – the name refers to the depleted soils of the area – presents something of a puzzle to anthropologists and archaeologists. The majority of the site consists of low mounds built in a concentric pattern. Since most of the mounds are only a few feet high, they are almost undetectable at ground level. Not until the 1950s, when analysis of aerial photographs showed a landscape with a pattern of low concentric mounds covering a large area, did anyone recognize it as an archaeological site.

From studying the artifacts the Poverty Point people left behind and the remains of their cooking fires, archaeologists have determined that they lived on the mounds. There is no evidence that they practiced agriculture. Living in a land of forests, rivers, and bayous, they had access to a large variety of animals and fish, as well as plant foods, and probably had little or no incentive to engage in agricultural labor. While we know nothing about their spiritual life, there is one high, large effigy mound on the site in the shape of a bird with its wings outstretched. It has been theorized that this mound could have been used for ceremonies, and may have been reserved for a priestly elite who lived on it. It is unknown what the Poverty Point people did with their dead, as no human remains have been found on the site. It has been speculated that bodies were buried off site or placed in the river.

In the Ohio River Valley about 2000 years ago, the people of the Adena-Hopewell culture also built mounds. Like the Poverty Point people, they did not practice agriculture. Their structures differed, however, in several key respects from those of the Poverty Point complex. Rather than many low mounds, the Adena-Hopewell people built quite large ones in which they buried their important personages along with impressive collections of grave goods, presumably intended for use by the entombed in the next world. The Adena-Hopewell culture vanished by the sixth century. Scholars have put forth a number of possibilities for the disappearance of the Adena-Hopewell people, including climate change and war.

Another group, the Mississippians, appeared about 1,400 years ago and differed from the mound-building cultures that preceded it in one key respect: while Mississippian people also hunted and fished, their primary source of food was agriculture. The Mississippians established their largest city, Cahokia, at the confluence of the Mississippi, Ohio, and Illinois Rivers, in about AD 700. The largest settlement in pre-contact North America, Cahokia's central location – and its proximity to three major rivers – made it the most important trading site in North America. Native American traders from all over the continent transported commodities there, exchanging goods such as obsidian from the upper Missouri River, copper mined in the Lake Superior region, and seashells that originated as far away as the Gulf Coast and the Chesapeake. Cahokia probably reached its apex in about AD 1200, with a population of about 30,000, which is comparable to large eighteenth-century American cities such as Philadelphia and New York. The population probably began to decline because the surrounding landscape could not support so many people. In time, the lands around the site lost their fertility, and firewood, essential for heat and cooking, would have become scarce. By about 1400, Cahokia had been largely deserted. Cahokia's large mounds can, however, still be seen today. In the nineteenth century, American historians and antiquarians, refusing to believe that native peoples could have created such impressive structures, often dismissed the mounds as natural formations. Still others made the rather amazing claim that advanced civilizations that pre-dated Native Americans had created the mounds.

Native American Population before 1492

Throughout much of the twentieth century, scholars of Native America spilled a great deal of ink in a heated debate as to the pre-contact population of North America. In the early twentieth century, ethnographer James Mooney placed the pre-contact population for the lands north of the Rio Grande at a little over one million. Mooney's estimate enjoyed wide acceptance by historians, archaeologists, and anthropologists, and remained the standard interpretation for nearly a half century. Since the 1960s, however, Mooney's figures have been challenged, as scholars have utilized more sophisticated techniques of estimating population size, such as determining the carrying capacity – that is, the ability of a given region to support a population – and by examining the remains of village middens, or refuse heaps.

In the 1960s, after conducting extensive research in Peru, ethnohistorian Henry Dobyns argued that prior to the arrival of Europeans, North America had a human population of approximately 16 million, and the Americas as a whole may have been home to anywhere between 90 to 112 million people. While Dobyns's figures are still not widely accepted, his work prompted many scholars to revise their population estimates upward, and many now believe that the total population of pre-contact Native North America north of the Rio Grande may have been between 10 and 12 million. Dobyns's other figures and assertions, as well as those of other academics who have entered this debate, remain the subject of dispute.

Obviously, the thorniest part of the population debate is that it is impossible to determine the precise pre-contact population. This is the case for several reasons. Native peoples did not conduct – and would have seen no need to – anything resembling a modern census. While European explorers and missionaries did make estimates of native populations, their numbers usually reflect local (and sometimes isolated) peoples and villages. In other words, they often counted the people they saw – not the multitudes they did not see. When Europeans attempted to extrapolate native populations, they most often based their estimates on unreliable native informants or on wishful thinking, which often made the numbers they fabricated little more than wild guesses.

The effect of European diseases on native peoples compounds the problem of attempting to determine the extent of pre-contact populations. Biologically separated from Asia and Europe for several millennia, the peoples of the Americas lacked exposure to a host of communicable diseases that had long plagued human populations in Europe, Africa, and Asia. This should not be taken to mean that native populations were disease free; that would be grossly inaccurate. Native people suffered from a host of maladies such as arthritis, beriberi, and pellagra. They had not, however, been exposed to the epidemic diseases that ravaged the populations of Europe, Asia, and Africa, such as measles and smallpox.

Native Americans and Old World Diseases

Most of the recorded observations made by Europeans of native people, including of their numbers, took place in the years well after contact. By that time, Old World diseases such as smallpox, measles, and influenza had killed off untold numbers of Indians. Most estimates of native mortality from this incredibly destructive disease event fall somewhere between 50 and 90 percent, but exact numbers do not exist. Another problem was that European diseases did not spread in a predictable pattern. When the French explorer Samuel de Champlain landed at what he named Cape de St Louys in 1604, he portrayed it as a region densely populated with Indians. In fact, he thought there were so many Indians that the French should abandon any thought of colonizing the region. Sixteen years later, English Separatists (often called Pilgrims in American history textbooks) landed at the same place, called it Plymouth, and found evidence of a demographic catastrophe: abandoned, unharvested fields of maize, wigwams falling into disrepair, and most tellingly, human remains lying above ground. They learned later that a European disease epidemic (no one knows which disease it was) had struck, killing most of the inhabitants. However, in a story that would be repeated over the next two centuries, European pathogens seemed to follow no rhyme or reason when they devastated native populations. Nearly all of the Pautuxet peoples of Cape Cod were wiped out. The Wampanoag people lost half of their population, yet their Narragansett neighbors – for the moment at least – remained unscathed by the sickness. In the future, the Narragansett (as would nearly all native peoples) would suffer from a visitation of European diseases.

The effects and rapid dissemination of European diseases could be attributed primarily to native peoples' lack of prior exposure to these pathogens. While smallpox, for example, killed approximately 30 percent of all Europeans who contracted the disease, they at least had some immunity so their odds of survival – particularly if they were not very old or very young – were far higher than those of an American Indian. In large part, this can be attributed to heredity. For several millennia, the ancestors of Europeans, Africans, and Asians had been exposed to the pathogen that causes smallpox. Their immune systems responded by developing antibodies which, in turn, were passed on to their offspring. While not totally successful in protecting one from the malady, the antibodies that Old

World peoples carried granted them somewhat better odds of surviving a bout of smallpox. Another factor was the extensiveness of native peoples' travel and trade networks. Smallpox, if not the most common perhaps the deadliest of European pathogens, had an incubation period of about 12 days, during which a carrier would show no symptoms. This was adequate time for a native person traveling from one region to another, or for a person fleeing an epidemic, to unwittingly expose others. Another factor was native treatment of disease. In most cases, New England's native peoples tended to gather around the sick individual, rather than isolating them.

The Columbian Exchange

The transmission of disease became the most important aspect of what has come to be known as the Columbian Exchange. The Columbian Exchange theory argues that Cristóbal Colón's landing in the Caribbean in October of 1492 initiated a series of global biological exchanges that have continued to this day. Of the three elements of the Columbian Exchange – plants, animals, and pathogens – pathogens, or disease causing organisms such as bacteria and viruses, had the most immediate and dramatic effects on human populations. While Europeans contracted New World diseases previously unknown in Europe – most notably syphilis – most of the exchange in diseases went the other way, with Native Americans being exposed to European pathogens that proved, in large part, deadly to them. The lethality of Old World diseases also made it impossible to enslave the native people of the Americas over the long term; what native people did best in the presence of Europeans was die. While Europeans did enslave native people, the enslaved individuals died quickly and had to be replaced, so Europeans turned to importing Africans, who shared with them a certain level of immunity to Old World pathogens.

The intentional portions of the other aspects of the Columbian Exchange largely benefitted both native peoples and Europeans. Most of the exchange in animals went one way, with Europeans importing domesticated animals such as cattle, sheep, hogs, and horses. Throughout the Americas, native people had domesticated only dogs, turkeys, and in some portions of South America, the llama. Horses began to filter onto the Great Plains in the late seventeenth century via native rustlers and traders in the Southwest, making possible the horse-buffalo-gun culture that would dominate the region for all of the eighteenth and much of nineteenth centuries.

Native people also appreciated other European livestock species. Sheep, for example, became very important in the Navajo culture and facilitated their transformation over time, from raiders to farmers and herders. Other forms of livestock were, however, less beneficial to native people. Extremely useful to Europeans as a means of bringing fresh meat along with them, pigs had several advantages over other European livestock species. They could forage for food on their own, often freeing humans from the chore of feeding them. They could also defend themselves from most would-be predators. Spanish sailors began the practice of turning a few pigs loose on small islands in the Caribbean, where, lacking predators, they quickly reproduced, providing passing vessels with a supply of fresh meat. In foraging for food, hogs found their way into native people's fields and destroyed their crops. When native people retaliated by killing and eating the offending animals, it often brought them into conflict with Europeans.

Europeans also unintentionally imported other species to the Americas that they would just as soon have left in Europe. The black rat, an animal that played host to the fleas that carried the bubonic plague or "Black Death" that decimated fourteenth-century Europe, often crossed the Atlantic in the hulls of sailing vessels. When ships anchored in the Americas, the rodents crept down anchor chains and ropes, and made their way ashore. Rats ate their way through European food stores, and nearly doomed the English colony at Jamestown, Virginia. In the winter of 1609, the Jamestown colonists placed their harvest of grain – primarily maize – in storage. When they became hungry during the winter, they opened their granary, and discovered that rats had consumed all of their food stores.

Likewise, European plant species could also inadvertently hitch rides to the Americas. Plants from Old World weeds easily found their way into hay or silage fed to livestock aboard ship. It is very likely that the seeds of these plants passed through the gastrointestinal tract of a cow or pig and, perhaps fertilized with the animal's leavings, had a good start in American soil. The importation of grain crops such as wheat and oats also contributed to the introduction of European weeds into the Americas. Sifting of seed for grain could not eliminate wild grasses that inadvertently found their way into the seed. Plants such as plantain, which native people called the "Englishman's foot" because of how rapidly it spread, and the dandelion, also made their appearance, probably first in European fields in the Americas but spreading later into native fields. Intentionally and otherwise, Europeans also imported crops that benefitted native people. Nearly all of the stone fruits found in the Americas, such as peaches, cherries, and plums, originated in the Old World. Likewise, citrus fruits such as oranges, limes, and lemons originated in the tropics of Africa and Asia.

As part of the exchange, however, plants also traveled from west to east, and Europeans also benefitted immensely from New World crops. Today, maize is the most widely grown and consumed grain on earth. It is also the primary food found on animal feedlots, meaning that the majority of meat consumed today is from animals fattened on corn. It is difficult to imagine Italian cuisine without tomatoes, which originated in Central America. In fact, the first recorded use of a form of salsa, made from peppers and tomatoes, may have occurred when the Aztecs, having briefly driven the Spanish out of their city during Cortes's conquest of their empire from 1519–1521, took a few Spanish prisoners, and after having sacrificed them, ate them after dousing them with a sauce made of tomatoes and peppers.

Perhaps the most important of all the New World crops is the potato, which became a staple food of peoples in the Andes Mountains in South America. Easy to plant, tolerant of poor soils, and able to grow in cold climates, the potato was exported to Europe, where governments hoped that its qualities would allow it to feed large numbers of the poor. After a rough start – peasants were initially suspicious of the unappetizing appearance of the plant – it succeeded spectacularly, and was re-exported to North America, where it also did well.

Despite the considerable (mostly posthumous) fame he gained for "discovering" the Americas, Cristóbal Colón's historical reputation has waxed and waned. During Chicago's 1893 Columbian Exposition, the United States celebrated the four-hundredth anniversary of his landfall, hailing him as a hero. A century later, during the five-hundredth observation of Colón's landing in 1992, his historical reputation had undergone a marked change. While some still viewed him as a fearless explorer and gifted navigator, others pointed out that his explorations instigated an invasion of Native American's homelands that would continue for 400 years, resulting in warfare, the introduction of

European diseases to the Americas, and the deaths – not to mention the mistreatment – of millions of Native Americans. This argument has been countered with the observation that while Colón began the European invasion of the Americas, he should not be held responsible for what followed. If anything, one can agree that Colón did have one indisputable achievement: he established the permanent linkage between *two* "old worlds" that had previously been unaware of each other's existence. But it cannot be denied that his "discovery" had grossly unfortunate consequences for Native Americans.

2

Encountering the Spanish

Pánfilo de Narváez

In April 1528, the Timucuan peoples of southwestern Florida watched apprehensively as five vessels carrying approximately 400 men under the command of Pánfilo de Narváez dropped anchor in what is now known as Tampa Bay. A veteran conquistador, Narváez had been dispatched to Mexico by the governor of Cuba in 1521 to apprehend Hernán Cortés. Lacking the *adelantado* (license) the Spanish Crown required would-be conquistadores to obtain before setting out on an expedition, Cortés had acted illegally when he sailed to the Yucatan, then central Mexico, and commenced his campaign against the Mexica (Aztec) Empire in 1519. In the process, he also defied the orders of the governor of Cuba – a Crown appointee – who had forbidden him to leave the island. When Narváez landed on Mexico's east coast, Cortés, despite having a numerically inferior force, sallied out of Tenochtitlan, the Mexica capitol, and defeated him in a pitched battle. After taking most of Narváez's men prisoner, Cortés offered them two choices. They could return in shame to Cuba as defeated men, or they could join him in the conquest of the rich empire that lay beyond the horizon. Not surprisingly, nearly all of Narváez's followers opted to join Cortés and went on, in varying degrees, to reap the rewards of the

"Times Are Altered with Us": American Indians from First Contact to the New Republic,
First Edition. Roger M. Carpenter.
© 2015 John Wiley & Sons, Inc. Published 2015 by John Wiley & Sons, Inc.

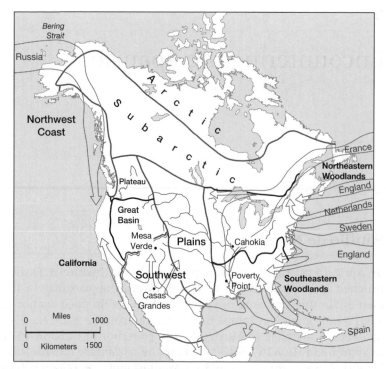

Map 2.1 Invasions of North America

conquest of the Mexica Empire. Only Narváez, who had been seriously wounded when an arrow struck him in the eye, rebuffed
Cortés's blandishments and remained loyal to the governor of Cuba.
By choosing to remain Cortés's prisoner, Narváez did not receive
any of the proceeds of the conquest of the Mexica. In the wake of
Cortés's spectacular success, the Spanish Crown apparently decided
to forgive his legal transgressions. Certainly the amount of treasure
that Cortés and his men captured – it instantly made Spain the richest nation in Europe – impressed the crown. Cortés also promised
the Crown one-quarter, rather than the customary one-fifth, of the
proceeds of the conquest. Cortés personally became very wealthy
from the conquest of the Mexica Empire (for a period, he may have
been the richest man in the world).

Humiliated in battle against Cortés, missing out on the riches of
the greatest of the Spanish conquests, and having lost an eye in the

process, Narváez is perhaps Cortés's polar opposite. Whereas Cortés is remembered as one of the luckiest and most successful of the conquistadores, Narváez is nearly forgotten, and would certainly rank among the unluckiest of the Spaniards who sought their fortunes in the Americas. His failure to apprehend Cortés did, however, result in his receiving something of a consolation prize. For nearly two decades, the Spanish had cast their eyes northward, hoping the lands they called *La Florida* – which now comprises the entire southeastern United States rather than just the peninsula we know by the same name – contained another rich empire. Failed, brief expeditions by Juan Ponce De León in 1521 (to the present-day Florida Peninsula) and Lucas Vásquez de Ayllón in 1525 (to present-day South Carolina) resulted in little more than dead colonists. Rewarding Narváez for his loyalty, the governor of Cuba helped him obtain the *adelantado* that authorized him to embark on a conquest (the Spanish used the term *conquest* to refer to their explorations in the Americas until 1573, when they replaced it with *pacification*) of the vast stretch of territory extending from the southernmost tip of the Florida peninsula, westward along the Gulf Coast, and into present-day northeastern Mexico.

Dividing his force after landing at Tampa Bay, Narváez put 300 soldiers and 80 horses ashore and left 100 men aboard the ships. Ordering the ships to sail roughly parallel to his line of march, Narváez planned to signal them by means of flags, smoke, or signal fires should he need resupply or reinforcement. However, soon after leaving the vicinity of Tampa Bay, the ships and the men ashore lost contact with one another. Despite remaining in the vicinity for more than a year, the men (and women) aboard the ships would never see Narváez again. Florida's natives had already had some negative experiences with previous Spanish expeditions. When, for example, Ponce de León landed on the peninsula nearly two decades earlier he had engaged in conflict with the Indians. In addition, Spanish slavers in search of labor for their burgeoning sugar plantations in the Caribbean made periodic raids along the coast, taking Indians captive. Fearing that Narváez and his men meant to carry them off, the native peoples of the region deserted their villages, fleeing into impenetrable swamps at the approach of the conquistadores.

As Narváez marched his men northward along the coast, they sought out precious metals and native maize fields. Like other Spanish conquistadores, Narváez and his men did not carry adequate provisions with them, and counted on being able to extort food from the Indians they encountered. In order to rid themselves of the armored and threatening strangers, the natives of southwestern Florida cagily directed Narváez and his men northward, telling them tales of a place called "Apalachen, where was much gold...[and]...of everything that we at all cared for." When the Spaniards reached northern Florida, they found small villages consisting of a dozen or so dwellings with nearby fields of ripening maize, but no gold. Unfortunately for the intruders, they also found Apalachee warriors, whom they described "as large of body," and who, they said, "appear at a distance like giants." Launched from stout bows as tall as a man and with staves as thick as a man's arm, the arrows fired by Apalachee warriors struck with so much force that they could pierce a red oak the thickness of a man's leg. Tipped with sharp, narrow points made of fishbone, Apalachee arrows sometimes penetrated Spanish armor. In addition, the thin reed arrow shafts often shattered, the splinters finding their way through links in the conquistadores' chain mail and inflicting painful wounds.

After a particularly bruising encounter with the Apalachee, Narváez ordered the expedition's treasurer, Alvar Núñez Cabeza de Vaca, to go to the coast to try to signal the ships. Unable to contact the ships and receive provisions or reinforcements, Narváez and his men took up residence in an abandoned Apalachee village, where they came under recurring, sporadic, harassing attacks by native warriors. Short of food and desperately hungry, the conquistadores slaughtered their horses – which had given them a key advantage over their native adversaries – for meat. Realizing that they must escape Florida or perish, Narváez and his men hatched a risky scheme to extract themselves from their predicament.

Despite lacking navigational instruments, maps, and tools, Narváez and his men decided to construct rafts and sail along the Gulf Coast, following it until they reached Spanish settlements in northern Mexico. Constructing a makeshift forge, the conquistadores melted their armor and spurs, and began converting them into nails and crude tools to build their rafts. Under the direction of a Portuguese carpenter who accompanied the expedition, they finished five rickety rafts over a period of several weeks. In late September 1528, the surviving 244 men cast the rafts – and their fates – into the Gulf of Mexico. Beset by thirst and hunger, the conquistadores dared not go ashore until they reached the Pensacola River (off the coast of present-day Alabama). There they met Choctaw people who fed them and took them back to their village. Distrustful of the Choctaw, or perhaps wishing to ensure they remained friendly, the Spaniards seized their leader as a hostage. The plan backfired when the Choctaw launched a successful nighttime attack and rescued their chief. Put to flight by the Choctaw, Narváez and his men fled back to their rafts and the waters of the Gulf.

The Spaniards traversed the Gulf Coast for approximately 600 miles, until a violent November storm flung all five of the rafts and their occupants ashore along the Texas coast, scattering them at sites between Galveston Island in the north and present-day Corpus Christi in the south. Shorn of their weapons, armor, and mounts – in short, everything that made them conquistadores and granted them military advantages over the Indians – the survivors feared what the local natives may do to them. To their great surprise, the local Karankawa people, upon encountering what by this time amounted to only 40 surviving Spaniards, took pity on the naked and shivering beings. The Karankawa built fires to warm Cabeza de Vaca and his men before taking them to their village to feed and care for them.

Recalling tales of Indian cannibalism and human sacrifice from Cortés's conquest of the Aztecs less than a decade earlier, several of the survivors – including Narváez – refused the Karankawa's offer of assistance, fearing they would be sacrificed and eaten. In a fine twist of irony, five Spaniards who refused the Indian's hospitality became what they feared most when they resorted to cannibalism. In a further bit of irony, the discovery that the small party of Spaniards became cannibals alarmed the Indians.

For most of the winter the largest group of Spanish survivors lived with the natives, becoming a drain on their hosts' food resources. Unable to contribute to the larder due to their lack of hunting skills and knowledge of local food plants, the Indians enslaved the Spaniards, putting them to work carrying water, cutting and collecting firewood, and digging for roots. After months of starvation and exposure, most of the surviving Spaniards died; so too, however, did many of the local Indians. New diseases (likely and unwittingly carried by the Spanish) raced through the indigenous communities of coastal Texas, killing almost half of the natives. Recognizing the close timing between the outbreak of disease and the arrival of the Spaniards, the natives deduced that the newcomers must have brought the sickness among them and so killed many of the surviving castaways.

Cabeza de Vaca

After six years of slavery among the Karankawa people of coastal Texas, only four of the 300 men who went ashore with Narváez in Florida had survived. The treasurer, Cabeza de Vaca, two other would-be conquistadores, and an African Moor named Estenbico (whose name is variously rendered as Esteban, Esteven, and Estenvico) escaped their hosts in the summer of 1534. During their years in coastal Texas, they had succeeded in making a reputation for themselves as healers among the Karankawa. Coerced into attempting to "heal" a sick person, Cabeza de Vaca and his companions at first refused, pointing out they did not know how to cure illnesses. The Indians responded by withholding food, forcing Cabeza de Vaca and the other Spaniards to take up the practice of "healing." Cabeza de Vaca described the healing ceremony he and his cohorts devised as a mixture of Christian and native practices:

> Our method was to bless the sick, breathing upon them, and recite a Pater-noster and an Ave-Maria, praying with all earnestness to God our Lord that he would give health and influence them to make us some good return. In his clemency he willed that all those for whom we supplicated, should tell the others that they were sound and in health, directly after we made the sign of the blessed cross over them. For this the Indians treated us kindly; they deprived themselves of food that they might give to us, and presented us with skins and some trifle.

Cabeza de Vaca and his men soon discovered they had further incentive to act as healers, once they realized that claiming to possess spiritual power and their alleged ability to cure sickness granted them a great deal of leeway among the native communities of coastal Texas – as well as with other natives they encountered much farther inland. It also gave them the freedom to go wherever they wished and obtain the food and provisions they would need to make it to Spanish settlements in Mexico. For eight years, Cabeza de Vaca and his men traversed much of present-day Texas and other parts of what is now the American Southwest.

Estenbico apparently developed a good command of native languages, so he began to serve as the advance man for the group. He would approach a native community – or would be introduced into a new one accompanied by native people of another – and negotiate for the provisions the castaways required to conduct their healings and assist them in their travels. Usually, Estenbico bartered the Spaniards' services as healers in exchange for food, shelter, and, sometimes, women.

Passed from one native community to another, the four men found that their reputation as medicine men preceded them as they traveled west through much of what is now central Texas and New Mexico before turning southward. Native people willingly offered them food, shelter, and assistance in exchange for healing. They soon had such a following that large crowds of native people (totaling 600 persons at one point) trailed along after them as they moved from village to village.

In 1535–1536, as Cabeza de Vaca and his cohorts moved west, and then south, they began to see signs among the natives that some of them had already encountered the Spanish. They found, for example, a native person using a metal sword belt buckle as an ornament. They also saw signs of devastation, such as burned villages and lands populated by native peoples too afraid to go out into their fields and plant, lest Spanish slavers fall upon them. Cabeza de Vaca described the scene:

> We passed through many territories and found them all vacant: their inhabitants wandered fleeing among the mountains, without daring to have houses or till the earth for fear of Christians. The sight was one of infinite pain to us, a land very fertile and beautiful, abounding in springs and streams, the hamlets deserted and burned, the people thin and weak, all fleeing or in concealment. As they did not plant, they appeased their keen hunger by eating roots and the bark of trees... they related how the Christians at other times had come through the land, destroying and burning the towns, carrying away half the men, and all the women and the boys, while those who had been able to escape were wandering about fugitives. We found them so alarmed they dared not remain anywhere. They would not nor could they till the earth, but preferred to die rather than live in dread of such cruel usage as they received.

In April of 1536, Cabeza de Vaca and his party encountered a Spanish slaving patrol in western Mexico. The patrol initially mistook Cabeza de Vaca and the three other Spaniards for Indians until they greeted them in Castilian. Shocked at discovering survivors of the Narváez expedition eight years and thousands of miles from their landing site in Florida, the patrol escorted Cabeza de Vaca and company to Mexico City. There they met the Viceroy of Mexico, who listened as they told the tale of their trek across the continent. Interrogated about the lands of New Spain's far northern *frontera* (frontier), Cabeza de Vaca and the others stated they had heard of, but not seen, rich empires to the north. They also made vague references to having seen traces of gold and silver mines. Cabeza de Vaca also claimed that the castaways at one time had five emerald-tipped arrows in their possession, but had lost them during their journey.

Cabeza de Vaca noted that the Indians who followed him and his companions had difficulty believing they could be Spaniards, since "we healed the sick, [whereas] they [the Spaniards the Indians had met previously] killed the sound; that we had come naked and barefooted, while they had arrived in clothing and on horses with lances; that we were not covetous of anything, but all that was given to us we directly turned to give, remaining with nothing; that the others had the only purpose to rob whomsoever they found, bestowing nothing on any one." To his credit, such a statement indicates a shift in Cabeza de Vaca's moral compass. At the time he landed in Florida with Narváez, Cabeza de Vaca, like other conquistadores, regarded native people as non-Christian savages who deserved to be conquered and exploited. Apparently, his long, unwilling sojourn among them changed his views.

Most Spaniards in the Americas simply ignored Cabeza de Vaca's assessment of their behavior – if they did notice it, they reacted with irritation – and focused instead on his ambiguous statements about a possible rich empire to the north and the tantalizing traces of precious metals that he mentioned in his report.

For a twenty-first-century American, the notion of rich golden empires is preposterous, and it can be difficult to understand why the Spanish did not simply dismiss it as such. Would-be conquistadores of the late 1530s and early 1540s, however, did not – could not – think in these terms, nor did they think of conquering a wealthy empire as a pipe dream. In the decade and a half before Cabeza de Vaca's return, the rich empires of the Aztecs and the Incas had been conquered and subjugated by the Spanish. In other words, Spain's recent historical experience demonstrated that some tales of rich New World empires and golden cities were real.

The De Soto Expedition

The mere chance that a rich empire existed to the north sparked two Spanish expeditions, both of which had long-term negative consequences for Native Americans of the Southeast and Southwest. Hernando de Soto, who served as a key lieutenant to Francisco Pizarro during the conquest of the Inca Empire in Peru in the early 1530s, undertook a conquest of what is now the southeastern United States. Reckoned to be among the six richest men in Nicaragua as a result of his role in the conquest of Peru, De Soto, according to his subordinates, possessed a sadistic streak, enjoying the "sport" of hunting Indians from horseback with a lance. Despite his wealth, De Soto wanted more. Upon hearing the tales of Cabeza de Vaca, De Soto acquired an *adelantado* to embark on a conquest of *La Florida* – in other words, the same stretch of territory that Pánfilo de Narváez had set out to conquer a decade earlier. De Soto attempted to recruit Cabeza de Vaca as a guide for the expedition, but he refused.

At the end of May 1539, De Soto landed about 600 men, more than 200 horses, and a herd of about 200 swine at Tampa Bay, the same spot where Narváez and his ill-fated expedition had waded ashore 11 years earlier. He also carried with him, rather ominously for the native people of the Southeast, a supply of chains and iron collars. Unlike the unlucky Narváez, De Soto had a stroke of good fortune soon after landing. A few of De Soto's mounted men pursued several Indians, who took cover in a thicket. The Spaniards pulled up short, however, when one of the Indians suddenly called out to them in somewhat rusty Castilian, "do not kill me, caviler; I am a Christian! Do not slay these people; they have given me my life!" De Soto had found Juan Ortiz, a member of Narváez's expedition who had been captured by Timucuan peoples and lived among them for a decade, first as a slave, and then as a free man. Ortiz joined De Soto and served him as an interpreter and provided intelligence about the native peoples of the Florida peninsula.

De Soto's initial observations of the Native American Southeast encouraged his belief that North America contained riches that rivaled those of Peru. While the southeastern peoples did not build the closely fitted stone structures that De Soto saw among the Inca in Peru, they did have large earthen mounds, the construction of which obviously had required some sort of central organization. The chroniclers of the De Soto's expedition described a southeastern landscape that consisted mainly of villages and vast cornfields situated in the river valleys of the region. He also learned from Ortiz that powerful paramount chieftains led most of these communities.

Often uncertain as to their location as they wandered through the Southeast, De Soto and his men extorted food and servants (bearers for supplies linked together with the iron collars and chains De Soto had brought along) by seizing local leaders as hostages when they entered a native community. De Soto also demanded that his men be provided with women, who would then be baptized by the expedition's missionaries before the Spaniards raped them. The expedition's secretary explained that the women served the Spaniards' "foul uses" and their "baptism" had more to do with making it permissible for De Soto's men to have "carnal intercourse with them than to teach them the faith." De Soto thought he could extort treasure from the natives in the same way. In nearly every case, however, De Soto did not obtain treasure from native people, mainly because they had none.

As De Soto moved from one native community to another in his quest for treasure, native peoples adopted varied resistance strategies. Recognizing that the Spanish had the advantages of horses, steel weapons, and armor, many native communities opted for passive rather than active resistance. Native leaders often informed De Soto that they had none of the riches he sought, but they knew where he could obtain them, and would direct him to a place hundreds of miles away, preferably in the direction of their enemies. On other occasions, after De Soto described the gold he sought, native people would tell him they possessed it, and offered to give it to him. However, De Soto went away disappointed when Indians presented him with copper instead of gold.

In one notable exchange, De Soto and his men encountered a female ruler he referred to as the "Lady of Cutifachiqui." The Cacica, as the chroniclers of De Soto's expedition referred to her, bestowed a number of gifts upon him, including freshwater pearls. This is one of the few times the Spanish found anything of value during this expedition – although De Soto did not consider the pearls sufficient. De Soto and his men displayed their gratitude by ransacking the temples and the tombs of chiefs in the Cacica's village. They found more pearls in the tombs as well as Spanish-made hatchets and tools – artifacts, in all likelihood, of the Ayllón expedition. Continuing his practice of taking native leaders hostage, De Soto then seized the Lady of Cutifachiqui as a captive (she later managed to escape by subterfuge) in order to extort bearers from her people and ensure their good behavior.

Mabila

De Soto and his men met their match, however, when they encountered the ancestors of present-day Chickasaws at Mabila, believed to have been located in what is now central Alabama. De Soto had taken Tascaluca, an important cacique, hostage. One of the regions' paramount chiefs, Tascaluca ruled over several villages and caciques who paid him tribute. Using their horses – which Tascaluca had never seen before – De Soto and his men attempted to intimidate him into coming with them. Apparently unfazed, Tascaluca nevertheless accompanied the Spaniards, who could not help but note the excessive deference other Indians along their route paid the paramount chieftain. However, Tascaluca, irked at his treatment at the hands of De Soto, had apparently managed to send word ahead to the village of Mabila to resist the Spaniards. Upon reaching Mabila in October of 1540, De Soto noted the village had a large number of warriors who seemed prepared to fight. Underestimating the natives' military capabilities, De Soto made the decision to enter the palisaded village anyway (the term *palisade* refers to a fence or fortress wall).

Once the Chickasaw lured De Soto and his men into the village, Tascaluca's warriors moved quickly to separate their cacique from his captors and launch a well-planned attack against the Spaniards. Targeting the horses first, the Chickasaw killed several of the animals and drove De Soto and his men from the village, destroying most of their provisions and the freshwater pearls (the only thing De Soto found during the expedition that he regarded as having value) and freeing the Indians forced to serve as bearers for the Spanish. In the close quarters of the village, the Indians exploited the advantage of surprise, numbers, and the fact that the Spanish had limited space in which to maneuver. After the initial shock of the attack, De Soto ordered his men to retreat to the grounds outside of Mabila's palisade, all the while pursued by the Indians. Once in the open, the Spanish were able to regroup, and their horses and steel weapons gave them the advantage.

Despite the shift in advantage, the battle turned into a difficult day-long fight for De Soto and his men. At the end of it, De Soto and his men burned Mabila to the ground while killing an estimated

2,500 Indians. The victory came, however, at a tremendous cost. Eighteen of De Soto's men perished in the battle and nearly all of the 150 survivors suffered multiple arrow wounds. The Chickasaw destroyed all of the expedition's medical supplies during the battle, forcing De Soto and his men to slice fat from the bodies of dead Indians in order to dress their wounds. Despite achieving victory, the loss of supplies and horses meant that De Soto's band now presented a much diminished military threat to most large native communities of the Southeast. Moreover, the loss of what little treasure they had found contributed to a loss of morale among most of De Soto's men and fueled their desire to go home.

De Soto, however, refused to leave until he found the rich empire he sought. When local Indians informed Juan Ortiz that Spanish ships in the Gulf of Mexico sought information about the fate of the expedition, De Soto ordered him not to share this knowledge with any of his men, lest they attempt to desert. In March of 1541, Chickasaws attacked De Soto's winter camp in what is now northern Mississippi. While De Soto and his men fended off the assault, they now realized they no longer overawed the natives.

The Death of De Soto

During his conquest of the Mexica (Aztec) Empire, Hernán Cortés sometimes attempted to pass himself off as a deity in an effort to awe the natives. Historians have debated just how effective (or ineffective) these attempts were. Taking a page from Cortés's playbook, De Soto claimed to be a divine being of some sort. This may have helped in keeping some native peoples at bay, and perhaps in extorting food and bearers in certain cases, but not all Indians could be so easily deceived. In an attempt to overawe a Natchez cacique, De Soto boasted that he was a child of the sun, and that all obeyed and paid tribute to him. The unimpressed Natchez leader scornfully called De Soto's bluff:

> As to what you say of your being the son of the Sun, if you will cause him to dry up the great river, I will believe you: as to the rest, it is not my custom to visit any one, but rather all, of whom I have ever heard, have come to visit me, to serve and obey me, and pay me tribute, either voluntarily or by force. If you desire to see me, come where

I am; if for peace, I will receive you with special good-will; if for war, I will await you in my town; but neither for you, nor for any man, will I set back one foot.

In the spring of 1542, De Soto took ill and died. While one of the members of his expedition eulogized De Soto as a "magnanimous, virtuous, and courageous captain," he also admitted that many of the men, now certain that their fruitless quest for riches had reached an end, "rejoiced at the death of Don Hernando de Soto." After burying De Soto in the Mississippi River, the surviving members of his expedition attempted to reach Spanish settlements in Mexico by an overland route. Unaware of the terrain that faced them and underestimating the distance involved, they opted to return to the Mississippi upon reaching the Red River. Once they made it back to the Big Muddy, De Soto's surviving men constructed boats and followed the same plan the failed Narváez expedition had used when they evacuated Florida. They sailed down the river, fending off near continuous attacks from native people along the way, and followed the Gulf Coast until they reached northern Mexico and safety.

The end of De Soto's life and expedition did not end the suffering of the native people of the Southeast. His herd of pigs grew to more than three times its original size, from a little over 200 to about 700. The hogs, some of which escaped and became the ancestors of today's wild boars across the South, invaded native fields and destroyed their crops. During their four years of tromping around the Southeast, De Soto and his men killed, tortured, and enslaved native peoples, and destroyed their communities. But their inadvertent introduction of European diseases had the greatest long-term effect on the native Southeast. Whereas the chroniclers of the early portion of De Soto's expedition described a densely populated landscape consisting of villages and vast fields, more than a century later, other European explorers encountered a region sparsely populated by native peoples that had largely reverted to wilderness.

Coronado

Cabeza De Vaca's wanderings and subsequent report encouraged expeditions other than De Soto's. Even as a worn-out Cabeza de Vaca sailed for Spain, the Moor Estenbico remained in Mexico, where he became a guide for an expedition led by a priest of the Franciscan order, Fray Marcos de Niza. Estenbico's command of native languages and customs made him invaluable to the expedition, and Fray Marcos sent him far ahead as a scout. At one point Estenbico apparently entered a Zuni village, where, it is speculated, he demanded food, turquoise (much valued by peoples in the Southwest), and women. Apparently not very happy about being ordered about, the Zuni killed him. When he learned of Estenbico's death, a panicked Fray Marcos fled back to Mexico City. Even though he had not personally entered the pueblo in which Estenbico met his end (he viewed it from a mesa at a distance), Fray Marcos brought back with him a wild story claiming he had seen the seven lost cities of Cíbola. The story of the seven lost cities relates to an old Spanish legend about a churchman who stole gold from the Holy See and made his escape by sailing to the west. More elaborate versions of the story claimed that the churchman constructed cities and temples made of gold. According to Marcos, the city he saw contained much wealth, with temples, not only made of gold, but studded with precious gems.

This fantastic report convinced the Viceroy of Mexico to organize an expedition commanded by one of his protégés, Francisco Vásquez de Coronado. Eager to believe the friar's wild story, Coronado had little difficulty raising a force of 100 Spaniards and 1,000 Indian allies. Guided by Fray Marcos de Niza, Coronado and his men marched northward to Cíbola, only to find a pueblo made of adobe brick, rather than the golden city they expected. Aware of the Spaniard's approach, the Zuni sent their women and children away, drawing lines in the earth with sacred cornmeal to protect their village and telling Coronado that he must not pass the line unless he wished to die. Coronado and his men responded by storming the village, putting the Zuni to flight. However, upon discovering that the pueblo contained no riches of any sort, Coronado's men cursed and threatened Fray Marcos de Niza. Angry with the friar, Coronado dispatched him to Mexico City,

> because he did not think it was safe for him to stay in Cibola, seeing that his report had turned out to be entirely false, because the kingdoms that he had told about had not been found, nor the populous cities, nor the wealth of gold, nor the precious stones which he had reported, nor the fine clothes, nor other things that had been proclaimed from the pulpits.

Still unwilling to leave until they found the riches they sought, Coronado and his men went from pueblo to pueblo over the winter of 1540–1541, seeking something of value. Like most Spanish expeditions, they did not carry sufficient provisions with them, forcing Coronado and his men to take food and clothing from the natives. When one pueblo put up a significant amount of resistance, Coronado decided to use it as an opportunity to give the other natives of the region an object lesson in the futility of resisting the Spanish. Smoking the defenders out of the pueblo, Coronado ordered 200 warriors bound to stakes and burned alive.

While appearing culturally similar to outsiders, the different groups of Pueblo people of the Southwest competed for scarce resources in a harsh landscape, and as a consequence often fought one another. However, the continued depredations of Coronado and his men united them. Realizing that the Spaniards had the advantages of steel weapons, armor, firearms, and horses, the Pueblo knew that they could not defeat them in battle. Instead, they decided to rid themselves of Coronado and his followers by subterfuge.

On to Quivera

Utilizing the aid of an Indian the Spanish called the "Turk" (because some of the conquistadores claimed he looked like one), Coronado and his men set out in a northeasterly direction for a place the natives called Quivera. The Turk told them wild stories about Quivera, claiming that its inhabitants ate off golden plates and its trees bore little golden bells that tinkled in the breeze. The Turk led Coronado and his men through present-day New Mexico, into North Texas, western Oklahoma, and finally central Kansas, where they saw vast herds of bison, which the Spanish referred to as "cattle." Several Spaniards went hunting for the animals, and discovered that the featureless character of the Great Plains made navigation difficult. Many of them got lost and Coronado and his men sometimes spent their nights blowing trumpets and firing shots into the air in attempts to guide the wayward hunters back to camp.

When they reached "*Gran Quivera*," the Spanish found a Wichita village consisting primarily of grass huts. Furious at not having found any riches, Coronado ordered that the Turk be tortured, forcing him to confess his role in a plan hatched by the Indians of the Pecos Pueblo. The plan had called for the Turk to lead the Spaniards out onto the Great Plains, get them lost, and then slip away from them, leaving Coronado and his men to starve to death. The Indians thought that once they expended their provisions, most of the Spaniards would perish. Should any of them find their way back to New Mexico, they would be so weak and so few that the Pueblo people could easily dispatch them. After garroting the Turk, the Spaniards found their way back to the Southwest, where they wreaked havoc on the Pueblo people. Having found nothing of value, Coronado returned to Mexico City in 1542 and the Spanish authorities wrote off his expedition as a failure.

Bartolomé de Las Casas

Most Spaniards remained unaware of the cruelties conquistadores inflicted on the natives of the Americas. Some individuals, however, not only aware of the abuses but deeply disturbed by them and wishing for them to cease, as the writings of a former conquistador turned Dominican friar, Bartolomé de Las Casas, attest, attempted to change this. As a conquistador, Las Casas had taken part in the conquest of Hispaniola in the late fifteenth century, becoming a large landholder on the island. His transformation into a champion of the Indians began on Christmas Day 1511, when he and other Spaniards attended mass. Rather than hearing the Christmas message they expected, the Dominican conducting the mass laid into the colonists, upbraiding them for their mistreatment of the island's Indians. Most of the colonists left the church unaffected, while in some cases perhaps, they may have been disgruntled with the priest who conducted the mass. Las Casas on the other hand, his conscience touched, sold his holdings and returned to Spain, where he joined the Dominican order.

The Black Legend

Returning to the Americas, Las Casas became a champion for the Indians, attempting to protect them from Spanish exploitation. He wrote several books, perhaps the most famous being *In Defense of the Indians*. Las Casas's works were translated and published outside of Spain, sometimes adorned with lurid illustrations of Spanish atrocities engraved by the famed Dutch artist Theodor de Bry. Perhaps unwittingly, Las Casas had instigated what came to be known as *La Leyenda Negra* (The Black Legend). Widely believed by other peoples throughout Europe, the Black Legend postulates that the Spanish were uniquely cruel to native peoples of the Americas. As Spain was the richest and most powerful nation in Europe at the time, and had a propensity for throwing its weight around, other European nations tended to believe these stories. In time, other writers would add to the Black Legend, sometimes writing factual accounts, but just as often composing pieces that blended truth and fiction. In other cases, accounts were wholly fictional.

Despite their failures to find mineral wealth in both *La Florida* and the Southwest, the Spanish, it turned out, could not desert both regions and their peoples entirely. Strategic considerations in Florida and religious motivations in the Southwest compelled them to return. Attacks by French and Dutch pirates on the ships that transported their treasure out of the Americas prompted the Spanish to establish naval bases in Florida in an effort to protect their fleets that sailed the channel between the peninsula and Cuba. Occupying promising harbors on the Florida peninsula, the Catholic Spanish displayed their intolerance of other European interlopers in their domain when they ruthlessly butchered a colony of French Huguenots who settled near their base at what later became St Augustine.

La Florida

From the Florida peninsula, Spanish explorers ranged northward along what is now the eastern seaboard of the United States, encountering more bands and tribes of native people in the process. In 1570, Spanish Jesuits established a mission in the Chesapeake Bay area, along what the English would later name the James River. Refusing military protection – they believed it would provoke the natives – the Jesuits relied on the advice of a young captive Powhatan Indian who had been baptized Luís de Velasco. Luís de Velasco had been taken to Mexico City for religious instruction, and the Spanish seemed to think he had been thoroughly indoctrinated. However, once he returned to the Chesapeake, he returned to his own people and led an attack against the mission, killing all eight Jesuits. A Spanish resupply expedition later took revenge by killing 34 natives, 14 of whom they hanged from the yardarms of their ships. Ultimately, having found nothing of value, the Spanish chose to desert the

Figure 2.1 A benign image of Spanish colonization. A Franciscan missionary and a Spanish soldier look over an Indian child. In reality, Spanish missionaries exploited native people for their labor, while the presence of soldiers in nearby presidios (forts) served to intimidate native people, discouraging resistance. Detail from *Amplissimae regionis Mississipi...*, Nuremberg, 1730. Courtesy of Darlington Library, University of Pittsburgh.

Chesapeake. As for Luís de Velasco, he returned to his people and it is believed by some historians that he later took the name Opechancanough, the man who later led two rebellions against English colonists in Virginia in the seventeenth century.

In Florida, the Spanish sought to make allies of the natives by trying, with limited success, to convince nomadic peoples to reside permanently in stationary missions. Attempts to convert them to what the Spanish claimed was a superior religion could not persuade the Indians to do so, but their increasing dependence on European trade goods could, and Franciscan friars established missions in northern Florida. Settled in one place and constantly exposed to European pathogens, many of the missionized Florida natives perished. But they also became Spanish allies who would become a bulwark against English incursions southward over the next two centuries.

New Mexico

Spanish secular authorities, taking note of the barrenness and what they regarded as the poverty of the Southwest, would just as soon have left the region alone, and not committed resources to it. The Franciscan order, however, argued that past commitments Spain had made to the Holy See obligated it to seek out and convert the native peoples they had encountered there. While the Spanish secular authorities wished to simply forget about its northern borderlands – they saw little or nothing there of economic value – the Franciscans would not let them, arguing that the Treaty of Tordesillas, in which the Pope divided the Americas between Spain and Portugal in the 1490s, mandated that the natives be converted, lest they be condemned to hell.

In 1598, Don Juan de Oñate, who had been appointed governor, *adelantado*, and captain-general, established and began the settlement of the colony that came to be called New Mexico. As with those who spearheaded other Spanish colonizing ventures, Oñate and his followers did not bring sufficient supplies with them, and they extorted food from the Indians in their newly declared colony, in this case the Pueblo. When the weather turned cold, Spanish solders literally stole blankets off the backs of Pueblo women. Not having constructed their own shelters, Oñate's solders evicted the Indians of the San Gabriel Pueblo. While the Pueblo may have been intimidated by Spanish weaponry and horses, they naturally resented the actions of the colonists and the soldiers.

Acoma

Matters came to a head in December of 1598 when Oñate dispatched a detail led by his nephew to extort food from the Acoma Pueblo. Known as the "sky Pueblo," Acoma sat (and still sits) atop a plateau that rose more than 350 feet from the desert floor. The people of Acoma delayed the Spaniards, telling them they needed time to grind the cornmeal the newcomers demanded, while they prepared to defend themselves. When 18 soldiers entered Acoma to demand the provisions, one of them stole two turkeys and another molested a young woman. Needing little provocation at this point, Acoma warriors attacked and slew 12 of the Spaniards, including Oñate's nephew. The survivors fled and reported the incident to Oñate.

Gathering a force of 70 men, which represented more than half of the Spanish soldiers in the province, Oñate arrived the next month, and stormed Acoma. In a savage three-day battle, the Spanish killed 800 Acomans. Oñate placed the surviving prisoners on trial and oversaw the proceedings himself. He sentenced all prisoners over the age of 12 to 20 years' slavery in New Mexico. To make a more graphic and terrifying example to other native peoples, Oñate additionally ordered that all Acoma males over the age of 25 years have one foot severed to prevent them from running away or resisting. In addition, Oñate released two Hopi men captured at Acoma, but only after cutting off one hand of each Hopi to serve as a warning to their people should they think of resisting the Spaniards. Oñate declared all the children of Acoma under the age of 12 to be innocent of taking part in the rebellion. However, they were to be taken from their parents and given to the Franciscan order, which would see to their religious instruction and train them to be servants in Mexico.

Converting the Pueblo

With the Pueblo people apparently pacified, the Franciscans settled down to convert them. To ensure the safety of the missionaries, nearby each mission the Spanish built a *presidio* (frontier fort) that garrisoned a small contingent of soldiers who could be called upon to force recalcitrant Indians back into line, and to ward off attacks from nomadic peoples who attacked the Pueblo. Not bothering to learn the native languages (although eventually many of the Pueblo learned Spanish), the friars attempted to teach Christianity by means of images and sign language. The language barrier created a situation rife with misunderstandings and, not surprisingly, the Pueblo misinterpreted the missionaries' message. Given inadequate explanations of the Catholic faith and presented with multiple images of the deity and near deities (saints), the polytheistic Pueblo people, quite naturally, interpreted things on their own terms, incorporating Christianity (or at least the parts they liked) into their own religious practices.

The Pueblo objected to the Franciscans' aggressiveness in their attempts to convert them. The Friars provoked anger when they destroyed the *katsinas* (images that represented spirits) as idols, and by using the *kivas* (subterranean, round rooms in pueblos used for religious purposes) to store supplies and stable animals. Most seriously, they violated Pueblo taboos by allowing women to enter the *kivas*. The effectiveness of the Franciscan missionary effort is questionable. The friars sometimes acted forcibly, seeking out and punishing Indians whom they thought profaned the mass. Aware that the natives often created idols and hid them, the friars sought the hidden objects out. At times they discovered idols secreted in their own chapels, raising the question as to which deity (or deities) the Pueblo worshipped during mass. Other times the friars found idols hidden in nearby caves. The caches of idols often surprised the friars, who found that the Pueblo made statues of Jesus, Mary, and various other Catholic saints, and often grouped them next to representations of their own deities. In other words, the friars realized the Pueblo had taken the religion to which they had attempted to convert them and made it into their own. This, not surprisingly, did not please the Franciscan missionaries.

Secularly, the presence of the friars and the intimidating soldiers that accompanied them benefitted the Pueblo in some respects. The Spanish forced the Pueblo people to build missions and churches, and frequently interfered with their social and economic life. But in something of a tradeoff, the presence of the soldiers also provided the Pueblo with military protection from their traditional enemies, Apache and Navajo raiders. The Spanish also improved the lives of Pueblo people in material terms by introducing them to new crops and livestock, such as sheep, and by giving them metal tools.

The Pueblo Revolt

For the first eight decades of the seventeenth century, the Pueblo people tolerated Spanish rule. In the 1670s, severe prolonged droughts throughout the Southwest caused food shortages among the Pueblo and other peoples. Pressed by the lack of resources, the Apache and Navajo, who long had relied on foodstuffs stolen from the Pueblo, stepped up their raids, and Spanish soldiers had difficulty protecting the villages. Believing that the Spanish god had failed to protect them, Pueblo people turned to their own traditional religious leaders. Enraged by what they viewed as the Pueblo people forsaking Christianity, the friars convinced the Spanish secular

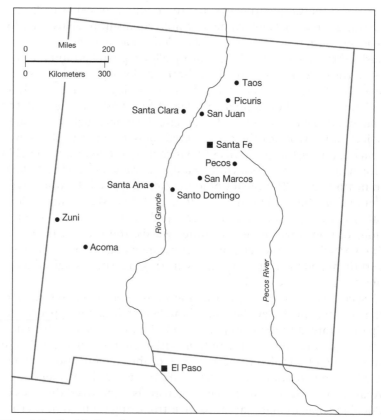

Map 2.2   Pueblo Revolt

authorities to arrest and punish native religious leaders. The Spanish seized 47 medicine men, and held them at the New Mexico capital of Santa Fe. After executing four of the native priests, the authorities whipped the others and released them.

One of the whipped priests, a Tewa medicine man named Popé, devised a bold plan to unite the Pueblo people and, together, drive the Spanish out of New Mexico. Popé could not convince every Pueblo community to join him – too many ancient differences still divided some of them – but most did become part of a grand conspiracy. In part, one can view this as a testament to Popé's abilities as an organizer and leader, but it also reflects the desire of many of the Pueblos to rid themselves of the Spanish. Even some Apaches, traditional enemies of the Pueblo, joined the plot. Realizing that his plan relied heavily on secrecy, Popé confided his entire scheme to only a few trusted lieutenants. Indeed, it is said that Popé suspected his own son-in-law of being a Spanish informer and ordered his followers to assassinate the young man. Popé dispatched runners carrying knotted cords to each of the 24 Pueblo villages involved in the plot. Those in each village would untie one knot each day. Once they had undone all the knots, the Pueblo would begin their coordinated attack on their Spanish overlords.

Despite the secrecy and the depth of planning, the Spaniards learned of Popé's plot when they apprehended two of the runners on August 9. Despite learning Popé's plans, the Spanish were still surprised when the Taos Pueblo began their revolt earlier than planned, on August 10, 1680. The Indians first fell upon the Franciscans, who actually lived in the churches and missions within or adjacent to the pueblos. Taken by surprise, the panicked surviving Spaniards withdrew into their provincial capital at Santa Fe. Popé laid siege to Santa Fe and cut off the water supply. After about 10 days, the Spanish capitulated and Popé granted them safe passage to leave for Mexico. Of the 2,500 Spanish colonists in New Mexico, 380 perished in the revolt, including 21 of the 33 Franciscan friars.

In the aftermath of the Pueblo Revolt, Popé led a movement to do away with all vestiges of Christianity. The Pueblo demolished the churches and the missions the Franciscan missionaries had forced them to build. Popé oversaw the destruction of crosses and images of saints and invalidated the Catholic marriages performed by the Franciscans, ordering couples to separate. Other Pueblos flung themselves into rivers, where they attempted to scrub from themselves their baptism and other trappings of Christianity.

Popé had overseen the most successful revolt by native people against a European power, and, apparently, his opposition to Christianity and the Franciscan friars won him much support from the Pueblos. However, when Popé also advocated the elimination of material items the Spanish had introduced, such as wheat, livestock, and metal tools, he met resistance from those very same people. While the Pueblo apparently had little use for the Spaniards and their religion, they very pragmatically wanted to keep the things that improved their lives.

The Spanish did not return to New Mexico until 1692. In the dozen years since the 1680 revolt, Popé had died and, freed of an external threat, the unity the Pueblos had displayed against the Spanish unraveled. Initially, the returned Franciscan friars attempted to reimpose the religious yoke on the Pueblos. However, they met resistance, and in 1696 the Pueblo people staged another revolt. But this effort lacked the level of secrecy and organization that characterized the 1680 revolt and Spanish troops suppressed it over a period of six months, following a strategy of destroying corn-fields in order to starve the Pueblo into surrender. The Spanish did not keep a careful record of the second revolt and it is unknown how may Indians died, although we do know five Franciscans lost their lives. The second Pueblo Revolt did, however, have long-term effects, as it forced the Franciscans to reappraise their approach. Rather than bully the Pueblo into conversion, the friars now attempted to convince them that conversion to Catholicism was in their best interests, and learned to simply "look the other way" when their Indian charges did something they considered religiously questionable.

The most successful rebellion ever undertaken by native people, the Pueblo Revolt drove the Spanish from the American Southwest and forced them to wait more than a decade before they attempted a return. The memory of the uprising caused the Spanish to take a gentler approach and to reach an accommodation with the Pueblo people. Granted, the relationship between the Spanish and native people would never be perfect. But as they moved to counter what they viewed as encroachments on the frontiers of their colonial domain by other European powers, Spanish administrators, soldiers, and missionaries would encounter native peoples who differed from the Pueblo, and learned to use diplomacy – albeit imperfectly – to induce these peoples to become their allies.

3

Encounters with the French

News of Cristóbal Colón's "discovery" – once scholars and cartographers ascertained that he indeed had *not* reached the Far East – sent shock waves through a Europe that never suspected that two vast continents lay between it and Asia. Taking advantage of its enormous head start, Spain took the lead in exploring and exploiting the wealth of the Americas, while the other European powers lagged behind. Conscious that their early explorations gave them a geographical and ethnographical knowledge of the Americas that their European competitors lacked, the Spanish treated such information as a state secret. While they successfully denied their European competitors' intelligence about the New World – particularly in terms of navigation – for a time, other details, perhaps spread by loose-lipped Spanish sailors during calls in European ports, began to appear in printed form throughout the continent. Some of the information that reached the public and navigators in other countries contained inaccuracies and amounted to little more than sailors' tall tales. However, some of the reports, despite their exaggerations and inaccuracies, did give navigators and sailors of other European nations a gleaning of what to expect from the peoples of the New World.

England became the second European nation to send an expedition to the Americas, sponsoring the 1497 voyage commanded by the

"Times Are Altered with Us": American Indians from First Contact to the New Republic, First Edition. Roger M. Carpenter.
© 2015 John Wiley & Sons, Inc. Published 2015 by John Wiley & Sons, Inc.

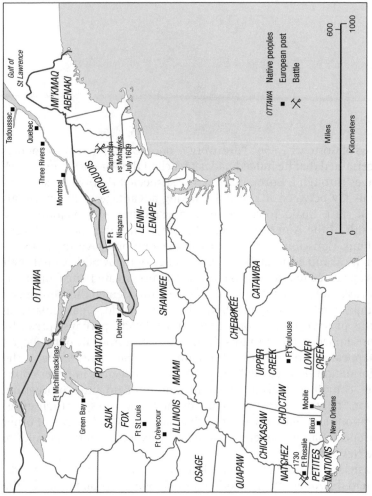

Map 3.1 Native people and the French

Venetian Giovanni Caboto (later anglicized to John Cabot). Cabot, looking for a way around the Americas to Asia, instead ran into Newfoundland and its offshore Grand Banks, a part of the ocean teeming with codfish. Domestic political and economic difficulties prevented the English from following up on Cabot's discoveries for more than a half century. Likewise, England's cross-channel rival, France, also found itself bedeviled by domestic political and religious strife, which diverted its attention from the Americas until 1524, when the Crown commissioned the Italian navigator Giovanni da Verrazzano to explore the coast of North America.

Verrazzano's Voyage

Traversing much of the present-day eastern seaboard of the United States, members of Verrazzano's expedition went ashore several times to make contact with the natives, with varied results. The recorded behavior of both the Indians and the French tells us much about cross-cultural misunderstandings. Somewhere in the vicinity of present-day coastal South Carolina, native people onshore made gestures of friendship to the French ship. One of Verrazzano's younger crewmen, underestimating the coldness of the water and roughness of the surf, attempted to swim ashore, intending to present some baubles and knick-knacks to the Indians. The rough seas buffeted the young sailor and cast him up on the beach, shivering and exhausted. Seeing him in this state, the Indians kindled a large fire, carried him over to it, and stripped off his clothes. Aboard ship, Verrazzano's crew – conditioned by the wild tales they had heard about the Americas – looked on in horror, certain that the Indians intended to kill, cook, and eat their shipmate. Instead, the Indians had built the fire merely to warm the young man and wanted to make sure he had not been injured. The paleness of the sailor's skin also intrigued them. Once the young man regained his senses, the Indians escorted him back to the edge of the surf and watched him until he had swum safely back to the ship.

Somewhere in present-day North Carolina, some of Verrazzano's men went ashore and found a native village. The villagers fled at their approach. Looking around, Verrazzano's sailors found an older woman with two small children hidden in the grass. They also found a young woman they described as being about 18 or 20 years of age and "very beautiful and tall." They gave the older woman some gifts and seized one of the children and the young woman, with the intent of taking both of them back to France. The young woman, however, shrieked continually, causing Verrazzano's men to leave her and take only the boy. Verrazzano offered no clues in his writings as to the eventual fate of the boy.

Proceeding north, Verrazzano and his men encountered friendly native peoples near the site of present-day New York City and Narragansett Bay in southern New England. However, when Verrazzano and his men dropped anchor off the coast of present-day Maine, relations with native people took a sharp turn. The local Abenaki people had already had encounters with Europeans, not all of which, apparently, had been positive. Upon seeing the French, the Abenaki loosened some arrows in their direction and retreated into the woods. Later they returned, indicating that they wished to trade. Sending their women out of sight, the Abenaki controlled the terms of exchange, refusing to allow Verrazzano and his sailors to come ashore. With the French remaining in their boats, they and the Abenaki swapped animal pelts and trade goods by means of a rope. The French also discovered, to their dismay, that unlike the childlike barbarians they had been led to expect, the Abenaki proved to be shrewd traders who drove hard bargains. Showing no interest in the beads and other trinkets the French offered, the Abenaki demanded useful metal items such as fishhooks, knives, and edged tools. Nor did the act of trade imply friendship between the Abenaki and the French. Once the French ran out of metal goods, the Abenaki left, making, Verrazzano later reported, "all signes of discourtesie, as was possible for any creature to invent."

Verrazzano's voyage yielded some information for the French, but it would be a decade before they would send another voyage to the Americas. Wary of provoking the powerful Spanish empire, the French sent an expedition northward to the mouth of the St Lawrence River, where they hoped they would find the fabled shortcut to the Far East that Europeans called the Northwest Passage. Spain learned about French intentions through its network of spies, but certain that nothing of value could be found that far north, made no move to interfere. The French and other Europeans already knew a little bit about the native peoples who lived near the mouth of the St Lawrence. Crews of European fishing vessels that plied the waters off Newfoundland's Grand Banks frequently traded with native people, who exchanged what they regarded as old worn-out beaver robes, which Europeans valued, in return for metal goods and cloth.

Figure 3.1 Native hunters and European fishermen. Many of the earliest interactions between Native Americans and Europeans took place in coastal regions in Canada and New England. Native people swapped animal pelts in exchange for items such as fishhooks and knives. Detail from *France occidentale dans l'Amérique Septentrional ou le cours de la rivière de St. Laurens,* Paris, 1718. Courtesy of Darlington Library, University of Pittsburgh.

Cartier

In 1534, French mariner Jacque Cartier set out to explore the St Lawrence to see if it did indeed lead to the hoped-for Northwest Passage. During this first voyage, Cartier limited his explorations to the mouth of the St Lawrence, where he encountered Mi'kmaq people who, like the Abenaki whom Verrazzano had encountered a decade earlier, obviously had prior experience with Europeans. Holding up furs on pieces of wood, the Mi'kmaq signaled their desire to trade with the French. So many eager Mi'kmaq traders approached Cartier's ship with their canoes that, fearing they would swamp his vessel, he ordered his men to fire cannon to frighten them away. The next day, Cartier went ashore and in what Europeans called a ceremony of possession – a scene that would play out over and over during the era of European exploration – he set up a 30-foot-high wooden cross bearing the arms of the French king near the mouth of the St Lawrence. While the cross obviously signaled a French claim to the region – and the natives recognized it as such – Cartier sought to soothe them by telling them that the object served to praise God and would be used as a navigational aid by French ships in the future. Apparently, this explanation did not satisfy all the natives. After Cartier and his men returned to their ship, Donnacona, the leader of the Iroquoian community of Stadacona, located further upriver, appeared in a canoe and harangued Cartier and his men, using sign language to point out that all the land for as far as they could see belonged to him, and that they should not have put up the cross without his permission. Using valued trade items, such as an axe, Cartier and his men lured the chief closer to their ship, seized him and hauled him aboard their vessel. According to Cartier, he convinced Donnacona (who may not have had much choice in the matter) that the French meant no harm and plied him with gifts. Cartier also persuaded Donnacona to allow his two sons to return to France with him.

Cartier's first voyage had taken only a little over four months. Exposed to European culture in France, Donnacona's sons, Taignoagny and Domagaia, learned a smattering of the French language. Cartier and the boys' other French hosts sought to learn as much as they could from them about the Americas and the commodities they could yield. They also hoped to train Taignoagny and Domagaia to become useful interpreters and guides. Many of the native people transported to Europe under similar circumstances wished to return home, and realized that telling Europeans what they wished to hear might hasten their return voyage. Such a desire probably fueled Taignoagny's and Domagaia's stories about rich mines and a route to the Pacific that lay in their homeland.

In September of 1535, Cartier returned to the St Lawrence with three vessels. He encountered Donnacona, accompanied by 16 warriors. For the first time the French saw the Huron Village of Stadacona, near the site of present-day Quebec. Cartier and his men remained at Stadacona for about 10 days and made preparations to sail downriver with the smallest of his three vessels to another Iroquoian village known as Hochelaga.

At this point, Taignoagny and Domagaia, who had promised to guide Cartier to Hochelaga, now attempted to discourage him from proceeding. Some historians have suggested that the reason the two changed their minds involved the influence of their father, who saw Stadacona and Hochelaga as rivals. It has also been argued that Donnacona feared that Cartier might become a military ally of the Hochelagans, who would then be turned against Stadacona. A more likely explanation is that Donnacona realized the advantage that he and his community would have if he could find a way to monopolize trade with the French. If he could convince Cartier not to travel downriver, the Hochelagans, and presumably other inland native communities, would be dependent on him to acquire European cloth and metal goods. In other words, Donnacona may have been thinking that he could act as a sort of middleman and control the trade; but for such a plan to work, he had to keep the suppliers of manufactured goods (Europeans) away from those who possessed the furs they sought (other natives).

Donnacona made several unsuccessful attempts to dissuade Cartier from going to Hochelaga. When Taignoagny informed Cartier that his father had forbidden him to serve as his guide, Cartier simply replied that he would go without him. Two days later, Donnacona gave a lengthy speech in which he presented Cartier with his 10 to 12-year-old niece and two young male children, including one of his younger sons, to take back to France. Taignoagny – who Cartier now referred to as a "crafty knave" – informed him that he could keep the children only if he did not proceed to Hochelaga. Cartier simply kept the children, giving Donnacona two swords and two wash basins in exchange. To Cartier at least, this may have altered the presentation of the children from an exchange of gifts to a trade.

The next day, the Stadaconans made a desperate (and somewhat comical) effort to convince Cartier to remain at their village. At dusk, three men, each with their face blackened, wearing animal skins and "hornes on their heads more than a yard long," approached the French ships, warning Cartier not to proceed upriver. Shortly after they left, Donnacona and his sons appeared, told Cartier that the appearance of the three "devils" had been a warning from their deity for him not to go to Hochelaga. Cartier and his sailors appear to have been more amused than alarmed by the incident. In a final effort to keep Cartier from heading upriver, the Stadaconans asserted (correctly) that the St Lawrence did not lead to a seaborne passage to a western ocean.

Ignoring all such efforts to change his mind, Cartier proceeded, in the smallest of his three vessels, down the St Lawrence to Hochelaga, where he received a joyous reception. With our knowledge of the internal communication and trade networks in pre-contact Native North America, we can be reasonably certain that the Hochelagans knew about Europeans and their trade goods long before they ever set eyes on them.

Upon greeting Cartier, the leader of Hochelaga – despite the obvious language barrier – launched into a long and seemingly pointed speech that Cartier (and other European explorers) referred to as a harangue. It also became obvious that in all likelihood the Hochelagans had no prior direct experience with Europeans, but their joy in meeting Cartier and his men became readily apparent:

> So soone as we were come neere Hochelaga, there came to meete us above a thousand persons, men, women and children, who afterward did as friendly and merily entertaine and receive us as any father would doe his child, which he had not of long timeseene, the men dauncing on one side, the women on another, and likewise the children on another: after that they brought us great store of fish, and of their bread made of Millet, casting them into our boates so thicke, that you would have thought it to fall from heaven.

After this exuberant greeting, the Indians picked up Cartier and carried him (from Cartier's description, it sounds like they gave him a piggy-back ride) into their village. Once inside the village, the Hochelagans carried out their sick and – as near as Cartier could tell – implored him to heal them. Cartier complied by praying over the ill persons. Obviously imperfect, communication between the French and the natives required some guesswork on both sides. Cartier somehow got the impression that the Hochelagans wanted him to teach them about his religion. Cartier replied that he could not, but would return the next year and bring people who could instruct them in Christianity.

Determined to spend the winter, Cartier sailed back up the St Lawrence to Stadacona. Despite recognizing that the region experienced severe winters, Cartier (as did other Europeans) underestimated the severity of the North American climate. Still unprepared when the first snows arrived late in the fall, Cartier and his men found themselves and their ships locked into the winter ice. They built a small palisade (fort) in which to live, but soon began to run low on provisions. Scurvy – a vitamin deficiency caused by a lack of vitamin C – broke out among both the natives and Cartier's crewmen, but the visitors apparently got the worst of it. By February 1536, only about 10 of 110 Frenchmen had not come down with the malady. Distrustful of the natives, Cartier and his men kept their distance from them, fearful that should the Stadaconans discover their weakness, they would attack and wipe out the expedition. In the meantime, the French, with no knowledge of the causes of scurvy (as with other diseases of the time) performed amateur autopsies on their own dead in an effort to learn what killed them. Naturally, their observations of their deceased shipmates' internal organs provided them with little useful information.

One day in February 1536, one of Donnacona's sons, who previously had contracted a bad case of scurvy, came to visit Cartier at his outpost. Astonished to see the young man completely cured of the disease, Cartier asked how this came about. The young Iroquoian told Cartier about a tree (probably white pine) in the forest, whose bark and leaves, ground and brewed into a drinkable concoction, cured the sickness. Gathering the ingredients and procuring the help of some native women who showed him how to prepare them, Cartier managed to save his remaining men. In the spring, when he sailed for France, Cartier took a total of 10 natives with him, including Donnacona, and did not return to the St Lawrence for six years.

None of the 10 natives who went to France with Cartier ever saw home again, but Donnacona, at least, made the most of his time in France. Like other Native Americans taken to Europe, he spun tales for his hosts, telling them that he knew where they could find the precious minerals they craved, or, failing that, the location of a rich golden (and conquerable) kingdom or, even better, a waterborne route to a western ocean, presumably the Pacific.

Cartier set out on his next voyage for the St Lawrence in 1541, intending to assist Sieur de Roberval in establishing a colony near the mouth of the river. In this endeavor the French encountered their first difficulties in recruiting colonists, a factor that would plague their efforts to establish outposts in the Americas for the next two centuries. Indeed, Roberval only secured a sufficient number of settlers by convincing the king to release a number of convicts into his custody. The convicts – who had been jailed for offenses ranging from the theft of bronze used to make church bells, to the far more serious crime of premeditated murder – could not have been the best stock with which to establish a colony.

Originally, Cartier and Roberval planned to sail at the same time. Cartier, having more experience in putting together an expedition, had his ships stocked and ready to sail in May 1541, while Roberval's preparations for the voyage lagged. Rather than having Cartier's ships remain in port, it was agreed that he should set sail, and Roberval would follow, once his vessels and crews were prepared.

Cartier left France in May 1541, establishing a colony near Stadacona. Roberval, beset by delays, did not leave France until nearly a year later, in April 1542. In June 1542, Cartier's and Roberval's ships met off the coast of Newfoundland. Cartier had decided to return to France, with some disgruntled colonists and barrels filled with what he believed to be diamonds and gold. Roberval asked Cartier to guide him to the settlement. Eager to return to France, Cartier refused, but he did provide Roberval with maps and charts that enabled him to navigate his way to the settlement. Taking his leave of Roberval, Cartier returned to France with his barrels of treasure – which turned out to be nothing more than quartz and iron pyrite (fool's gold).

Roberval's colonists, like Cartier's men several years earlier, also suffered the travails of scurvy. But unlike Cartier's men, they did not know how to cure it, despite having received instruction from Cartier before he departed for France. In their weakened state, they also managed to arouse the ire of the Indians by stealing food from them. Within a few years, Roberval's colony failed. Most of the colonists perished and the survivors returned to France. With a new king who had little interest in American exploration, and beset by internal religious conflict, this time the French would not return to the St Lawrence for nearly 40 years.

Huguenots in Florida

Yet that did not mean they would suspend all contacts with the natives of the Americas. The next colonizing venture of French persons would land far from the St Lawrence – and into far riskier circumstances. In 1564, French Huguenots (Protestants), fleeing the Wars of Religion in their homeland, established Fort Caroline at the mouth of St John's River (near present day St Augustine) on the east coast of the Florida peninsula. Alarmed at the French presence, the local Spanish commander wasted no time in assaulting their fort. When the survivors asked for quarter, the Spanish commander stated he would do as his god commanded him. Apparently reassured by this statement, the French surrendered. Unfortunately for the French, god apparently told the Spanish commander to tie their hands behind their backs and put all of them to the sword. Shortly after this incident, and concerned by recent attacks of French and Dutch pirates on their Caribbean treasure fleets, the Spanish established a naval base at St Augustine, which became the first permanent European settlement in North America.

The Fur Trade

Beginning around 1580, European traders, primarily French, began to journey regularly to the mouth of the St Lawrence to trade with the natives. French contact most affected the Mi'kmaq, Abenaki, and Montagnais peoples of present-day Maine and the Canadian Maritimes. The French established a trading post at Port Royal on the Acadian coast and at Tadoussac on the St Lawrence. There, French traders acquired animal pelts in exchange for woolen cloth and metal goods.

The native people of the Northeast did not initially regard many European goods as finished products. Instead, they often treated the goods they acquired in this early phase of exchange with Europeans as raw material that still required manipulation by human hands before they reached a finished, usable state. Valued for their obvious warmth, European woolens also offered other advantages over animal skins as clothing. Unlike leather garments, woolens dried much more quickly once wet. With the use of scissors and other metal cutting tools provided by European traders, woolens could easily be made into specific garments. Native people also found woolens quite versatile. Jesuit missionaries noted that a native person would sleep in a woolen blanket, and, with a few adjustments, quickly transform it into a garment to wear for the entire day. While native people valued other European trade goods, cloth became the single most exchanged item. This is a fact that tends to elude our attention for several reasons. A prosaic item used in mundane, day-to-day settings, cloth seldom appears in the archaeological record and did not create the problems that other European goods such as guns or alcohol did, which tends to make the latter stand out in the historical record.

The metal goods that native people demanded do appear in the archaeological record and, as the historical record makes clear, Indians quickly realized the distinct advantages that steel knives and hatchets had over stone tools. Far more durable, less brittle, and able to hold an edge, metal tools quickly supplanted their lithic counterparts. Native people also desired metal goods that could be transformed into other objects, such as the copper pot.

Archaeologists working in the Northeast have found on the sites of Indian villages the remains of copper pots that lack scorch marks, indicating they had never been set over a fire. Instead, native people transformed the first copper pots they received from French traders into other objects, such as jewelry, arrowheads, hide scrapers, and knife blades.

Over time, the copper pot assumed an important role among native peoples who lived near the mouth of the St Lawrence, such as the Abenaki and Mi'kmaq. Prior to contact with Europeans, these peoples had been limited to clan-defined hunting areas. Their reliance on communal cooking vessels, usually a large, burned-out stump, also limited their movement. The standard cooking method usually consisted of filling the stump with water (or bark vessels), putting in the meat, and adding red hot rocks until the water heated up (although it seldom reached a boil). Missionaries described food prepared in this manner as being "somewhat cooked." The copper pot changed that. Light, portable, and durable, it could easily be transported (as opposed to the unfired clay vessels native people used) without fear of breakage. It could also be hung over a fire, and the food placed therein would be rendered thoroughly cooked. It also freed people dependent on hunting from being chained to an immovable communal cooking vessel, allowing them to expand their hunting territories, which in some cases resulted in conflict with other native people upset by the intrusion into their traditional hunting territories.

Native people also valued European goods – particularly colorful and shiny items like copper pots – for the spiritual properties they imagined they possessed. French trader Nicolas Denys recorded a story wherein several traders, aghast that the natives buried their dead with large quantities of beaver pelts, attempted to convince them that the goods did not accompany the deceased to the next world. Convincing the natives to open a grave, the Frenchmen pointed out that the beaver pelts remained moldering in the ground, and had not gone to the other world. However, one Indian, not convinced, drew a corroding copper pot from the grave and rapped it sharply with his knuckles. Noting that it did not ring, he declared that the spirit of the pot had left to join its owner in the next world, as had the spirit of all the other items in the grave.

Champlain

The French made their next serious attempt at colonization in the early seventeenth century. Cartographer and explorer Samuel de

Champlain spearheaded this effort. Exploring what later became known as New England in 1606, Champlain accompanied an expedition to a body of water just off Cape Cod Bay that the French called Cape St Louis. Sixteen years later, English Separatists (frequently referred to as "Pilgrims" in American history texts) would establish their colony in the same region, and know Cape St Louis as Plymouth Harbor, finding a landscape and people greatly altered from that encountered by Champlain.

Shortly after landing, Champlain and some sailors traded with the local natives, who wanted glass beads and, most of all, items made of metal. However, the French also did things that made them unwelcome to the natives, such as taking crops without asking. During the trading, an Indian and a Frenchman came to blows over the ownership of an iron pot. The conflict over the pot, and the taking of crops, may have been the impetus for an Indian attack on the Frenchmen. The French noted that the Indians took down their huts and sent their women and children away, causing them to believe that an attack was imminent. Nevertheless, a few Frenchmen remained ashore, tasked with baking a 15-day supply of bread for the expedition. That night, they came under attack by more than 400 Indians. Champlain led a force that quickly came to their rescue, and compelled the natives to retreat. However, the French lost several men, and in his report to the crown Champlain argued that the region's dense Indian population precluded its successful colonization. Champlain's maps of the area reinforced his argument, portraying a heavily populated landscape consisting primarily of Indian villages and cornfields.

Tasked with settling the St Lawrence, Champlain established the first permanent French outpost in North America at Quebec in 1608. He chose the site because it could be easily defended and because it moved the French closer to the native peoples of the interior, with whom they wanted to trade.

Surprisingly, in his earliest reports on the commodities that the French could expect to extract from Canada, Champlain placed furs well down the list. But it soon became apparent that furs held more value than any other commodity the Canadian wilderness could offer. While fur did not have the monetary value that gold yielded to the Spaniards in their colonization ventures, it did have some marked advantages. European fashion, in the form of beaver felt hats for men, would drive the market throughout much of the seventeenth and into the eighteenth century. While Canada did not have mineral wealth, its furs, far lighter and therefore easier to transport than gold, brought in large profits. Unlike the Spanish, who had to marshal a large naval force to protect their annual treasure fleet on its voyage from the Americas to Spain, the French (and other colonizing powers that entered the fur trade) incurred no such expense in exporting furs. Most important, the French discovered that, unlike the Spanish, they had no need to coerce or enslave the natives in order to procure the commodity they sought. They found that establishing trade agreements, military alliances, and diplomatic relations with native peoples made for a willing work force, one that made the fur trade both possible and profitable.

In this set-up, native men did the bulk of the hunting. They knew the best places to find fur-bearing animals, and native women, finding their traditional labor patterns altered somewhat, preserved and processed the pelts of beavers and other animals. In exchange, the French offered them goods such as knives, hatchets, pots, kettles, and woolen cloth.

Located on the eastern shore of Lake Huron, the Wendat people, or Huron, became the key trading partners of the French in the 1630s and 1640s. Sowing vast quantities of maize, the Wendat used their harvest partly as a hedge against famine, but also traded the surplus to peoples farther north where short summers precluded agriculture. In exchange for maize, the Wendat acquired pelts from the upper Great Lakes and Hudson's Bay region, where fur bearing animals developed thicker, and hence to humans more luxurious, coats than their cousins to the south. Acquiring these furs from peoples such as the Ottawa, the Wendat funneled them to the French in Quebec, and later Montreal, in exchange for manufactured goods.

War with the Iroquois

In early 1609 however, Champlain – still learning his way around native diplomatic forms and practices – found that the Wendat, Algonquin, and Montagnais peoples who traded with the French did not regard the relationship in strictly economic terms. To them, economic relationships also implied a military and diplomatic alliance. Informing Champlain of the depredations of the Mohawk – the easternmost of the Iroquois Five Nations – the Algonquin asked that he provide them with military assistance. Feeling that he had to comply in order to maintain their friendship and cooperation in trade, Champlain in July of 1609 accompanied a joint Algonquin-Wendat war party southward into the lake that now bears his name. As they moved south, Champlain noted that the Algonquin and Wendat warriors, wary of being in Iroquois country, grew notably apprehensive and cautious. Knowing that many native peoples believed that dreams foretold the future, Champlain claimed he had one in which he saw the Iroquois warriors drowning while the Wendat and Algonquin watched them die. After relating the details of his dream to his allies, Champlain noted their renewed confidence.

Toward the end of the month, Champlain and his allies happened across a Mohawk war party. In the gathering darkness, the two sides parlayed and agreed to fight each other in the morning at first light. The Wendat and Huron warriors drew their canoes up to the shore and built a hasty barricade to prevent the Mohawk from surprising them during the night. The Mohawk did likewise, and throughout the night, the two sides, well within earshot of one another, shouted insults and boasts, describing how they would rout each other in the morning.

Champlain's allies had, however, taken care to keep him and the two other Frenchmen accompanying them out of sight of the Mohawk. In the morning, bearing wooden shields and wearing wooden armor, both sides came out of their makeshift palisades and lined up to fight. Champlain remained in the rear of his allies and sent the two other Frenchmen into the woods. As the two sides stood facing each other, the Wendat and Algonquin ranks parted and Champlain walked to the front of them, dressed in European metal armor and carrying a harquebus (an archaic type of musket), which he had loaded with four balls. The Wendat and Algonquin warriors previously had pointed out to him the Mohawk chiefs, and Champlain promised to "do what I could to kill them." For their part, the Mohawk stopped and looked at Champlain, probably having never seen a European in armor or a musket. Champlain fired, killing two Mohawk chiefs instantly and mortally wounding a third. When the other Frenchmen fired from the woods, the Mohawk dropped their shields, shed their wooden armor, and ran for their lives. Rather than pursue the fleeing Mohawks as Champlain encouraged them to do, the Wendat and Algonquin warriors claimed their enemies' shields as trophies and took prisoners they planned to kill slowly through torture.

While this resulted in a victory for Champlain and his allies, the Frenchman had unwittingly created an implacable foe that would torment New France for the next 150 years. Until the expulsion of the French from North America in 1763, the Iroquois League would launch periodic wars against French Canada, interspersed with periods of peace usually initiated by the Five Nations, and usually timed to benefit them.

A serious obstacle to French colonization of the Americas was that very few Frenchmen desired to go to North America, and as a result of religious strife at home, the crown usually forbade or restricted immigration by French Huguenots. Unable or unwilling to send sufficient numbers of colonists, the French relied very heavily on native people as military allies and cultivated good relations with them. French traders learned native languages and married native women – not as part of French policy; they found these things essential to conduct trade.

For many French traders, marriage to a native woman became a life insurance policy of sorts. Possessing European manufactured goods highly valued by native peoples, traders could be targeted by individuals who would rob or kill them. But many of those French traders who married a native woman found that their marriages granted them a measure of protection, by making them kin, or a relative of a native clan. A native person who might think of waylaying a lone trader, now had to consider the consequences; attacking and killing, or simply robbing a trader, may lead his clan relatives to seek revenge. Native women often entered into such unions willingly and with the approval of their clans, who realized that such unions meant they, on the other hand, would enjoy superior access to European trade goods. The trader not only received protection, he also gained instruction from his native spouse or her relatives in proper protocol, and he also had a personal instructor in native languages.

While appreciative of the sorts of trade goods Europeans offered for what they regarded as smelly old beaver robes, native people could not help but wonder if they lacked intelligence. An Abenaki person showed a "very fine knife" to a French Jesuit, stating "the English have no sense. They give us twenty knives like this for one beaver pelt."

The Jesuits in Canada

The French, like other Europeans, justified their North American colonization efforts by claiming they intended to convert native people to Christianity. While a few Jesuits appeared in the Port

Royal region in the early seventeenth century, French missionary efforts did not begin in earnest until the 1620s, when the Récollects, the French offshoot of the Franciscan order, sent a few friars to Canada. One of these missionaries, Gabriel Sagard, related how he studied the Wendat (Huron) language while in France, and continued to study it during his voyage to the New World and during his stay in Quebec. Upon arriving in the Huron country, which the French dubbed Huronia, Sagard discovered that he was "deaf and mute." The Wendat people and Sagard could not understand each other. While Sagard could not always understand the natives, he could observe them, and his observations of Wendat life and culture proved valuable to later missionaries. Among the first Europeans to witness and record the Huron feast of the dead, Sagard also noted the productivity of Wendat agriculture when he became lost in one of their vast cornfields. However, the inability of Sagard and other Récollects to master the Wendat language hampered their missionary efforts, and they made very few converts.

In 1628, a small English fleet sailed up the St Lawrence River and compelled the miniscule French garrison at Quebec to surrender. France regained Canada in 1632 through treaty. Appalled to discover that most of the Indians the Récollects had presumably converted actually knew very little about Christianity, Cardinal Richelieu, the regent for the minor French king, Louis XIV, forbade them from returning to Canada. In light of this, Richelieu allowed only the Jesuit order to serve as missionaries to the native people of New France and gave them a free hand. For the next four decades, the Jesuits would be the only missionary order in Canada. Well financed and well educated, the Jesuits, or the Society of Jesus, had extensive experience as missionaries in China, Japan, and the Caribbean. Unlike the mendicant Récollects, many of the Jesuits came from the upper levels of European society. Emphasizing the mastering of foreign languages, the Jesuits differed from other missionary orders by making it a point to learn the religious beliefs of the peoples they attempted to convert, seeing this as an important key to understanding how their prospective converts thought about spiritual matters.

Despite their extensive training, the Jesuit missionaries that arrived in New France thought they would be converting simple savages; they quickly learned otherwise. Many Jesuits regarded the Wendat language as more difficult to master than European languages. In their annual *Relations,* the reports the Jesuit order published each year, the missionaries were often brutally honest regarding their inability to learn native tongues. Many Jesuits regarded themselves as only marginally successful, but a few mastered native tongues and communicated effectively with native people. They discovered, however, that Christian concepts could be difficult to translate to Native Americans. For example, when working among the Wendat, Jesuits found no equivalent terms in their language for angels. They also discovered that they could not use the term *father* in the presence of a person whose parent had died, meaning that the term "Our Father," often used in Christian prayers, had to be omitted. The Wendat also had taboos that forbade the mentioning of the term *ghost*, meaning a Jesuit could not utter the phrases "Holy Ghost" or "Holy Spirit." All of these cultural prohibitions made it difficult for the Jesuits to instruct native people in the concept of the Trinity.

The Jesuits did, however, make valuable observations about native societies in Canada. They found native people, unlike Europeans, to be relatively free of the vices of ambition and greed. They also noted their form of government did not rely on autocratic commands from a king or other such leader, but on communities reaching a consensus. While native communities did have chiefs, people only followed them through their own good will and, later, through their ability to acquire European trade goods and distribute them to their followers. They also noticed that in the small face-to-face societies of North America, native people seldom showed anger to one another, but they suspected (correctly) that they often suppressed it.

The Jesuits did far more than other Christian missionaries in recording native religious beliefs. They learned that native communities often had generally agreed upon sets of spiritual beliefs, but each individual seemed to be free to deviate or elaborate on them as he or she saw fit. For example, in Wendat communities most people agreed that the village of the dead existed somewhere far to the west, and agreed as well as to the necessity of performing the periodic feast of the dead. Nevertheless, spiritual beliefs could vary greatly from one community to another, and even within the same community, just as beliefs could vary from one individual to another.

Like the Récollect Gabriel Sagard, the Jesuits also observed and recorded the Wendat feast of the dead. However, because many of them had mastered – or at least had a much better understanding of – the Wendat language, the Jesuits could better explain the practice and the spiritual significance surrounding it. The ceremony took place every 10 to 12 years, or whenever a village had to move because its fields had lost their fertility and could no longer produce enough maize. A cemetery consisting of small lodges erected over the bodies of the deceased abutted nearly every Wendat village. Prior to moving the village, the inhabitants would go to the cemetery and disinter their loved ones. They then cleaned the remains, stripping all of the flesh from the bones. The Jesuits who observed this process noted the intensity with which the Wendat grieved over the remains of their loved ones, and that they took great care in cleaning them, even as they sometimes swarmed with maggots. Indeed, the missionaries favorably compared the manner in which the Wendat cared for their dead with Europeans' treatment of the sick. Afterwards, they wrapped the cleansed remains in new beaver robes and dug an ossuary where all the bodies would be deposited together. They also included many gifts for the dead, often in the form of new knives, hatchets, and kettles. The Wendat then covered the ossuary, and for the next several days the living would feast and present each other with gifts, often in the name of a deceased person. At the conclusion of the feast, the villagers would relocate elsewhere.

The Jesuits questioned Wendat persons closely regarding their spiritual beliefs and often received more than one answer. Moreover, most Wendat subscribed to the belief that they had more than one soul. They believed that immediately upon death, one soul would depart and go to the village of the dead. The other soul would stay with the remains and rejoin the other soul later. The Wendat avoided saying a dead person's name aloud, fearing that the undeparted soul could develop an attachment to a living person. Should this happen, when it came time for the second soul to go to the land of the dead, it may try to take the living person with them.

While most of the native peoples of Canada believed the village of the dead to be located somewhere to the west, they frequently disagreed as to its nature. Most Wendat asserted that life there resembled life on earth, only somehow better. There, they believed, they would encounter the souls of loved ones who had passed on and find the souls of many of their cherished possessions. In the afterlife, a man who had been a hunter would find himself once again hunting the souls of animals that he slew in life.

As the Jesuits attempted to convert native people to Christianity they encountered a great deal of resistance, primarily from medicine men and shamans. Father Claude Allouez became locked in a quarrel with a Pottawatomie medicine man during the winter of 1666–1667 over the best way to cure a sick young man who had converted to Christianity. Allouez bled the young man (a common European medical practice in the seventeenth century), showed the supposedly bad blood to the village medicine man and told him that it caused the illness. Sometime later, the medicine man and other Pottawatomies claimed to have extracted two dog's teeth from the young man's body and argued that these caused his malady. When the medicine man compounded a concoction and gave it to the patient, it almost killed him (according to Allouez) and the Jesuit admonished the young man's family, arguing that their lack of faith may have resulted in the young man's eventual death.

More than any other single factor, the fur trade linked the French and native people together. Believing that shiny items such as copper pots and glass beads possessed what the Algonquin called *Manitou* and the Iroquoians called *Orenda* – a living spirit that Eastern Woodland peoples believed resided in all things – they attracted the attention of native people, for their spiritual as well as their utilitarian functions. The notion of *Manitou* and *Orenda* extended to what Europeans regarded as inanimate objects such as trees and rocks. Jesuit missionaries observed Wendat people giving offerings of tobacco to a rock near a lake, asking it to grant them a safe voyage. Some years later, a Dutch trader drowned near the site after mocking the rituals the Mohawk performed for the rock's *Orenda*. The Indians claimed that the *Orenda* caused his boat to capsize.

Alcohol and Native People

Missionaries and traders could not help but note how quickly native people took to alcohol. Put off by its bitter taste at first, they learned to enjoy the strange sensation it produced, seeing it as a sort of shortcut to encounters with the supernatural. Traditionally, if a native person sought a supernatural encounter, he had to go on a quest in which he deprived himself of food, water, and rest. Such deprivation often did result in the person hallucinating, and with any luck he would have a vision that would guide him through the rest of his life. One young man, for example, after fasting for several days claimed to have seen an old man with long white hair descend from the heavens. The old man warned him about many evil spirits who could have waylaid him. The old man then held out a piece of human flesh; seeing the young man recoil, he withdrew it and offered him bear's meat instead. The young man took the bear's meat and ate it. Years later, he attributed his success as a hunter to his accepting the bear meat, rather than the human flesh. Had he taken human flesh, he believed he may have been more successful in war.

In addition to providing a shortcut to the supernatural, alcohol loosened social restrictions in native communities. In the small, close-knit communities of the Eastern Woodlands, native people often strove for harmony and repressed animosities. Alcohol, however, gave individuals an excuse to act on their animosities and repressed hatreds. Since native people regarded alcohol as a spirit, drunken individuals could not be held responsible for any mayhem they might cause. The fault, native people believed, lay with the alcohol that he or she had ingested.

At first, chiefs controlled trade with Europeans. Natives thought of the trade as the gifts that would be given to their community leaders and then distributed. The French quickly learned that they had to adopt the trade protocols of native people. To native people, trade went beyond a mere commercial exchange. They regarded it as part of a friendship and alliance. European missionaries and diplomats noted that trade goods, often in the form of presents, had to accompany words in order for the latter to have any weight in native diplomacy. Native people soon learned, however, how to play off one trader against another and how to drive the best bargain for themselves. During their earliest exchanges with Europeans, native people often took whatever metal goods a trader offered, but once they realized that one trading vessel would be followed by another, they learned to be patient.

La Salle and Louisiana

The French did not begin to think in terms of colonizing what is now the southeastern United States until the latter part of the seventeenth century. Committed to a strategy of controlling and occupying the interior of the continent, the French sent expeditions under Robert La Salle to explore the Mississippi River and the Gulf Coast. In the 1670s, expeditions down into the Mississippi Valley by La Salle and Père Marquette found a landscape with a sparse Native American population. While La Salle did not reach the Gulf Coast during this initial exploration, he correctly surmised that the Mississippi flowed all the way to the Gulf of Mexico. Grasping the strategic significance of controlling the Mississippi River, the French Crown approved of La Salle's plan to establish a colony on the Gulf Coast. La Salle's naming the region Louisiana in honor of King Louis XIV may have helped him in gaining approval for his plan.

In 1684, La Salle returned to North America via the Gulf of Mexico. However, never having approached the Mississippi from the seaward side, he missed the entrance to the river and his ship, *La belle,* eventually ran aground and wrecked at Matagorda Bay off the coast of Spanish Texas, more than 400 miles west of his intended destination. Uncertain as to his location, La Salle established a settlement that he dubbed Fort St Louis. La Salle made several failed attempts to reach the Mississippi by a landward route. Frustrated with what they perceived as La Salle's incompetent leadership, some of his own colonists ultimately murdered him. Soon after La Salle's death, the local Karankawa Indians killed or captured most of the failed colony's survivors.

Despite La Salle's failure, the French remained determined to link Louisiana to Canada. In the late seventeenth and early eighteenth centuries, the French established posts along the length of the Mississippi River. In the south, they constructed the Arkansas Post among the Quapaw people, while building small military posts and trading establishments along the Gulf Coast at Biloxi and Mobile Bay. Unlike their efforts in Canada, the French made almost no attempts to convert the native people of the Southeast to Christianity. Instead, they concentrated on trade and securing native people's loyalty as military allies against potential English westward expansion efforts. The French also attempted to insert themselves as peace mediators in an attempt to end a conflict between the Choctaw and Chickasaw that they viewed as detrimental to trade.

Unlike Canada, which depended heavily on the fur trade, the Louisiana colony imported Africans to work in tobacco and indigo. Fearful that Indians and enslaved Africans might unite against them, the French assigned many blacks to their militias who fought Indians. To further sow antipathies between Africans and Indians, the French turned rebellious slaves over to the natives to be burned to death.

In another sharp departure from their behavior in Canada, the French treated many of the smaller Indian nations along the Gulf Coast and the lower Mississippi with contempt. Like their English counterparts in the Carolinas, the French developed a slave trade in the Southeast that relied heavily on Indians turning over captives to them. The majority of these captives from smaller Indian nations would then be shipped off to sugar plantations in the French West Indies, where, like their counterparts in the English possessions of Barbados and Jamaica, they would quickly be worked to death.

However, the French encountered difficulties with the Natchez people. The last vestige of the Mississippian culture, the Natchez still had powerful central chiefs, thought to be relatives of the sun, who had the power of life and death over their subjects. In the 1720s, the French commandant at Fort Rosalie demanded that the Natchez move their grand village to make way for a tobacco plantation. French livestock, permitted to run free, soon wandered into unfenced Natchez maize fields, destroying their crops. The Natchez retaliated by killing and eating the offending animals; the enraged French demanded compensation for their lost livestock.

In 1729, the Natchez revolted, carrying out a carefully planned attack in which they slew most of the garrison of Fort Rosalie. In the attack, 240 French lost their lives, including the some 140 soldiers that comprised the garrison. The Natchez also seized 50 French women and children as captives, as well as 200 African slaves, many of whom later chose to ally themselves with their captors. The losses at Fort Rosalie amounted to about 10 percent of Louisiana's French population. Lacking sufficient troops, the French persuaded their Choctaw allies to go to war against their traditional Natchez enemies in return for generous presents. In the early 1730s, the Choctaw destroyed most of the Natchez villages and turned over hundreds of captives to the French, who transported them to the West Indies. Some of the Natchez managed to escape to the villages of other native peoples, such as the Creek, Catawba, and Chickasaw, where they would be incorporated into those nations. While the French succeeded in destroying the Natchez, the conflict emphasized their dependence on native allies.

Numerous and powerful, peoples of the southeastern interior such as the Cherokee, Catawba, Creek, Chickasaw, and Choctaw, unlike many of the peoples of the Gulf Coast and lower Mississippi, could not be bullied by the French; indeed, they realized that the French competed with their English foes for influence and alliances with native peoples. Both sides would frequently employ Indians as military proxies. For much of the seventeenth and eighteenth centuries, these powerful groups of native people formed a sort of buffer zone between the French and English colonies in the southeastern interior, a region few Europeans ventured into.

French relations with native peoples in Canada differed significantly from those in the American Southeast. In Canada, the French found themselves dependent upon native people as willing laborers in the fur trade. Rather than dictate to native people, the French secured their cooperation by offering trade goods that they first desired, and later became dependent upon. While the French attempted to convert the native peoples of Canada to Christianity, they also discovered that this weakened their native allies and made them susceptible to assaults by their native enemies. Unlike their countrymen in Canada, the French in the Southeast hoped to grow crops such as tobacco and indigo for a worldwide market. Whereas in Canada the French followed a policy of friendship, even kinship, with native people, in Louisiana they pushed native people aside and held them at arm's length. However, the French also recognized that they needed larger, more powerful groups of native peoples as allies against the English, who competed with them for the resources of the American Southeast.

4

English and Native People in the Southeast

Only five years after Cristóbal Colón's landfall in the Caribbean, England became the second European nation to launch expeditions to the New World. In 1497 and 1499, the English sent their first explorations, under the command of the Italian mariner Giovanni Caboto, which skirted the coastline of North America near what is now the mouth of the St Lawrence River, where he "discovered" Newfoundland – a misnomer that indicates how Europeans thought about the New World and their level of ethnocentrism. Surely as old as any other piece of real estate on the globe, Europeans classified Newfoundland as "new" simply because they did not previously know about it. Caboto also discovered the Grand Banks, the rich fishing grounds off Newfoundland's shores that teemed with cod – a find of great interest in Europe, which had a great number of meatless days on the Church calendar (fish did not count as meat). A contemporaneous second-hand report about Caboto's voyage asserted "that sea is covered with fishes, which are caught not only with the net but with baskets, a stone being tied to them in order that the baskets may sink in the water ... they will bring so many fishes that this kingdom will no longer have need of Iceland, from which country there comes a very great store of fish." Some historians suspect that it is possible

"Times Are Altered with Us": American Indians from First Contact to the New Republic,
First Edition. Roger M. Carpenter.
© 2015 John Wiley & Sons, Inc. Published 2015 by John Wiley & Sons, Inc.

that at least a few European fishermen already knew about the Grand Banks even before Cristóbal Colón's voyage. However, no records exist to confirm these suspicions. Given the competiveness of the European fishing industry of the time, it is highly unlikely that fishermen shared secrets about rich fishing grounds with their rivals.

Despite Caboto's report about the Grand Banks and his assertion they could provide food for England's swelling population, the island nation found itself preoccupied with domestic political, economic, and religious strife for the next six decades, hampering its willingness and ability to mount overseas ventures, with the notable exception of their incursions into Ireland.

Ireland, the Foundation of English Colonial Strategy

Just as the Spanish and Portuguese used the Canary Islands off the coast of North Africa to stage what amounted to dress rehearsals for their invasions of the Caribbean and the Americas, so would the English use Ireland to form the rough outlines of the set of strategies their colonists later employed against native people in North America. One of these strategies involved the use of "plantations and palisades." In short, this strategy called for the English to build palisades, or forts. Large landholders received title to the lands between the forts and imported Englishmen of lesser means to till the soil for them. In effect, this created an "oil blot" strategy; colonists, if all went well, slowly filled in the land between the palisades, gradually making the island (at least according to the English) into a replica of England.

In order to achieve these goals, the English took a page from Spain's strategy of New World colonization, namely terrorizing the inhabitants. As practitioners of terror, few English commanders exceeded Sir Humphrey Gilbert. A favorite of Queen Elizabeth, Gilbert quickly made a name for himself as one of the most successful commanders of the English campaign in Ireland. Once, when preparing to parley with Irish chieftains, Gilbert made it a point to have the path to his tent lined with Irish heads. Besides his success in subduing the Irish, Gilbert also became a member of a group of investors who advocated English settlement of the Americas called the "west countrymen."

The West Countrymen

The west countrymen – despite possessing imperfect knowledge about the New World – advanced several arguments as to why England should establish colonies in the Americas. The best-known collection of these arguments appeared in *Discourse of Western Planting* by Richard Hakluyt the Younger (his uncle, Richard Hakluyt the Elder, an armchair navigator like his nephew, was just as staunch an advocate of English overseas colonization). The Hakluyts advanced several key arguments. The English needed territory in the Americas in order to compete economically and strategically with Spain. Colonies would help solve the nation's seemingly intractable economic problems by shipping large numbers of idle Englishmen and women overseas where they could be put to work. It would also give the English the opportunity, as the Hakluyts put it, to "plant sincere religion" in the New World. The Hakluyts also speculated (basing their argument on the Black Legend) that the native people of the Americas would welcome the Protestant English, preferring their friendship, trade, and religion over that of the Catholic Spaniards, who had so grievously mistreated them.

In the 1560s, voyages led by Martin Frobisher attempted to find the hoped-for Northwest Passage. Frobisher did not find such a passage, but he did manage to capture an Inuit man, bring him back to England, and place him on exhibit as a curiosity. On a voyage that took him to Baffin Island, off the coast of Canada, in 1578, Frobisher noticed large numbers of spiders. Having read that spiders indicated the presence of gold, Frobisher had his crew load his vessel with tons of the black rock that seemed to be the only resource on Baffin Island. Arriving back in England, Frobisher ordered the rock to be assayed, fully expecting that it would contain gold. It turned out to be nothing more than what it appeared to be: black rock.

Roanoke

Queen Elizabeth rewarded Sir Humphrey Gilbert for his services in Ireland with a "patent" or license to establish colonies in North America. Expansive and wholly unrealistic, the patent granted Gilbert the whole of present-day Canada. But in 1583, while on an expedition, Gilbert's ship disappeared. With his death, his patent passed to another of the Queen's favorites, his half-brother, Sir Walter Raleigh.

More determined (at least at first) than his late half-brother in establishing a New World colony, Raleigh sponsored a reconnaissance expedition in 1584. Commanded by Arthur Barlowe, the expedition explored present-day coastal North Carolina. Barlowe encountered friendly native people whom he described as living "after the manner of the golden age" and offered a very favorable account of the country that emphasized its fertility. While the peaceful encounter seemed to confirm the Hakluyts' notions that native people would welcome the English as a counterweight to the wicked Spanish, misunderstandings could not be avoided. When the English asked the natives the name of the country, they replied "Winganagoa," which really meant "you wear fine clothes." Praising the good manners of the coastal Algonquians in his report, Barlowe thought that relations between the English and the natives had gotten off on the right foot.

Sir Walter Raleigh's next move, however, caused relations to take a giant step backward. Rather than dispatching colonists on the next expedition, Raleigh sent soldiers. The next year, 1585, 100 troops under the command of Ralph Lane arrived. Perhaps taking the hospitality the natives extended the previous year for granted, Raleigh made no provision for resupplying Lane and his men. The English – much like De Soto four decades earlier – fully expected the Indians to feed them. The arrival of so many Englishmen – and they were all men – taxed native food resources. The notable absence of women and children – and the presence of European weaponry – probably caused the natives to question the intentions of these strangers.

Their choice of where to set up their colony must have caused further questioning among the natives. In a coastal region of rivers that teemed with fish and had rich, fertile soils, the English chose to set up their colony on a small sandy island called Roanoke off the North Carolina coast. The English did not consider the island's poor soil to be a drawback, since they did not intend to plant crops. Rather, the English chose Roanoke because they thought it would be easier to defend. However, the possibility of an Indian attack did not worry them; Lane worried more about the Spanish detecting and assaulting the colony. Pinched between the coast of North Carolina on the landward side and a chain of barrier islands on the seaward side, Roanoke would have been difficult for the Spanish to find and attack. But the same difficulties that the sandbars and shoals in the waters around Roanoke created for potential enemies also created hazards for the English in terms of resupplying the colony.

A veteran of the English campaigns in Ireland, Ralph Lane thought he could employ the tactics he had used there against the American "savages." In the spring of 1586, weary of English bullying and running short of food for his own people, Wingina, the leader of Roanoke's Algonquians, refused to continue to provision Lane and his men. Lane resorted to the tactics that had served him so well in Ireland: if the natives would not do what he wanted them to do, he would terrorize them into compliance.

Launching a surprise night attack that killed Wingina and several other Indians, Lane succeeded in his goal of terrorizing the natives; however, he soon discovered that he had succeeded all too well. In Ireland, the outcome of such a raid would have seen the natives providing Lane and his men with the provisions they demanded to avoid further reprisals. But the Roanoke natives reacted in a way that Lane could not have anticipated: they left. Belatedly realizing that they had managed to chase away the people who had provided them with their only source of subsistence, Lane and his garrison began to starve. Fortunately for them, English ships arrived at Roanoke late in the spring of 1586, and Lane and his hungry men begged the captain of the flotilla to take them back to England. The captain refused, pointing out that he had brought a ship laden with supplies for the colony. That night however, a storm came up, sinking the supply ship. Unable to supply the colony, the captain yielded to the entreaties of Lane and his men, and evacuated them.

The next year, 1587, Sir Walter Raleigh sent another contingent, this time consisting of colonists rather than soldiers. The 94 English included 17 women and nine children. Raleigh had chosen John White as the leader of the colony. White appears to have been an odd choice for the job. Insofar as can be determined, he had never governed anything. He had some slight experience in overseas exploration, having accompanied Martin Frobisher on one of his expeditions. He did, however, have a reputation as an artist. When Frobisher returned from an expedition with a captured Inuit man, woman, and infant, White rendered them in watercolors in their native garb. He would take his watercolors with him to Roanoke, where he would paint images of North American flora and fauna. Most significantly, he would be the first European to make artistic renderings of native peoples from life.

Unaware that Lane and his soldiers had been evacuated, the colonists and their neophyte leader were at first perplexed – and possibly alarmed – to find them missing. However, they soon deduced what had happened. The colonists discovered, however, that even though Lane was gone, they had to live with the consequences of his actions. Relations with native people ran the gamut from occasional friendship (but more often avoidance) to, at times, outright hostility.

Running short of supplies, White made the decision to return to England to acquire provisions. Bidding farewell to his daughter and granddaughter (Virginia Dare, the first English child born in the New World), White returned to England in late 1587. He picked a bad time to return. Fearful of the armada that the Spanish were constructing (easily the worst kept secret in Europe, the construction of the Spanish Armada could not be concealed; everyone knew about it and where it would be going once it embarked) the English, anticipating that they would need every ship they could get their hands on, embargoed all vessels entering their ports. White appealed to Sir Walter Raleigh to use his influence with the Queen to allow him to set sail for Roanoke with supplies, but Sir Walter, like much of the Queen's inner circle, found himself absorbed in preparing for the impending Spanish attack.

Even after the dispersal and defeat of the Armada in 1588, White still had difficulty securing supplies and a ship to carry them – and him – back to Roanoke. White finally returned to Roanoke in August 1590. Arriving off the coast of the island at night, White and the crew of the ship sought to signal the colonists by playing familiar English tunes on horns and other instruments. The next day, White led a group of sailors ashore, who found a silent, deserted palisade. The cabins within the palisade had begun to deteriorate and wildlife lived on the grounds. White and the sailors who accompanied him saw no signs of violence, and he found that his books and maps had been placed in chests and buried (presumably by the colonists as they made ready to evacuate Roanoke), then disinterred and scattered about (presumably by the Indians after the colonists had left). White also found his armor, which had nearly rusted through.

More significantly, the party discovered the word "Croatan" carved into a tree. Croatan signified a nearby island and the native people who lived there. White took this to mean that the colonists could be found there. The lack of a Maltese Cross – the sign the English agreed they would use should they be forced to leave Roanoke under duress – next to the word Croatan gave White hope that he would find the colonists alive and well. However, White had difficulty convincing the captain of the vessel to sail to Croatan. The issue became a moot point that evening as a storm blew up, damaging the vessel and causing her to snap two of her three anchor chains. Unable to remain safely in the waters around Roanoke in this condition, the ship, with John White still aboard, made its way back to England, the wistful White looking west at the retreating shoreline and wondering what had become of his daughter, his grandchild, and the other colonists.

After 1590, a veil of silence fell over Roanoke; the English made no effort to ascertain what had befallen the colonists. Sir Walter Raleigh, the sponsor of the colony, became interested in other colonizing ventures in South America and the Caribbean. With the death of his patron Queen Elizabeth in 1603, he found himself at odds with the new monarch, James I. Accusing Raleigh of being a member of a conspiracy against the King, James I had him placed on trial for treason. Convicted and sentenced to death, Raleigh was granted parole by James to lead an expedition to Venezuela. However, Raleigh's men assaulted a Spanish fort in Venezuela, taking England to the brink of an unwanted war. After the Spanish ambassador demanded that Raleigh be executed, James reinstated his death sentence and sent him to the gallows in 1618.

As for the Roanoke colonists, their fate continues to intrigue historians to this day. No trace of the missing colonists has ever been found. When the English finally mounted their next attempt to establish a colony in North America in 1607, some of the native peoples of the Chesapeake region stated that the Roanoke survivors had lived in one of their villages for years. However, with the arrival of another colonization effort that established itself next to the James River, Powhatan, the paramount chief of the coastal Algonquians, ordered all of the Roanoke English to be slain.

The Powhatan Confederacy

The Powhatan people of coastal Virginia took their name from the man who governed them as their paramount chieftain. Powhatan (Wahunsonacock) did not enjoy the strong central control exercised by the Mississippian chiefs whom the Spanish encountered in the American Southeast in the previous century, and unlike Mississippian chiefs, Powhatan did not claim descent from or a blood relationship to a deity. Nevertheless, he exercised a great deal of power over the 20,000–25,000 people who lived between Virginia's Atlantic coast and the Piedmont.

Consisting of about 30 tribes, the peoples of the Powhatan Confederacy, much like other native peoples of the Eastern Woodlands, followed a seasonal round of subsistence. In the spring, they set up camps near the coast and rivers where they fished, gathered shellfish, and collected edible aquatic pants. In the summer,

Figure 4.1 A Virginia Indian. This image appears to be loosely based on illustrations by English artist John White, who painted some of the first images of native people from life. Detail from *Nova Virginiae tabula*, Amsterdam, 1633. Courtesy of Darlington Library, University of Pittsburgh.

they gathered in villages of 20 to 30 houses that held between 100 and 200 people. In these villages they planted and tended their fields of maize, beans, and squash. In the fall, the men went on deer hunts, while the women and children gathered edible nuts and berries.

Much like other native peoples of the Eastern Woodlands, the Powhatan practiced a gendered division of labor. Men hunted, fished, waged war, and conducted diplomacy. Women performed agricultural tasks such as planting and harvesting crops, prepared food, took care of the village and the children, and gathered wild edible and medicinal plants. Men occasionally assisted women in the heavier work of their agricultural endeavors, such as clearing new fields for planting.

While Mississippian chiefs rested their claims to authority on their supposed relationship with native deities – specifically, the sun – Powhatan accrued power through more secular means, by employing his status as the head of a large and extended kinship network. When he defeated other chiefs, rather than remove them, Powhatan often co-opted those he trusted by bringing them into his kinship network by having them marry one of his daughters, or alternatively, Powhatan (who had many wives) would marry one of their children. By marrying subordinate chiefs off to his many children, Powhatan placed them in a position where they would enjoy the mutual benefits of kinship. If a subordinate chief later proved resistive, Powhatan could replace them with one of his blood relations.

A loosely organized affair in comparison to the Mississippian chiefdoms of the previous century, the Powhatan Confederacy worked by subordinate chiefs taking tribute given to them and channeling it to Powhatan, who then redistributed it to other villages in the form of maize or other foodstuffs. Powhatan also consolidated power by requiring lesser chiefs to provide men for war parties against Siouan speaking peoples to the west. Since proving oneself as a warrior allowed men the highly valued opportunity to gain stature in this society, Powhatan and his subordinate chiefs had little trouble finding willing volunteers.

Jamestown

It is difficult to ascertain what Powhatan and his followers thought of the English when they built their fort named Jamestown in just about the worst possible location in the Chesapeake region; one would think that the absence of an Indian village in the area would have told them something. As it is, Powhatan's thoughts regarding the initial English landing are not recorded. It is possible that he may have initially regarded the English as another tribe that could be incorporated into his confederacy.

Coastal Algonquians already had some experience with Europeans. European ships had put into Chesapeake Bay, sending parties ashore in search of fresh water and other provisions. At times, the crews of European ships kidnapped Indians, shipped them to Europe, and sold them into slavery. Opechancanough, Powhatan's half-brother or uncle (depending on the source one consults), may, as mentioned in Chapter 2, have been captured by the Spanish in the 1570s. Taken to Mexico City, he took the name of Luís de Velasco (after his Christian godfather, the Viceroy of Mexico). However, by convincing his captors that he had converted to Christianity, he returned to the Chesapeake, where the Spanish intended to put him to work as a guide and interpreter for a Jesuit mission. Once on his own turf, however, Opechancanough convinced his tribesmen to join him in slaying the missionaries.

Yet, as in the case of the St Lawrence Iroquoians and the French, Powhatan recognized that the English had superior technology, and he probably hoped they would be willing to trade with the natives. At first, the Powhatan people kept their distance from the English, probably until they could ascertain why they had come and what they wanted.

As had been the case with Roanoke, the English allowed military considerations to override all other concerns. Fearful of an attack by the Spanish – but not the Indians – the English sited Jamestown next to a swamp, thinking the Spanish would find it too difficult to attack from that direction, allowing the garrison to leave that sector of their palisade lightly defended.

The Powhatans must have regarded the English as crazy for selecting such a site. Not only did the nearby swamp teem with disease-carrying mosquitoes, but the James River, for eight or nine months of the year, flowed slowly and sluggishly. In the summer months, it developed at its mouth a "salt plug," where sea water entered the river, raising the saline content of the river water, the source of drinking water for the colonists. The sluggishness of the James contributed to the misery that the colonists experienced at Jamestown, since they deposited their bodily wastes into the river. Believing the old European adage that running water purified itself, it seems not to have occurred to them that the indolent waters of the James meant that the waste stayed near Jamestown – and hence in their drinking water.

Watching all this, the natives must have been perplexed and certainly unimpressed by the strangers' apparent stupidity and weakness. Nine months after the first colonists arrived in April 1609, 66 of the original 104 had perished, mostly from disease. The Powhatans probably thought that if hostilities between themselves and the colonists should break out, defeating them would be easy; they seemed to do a good job of dying without any help from the natives.

During the time when Powhatan was apparently still taking a wait-and-see approach with the English, there occurred the famous, some say fabled, incident in which Pocahontas, Powhatan's favorite daughter, rescued John Smith, then the governor of the Virginia colony. Smith had been captured by Opechancanough and taken to Powhatan. According to Smith, Powhatan sentenced him to death. But it is possible that Smith may have wholly misinterpreted events.

Pocahontas, whose name, roughly translated, can mean "little mischievous" or "little wanton," had already come to the attention of the English. She sometimes hung around the fort and as a girl of about nine or 10 years of age attracted attention by turning cartwheels in the nude. Smith related that at the last minute, Pocahontas threw herself between him and the club-wielding executioner. Powhatan then relented, and allowed Smith to live.

While this incident became very famous – being portrayed in nineteenth-century engravings and in twentieth- and twenty-first-century films – there are different ways of interpreting it. One distinct possibility is that even if events did unfold in the manner in which Smith claimed, he may have been an unwitting participant in a ritual that (at least to the natives) made him into one of Powhatan's subordinate chiefs, who would rule the English in Jamestown on his behalf. The intervention of Pocahontas (a member of Powhatan's family) on Smith's behalf, and the paramount chief's forbearance in giving Smith his life, would have signaled Smith's transformation into a subordinate of Powhatan who should accept his role as such. If that is what happened, the significance of the event (beyond that he did not die!) appears to have been lost on Smith, who seems to have been wholly unaware that he took part in a ritual, and his life may have truly never been in danger. He certainly did not regard himself as a vassal of Powhatan.

Another likely explanation is that the incident did not happen at all, and that Smith had a healthy imagination. Later in life, he wrote that he had been captured by the Turks while serving in Eastern Europe. There, a Turkish princess – a la Pocahontas – intervened to save his life and later to help him escape. Smith also did not relate the tale of his rescue by Pocahontas until 1625. By that time, anyone who could have confirmed – or debunked – his version of events – such as Pocahontas or Powhatan – had died.

Soon after the English established Jamestown, they came under attack. The Paspahegh people, one of Powhatan's subordinate tribes, and the one closest to Jamestown, may have been ordered to contain – but not kill – the English. But by making the colonists fearful of leaving the confines of their stockade, the Paspahegh indirectly killed many English by forcing them to remain in the diseased environment of their settlement.

Unable to leave Jamestown, the English ran short of provisions and resorted to eating whatever plants, roots, and small animals they could find. When they depleted the grounds of the settlement of edible plants, the situation became really gruesome, as the desperate colonists went so far as to disinter and consume their own dead. One colonist slew his wife and salted her remains to ensure that he would have a steady supply of meat. Once the authorities discovered his crime, he was tortured (to extract a confession) and executed.

When Powhatan could not subordinate the English, he resorted to other stratagems. A low-intensity conflict simmered from time to time, with inexplicable truces in which the Powhatans provided the colonists with maize before resuming hostilities. Severely burned in a gunpowder accident in 1609, John Smith returned to England to recover. His successors fell back on what they viewed as the tried and true (even though it had failed) Ralph Lane tactic of terror. In 1610, Captain George Percy led an attack against a Paspahegh village located along the James River. After slaying more than 60 Indians, and burning their wigwams and their maize fields, Percy took a native woman and her children prisoner. As the expedition sailed back to Jamestown, Percy had the children flung overboard, so that his men could use them for target practice as they swam for their lives. Upon reaching Jamestown, Percy had the woman put to death by the sword. Unfortunately for the English, the expected result of this raid – that the natives would be so terrorized that they would willingly provide foodstuffs to assuage the colonists' fury – did not materialize. Instead, the Indians retreated even further into the interior, a move that made their lives more difficult, as it distanced them from food sources on the coast, but also made it more difficult for the English to pursue their military campaign against them – and to secure the food that they needed.

English leadership employed violent strategies, probably because their prior experience in Ireland taught them that terror could keep other peoples in line. Terror could also be used, it turned out, not only against Indians but against resistive Englishmen at the lower end of the social and economic strata. A number of colonists – primarily servants – fled Jamestown to live among the Indians. While the Indians had things the runaways desired – a less restrictive environment and, most important, food – the Powhatan did not always welcome them. Englishmen who showed up at native villages expecting to be fed usually met with death instead. However, those who brought useful metal tools with them or, even better, firearms, were usually welcomed. In response, when the English recaptured the runaway servants, they put most of them to death in particularly painful and public ways as a warning to others who may be tempted to flee to the Indians.

The on and off again conflict between the colonists and the Powhatan continued for six years, ending when Pocahontas fell into English hands after being coaxed aboard a ship in 1613. Kept as a hostage to insure her father's good behavior, Pocahontas learned the English language. Converted to Anglicanism – there is some question as to the quality of her conversion – the English rechristened her "Rebecca." She also married the English planter John Rolfe. Powhatan consented to the marriage, which ushered in a period of peace between the Powhatan people and the Virginia colony. Taken to England by the Virginia Company in an effort to gain support for their enterprise, Pocahontas impressed the royal court. However, as the Rolfes departed England, Pocahontas, then about 20 years old, fell ill and died. Within a year, her father Powhatan would join her in death, and leadership of the confederacy that he built would pass to his kinsman Opechancanough.

Opechancanough's Wars

While John Rolfe helped bring about peace by marrying Pocahontas, he also helped bring about the economic salvation of the Virginia colony. In 1612, Rolfe imported a strain of tobacco more pleasing to European tastes than the native *nicotinus robustus*. Tobacco consumption had become something of a craze in England, despite King James's criticism of the habit. Nearly all of the tobacco consumed in the British Isles came from Spanish Colonies. By growing and exporting a flavorful and pleasing form of tobacco, Virginia had found its economic salvation. Colonists discovered they could make more money by growing tobacco for one year in Virginia than they could in five or 10 years in England. In order for tobacco cultivation to be profitable, however, planters needed large tracts of land as well as a sufficient number of laborers – which, of course, meant more Englishmen.

Biding his time, Opechancanough saw his opportunity to weaken the colony by inviting the English to take whatever land the Powhatan did not happen to be using at the moment. This cunning strategy dispersed colonists in isolated homesteads all over the landscape of coastal Virginia. Relations between the English and the Powhatan remained amicable until March 22, 1622. On that day, Opechancanough's warriors launched a well-coordinated surprise attack, killing approximately 350 Englishmen in a single day, which represented about a third of the colony's total population. The terrified survivors sought refuge in Jamestown, where after recovering from the shock and horror of the attack, they realized they now had the perfect excuse to exterminate the coastal Algonquians.

For his part, Opechancanough expected the sudden and stinging defeat to chastise the English and to force them to evacuate Virginia. But while Opechancanough's men burned plantations and tobacco fields, the English prepared to retaliate. Over the next decade the English and the Powhatan Confederacy engaged in a low-intensity, yet savage conflict. Determined to either capture or kill Opechancanough, the English convinced a number of native leaders to gather for a purported peace conference in 1623. Proposing a toast of sack – a cheap, watered-down wine – to open the proceedings, the English drugged the Indians. As the native chiefs lay on the floor incapacitated, the English drew their swords and finished them off. Unfortunately for the English, the wily Opechancanough avoided this conference. The conflict dragged on until 1632 when the English finally offered a real peace, forcing Opechancanough to surrender vast tracts of land along the Rappahannock and Potomac Rivers.

In April 1644, Opechancanough tried again, launching another surprise attack that killed over 400 colonists. By this time, however, the English population of Virginia stood at over 10,000. The colonists quickly recovered, went on the offensive, and defeated Opechancanough and his warriors in fairly short order. Reputedly over 100 years old at this time, Opechancanough had to be carried from place to place on a litter. When visitors wished to speak to him, a young assistant whom the old chief kept on hand had to hold Opechancanough's eyelids open so that he could see who he was talking to. Captured in 1646, the English took Opechancanough to Jamestown, caged him, and placed him on public display. Opechancanough complained bitterly to Governor Berkeley that had the fortunes of war been reversed, he would not have made a spectacle of him. A soldier assigned to guard Opechancanough shot him dead, killing the last of the Powhatan paramount chiefs. In the treaty following the war, the English restricted the natives to lands north of the York River. But in time, the colony would require more land. The next spurt of English colonial expansion in Virginia would result in a civil war among the English themselves, but native people would be drawn into this conflict as well.

Bacon's Rebellion

In the three decades after Opechancanough's death, native people and Virginia colonists coexisted in relative peace. To be sure, the two peoples kept their distance from one another for the most part. The 1646 treaty that ended Opechancanough's second war against the colony guaranteed Virginia's Algonquian lands north of the York River. However the colony's English population had increased markedly in the three decades following the treaty. Unlike the desperate early days at Jamestown that saw the majority of new colonists perish from disease and starvation, most new arrivals – the great majority of them indentured servants – now survived their terms of indenture, which entitled them to their "freedom dues." These dues, a final payment to the indentured servants upon the completion of their indenture contract, consisted of tools, clothing, seed for planting, and, best of all, land.

By the 1670s, large planters – mainly those who arrived early or their descendants – owned the majority of the land on the Chesapeake's eastern neck. Newly freed indentured servants often had to settle for land farther west, on frontier, which placed them at a disadvantage. They ended up on land that bore soils unsuited for growing tobacco and lacked access to waterways that would enable

Figure 4.2 A Susquehannock Village. The European artist was apparently unfamiliar with North America, placing what appears to be a coconut tree in this scene. While native people would not have been unfamiliar with European livestock by this time, they were not herding the animals, as is indicated in the lower right-hand portion of this image. Detail from *New map of the north parts of America*, London, 1720. Courtesy of Darlington Library, University of Pittsburgh.

them to transport their crops to the port at Jamestown. In other words, they could settle in areas granted to the Indians by the treaty of 1646 – but at their own risk.

Enjoying a profitable deerskin trade with the natives, Governor William Berkeley sought to keep peace with the natives north of the York River. In order to do so, Berkeley forbade settlement north of the York. The peace, however, came to an end one Sunday morning in April 1676 as a group of colonists made their way to church. Passing a plantation, they saw the overseer sprawled across the front porch, bleeding profusely. Going to the man's assistance, they heard him gasp out "Doegs, Doegs" before he expired. A small group of native people, the Doegs, had previously had altercations with the overseer that usually revolved around the plantation's hogs invading and destroying the Indians' cornfields. In retaliation, some Doegs appeared at the plantation with the intent of liberating (and probably eating) some of the offending pigs. The overseer intervened and violence ensued.

Responding to this episode, the militias of Maryland and Virginia quickly mobilized and set off in pursuit of the culprits. But rather than finding the offending group of Doegs, the militiamen attacked a Susquehannock village. One of the Maryland officers quickly realized the mistake – the Susquehannock had alliances with both colonies – and ordered his men to cease fire. Now the Virginia militia officers demanded a parley, to which the Susquehannock sent five of their leaders to negotiate. Rather than beginning negotiations, the English executed the Susquehannock chiefs. Realizing what had happened to their headmen, the Susquehannock refused to surrender, forcing the ill-disciplined colonial militias to lay siege to their palisaded village. Over the next several weeks, many of the Indians slipped through the militia lines at night. Finally, the remaining Susquehannock waited until a particularly dark night and made a mass breakout, which resulted in nearly all of them escaping. Retaliating for the slaying of their five leading men, the Susquehannock launched a war against the Virginians, attacking farms and plantations on the frontier.

The colonists on the frontier demanded that the government of the colony allow them to go on the offensive against the Indians. Turning aside their demands, Governor Berkeley instead suggested building a series of nine forts to protect the area. Virginians on the frontier responded angrily to this proposal, claiming that the forts would be little more than traps and that Berkeley and his cronies would benefit financially from their construction.

At this moment, Nathaniel Bacon stepped into the scene. Recently arrived from England, and related to Governor Berkeley by marriage, Bacon had used his wealth and connections to set himself up with a plantation rather quickly. Unlike wealthy Virginians who arrived earlier in the century, Bacon had to settle for a plantation situated in the backcountry, among many of the frontiersmen who wished to embark on a campaign of extermination against the local Indians. In many respects, England's elitist class society had been transported to the Chesapeake; while the settlers and the small planters on the frontier resented Berkeley and the larger planters in the eastern portion of the colony, they still sought someone from the upper classes to lead them.

Bacon offered to lead the vigilantes in a campaign of extermination against the Virginia Indians. While the Susquehannock had, understandably, launched assaults against the Virginians, Bacon and his vigilantes did not discriminate in their choice of targets. Bacon and his men attacked all Indian peoples they encountered, including Pamunkeys, Occoneechee, and other groups who had never engaged in hostilities against the colony. In one instance, Bacon convinced a group of Indians to attack a band of Appomattox Indians. After their successful assault, Bacon and his men turned on and slew their new native allies, taking, in turn, the valuable packs of furs that had been seized from the Appomattox. Bacon and his men also ransacked native villages, taking with them anything of value, including Indians, whom they then sold into slavery.

All of this took place in defiance of Governor Berkeley, who ordered Bacon and his followers to desist. In response, Bacon and his men attacked Berkeley and his followers, transforming an Indian war into a civil war among the Virginia colonists, a conflict heralded in US history texts as Bacon's Rebellion. Although Bacon and company successfully drove Governor Berkeley and his followers from Jamestown, Bacon did not succeed in his revolt. In October of 1676, he fell ill from some sort of fever and died. Thereafter his leaderless army dissolved and the rebellion dissolved with them.

The next year, after a royal commission decided that Virginia had wronged the native peoples within its borders, English representatives and native peoples signed what became known as the Treaty of Middle Plantation. The new treaty stipulated that native peoples would henceforth be English subjects, prohibited colonists from settling within three miles of a native village, and in effect created the first Indian reservations. The treaty also forbade native people from leaving their villages or reserves without first obtaining permission from the local magistrate.

The Indian Slave Trade

When the English began to settle the region of the present-day Carolinas and Georgia, they found, as they had elsewhere, that native peoples eagerly sought to acquire European goods, particularly metal wares. While native people thought they saw what Algonquin termed *Manitou* in the shininess of metal goods, they also realized that they served a practical purpose. Steel knives and hatchets gave

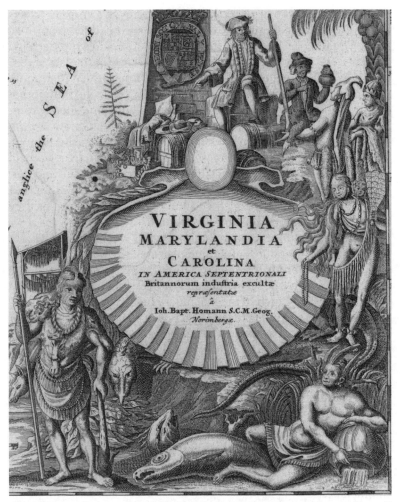

Figure 4.3 Natives and English traders. North America, its peoples and animals are portrayed as exotic in this illustration. The viewer also gets the impression that native people regarded English goods as exotic. While Native Americans may not have thought of European goods as exotic, within the space of a generation or two, they regarded woolen cloth and metal goods as necessities. Detail from *Virginia, Marylandia et Carolina in America Septentrionali*, London, 1714. Courtesy of Darlington Library, University of Pittsburgh.

coastal peoples – who usually came into contact with European traders first – a decided advantage over their native enemies who lived farther inland. In the 1670s, the primary commodity the Carolina Indians could offer English traders was deerskins. In the late seventeenth and early eighteenth centuries, the English exported more than 50,000 deerskins per year from the Carolinas to the mother country, where they became gloves, book bindings, and shop aprons.

The advent of the deerskin trade shifted native men away from hunting for food to hunting to supply a distant market. By hunting for deer hides, native men increased the workload of native women, obligating them to process the hides by cleaning the tissue and hair from them, and then tanning them to prevent rotting. Both native men and native women benefited from the trade, however, as they became part of a new consumer revolution.

It turned out, however, that English traders would pay even more for another commodity: human beings. Like the Spanish, French, and Dutch, the English discovered that immense profits could be realized through the growing and processing of sugar in the Caribbean. While much of the machinery on Caribbean plantations, such as the grinders that crushed sugar cane, depended on animal or wind power, the vast majority of labor had to be done by human beings.

Shortly after Cristóbal Colón's landfall in the Caribbean, the Spanish dreamed of finding vast quantities of gold there. In less than a decade, the Spanish realized the islands contained only minute quantities of the precious metal. However, the Spanish had already experimented with growing sugar, a profitable Old World crop they had raised successfully in the Canary Islands. Originating in the Far East, sugar cane had been introduced to Europe by the explorer Marco Polo, and there it became one of the most sought-after commodities.

At first, Spaniards in the Caribbean forced the native people of the islands to plant, care for, and harvest sugar cane and then process it into a finished product for export. Unfortunately, thanks to one of the key factors of the Columbian exchange – European pathogens – most Caribbean natives who worked in the sugar fields perished in short order. This led to the importation of African slaves, peoples who had the advantage of sharing with Europeans a certain level of immunity to Old World diseases. Still, the immense profitability of sugar meant that even laborers who died quickly could still be useful.

The slaughter of enormous numbers of deer resulted in a dwindling of the white-tailed deer population, followed by a dwindling in the trade of their hides, so English traders and their French counterparts sought new ways of making a profit, by turning to the trade in human beings. With the reduction of the southeastern deer herds, native peoples also had to find a new commodity to trade for the metal items and cloth on which they had become dependent. Most significantly, native warriors in the Southeast had by this time also become dependent upon European firearms. European traders recognized that trading firearms to native people made them into repeat customers. Once a native warrior had a firearm, he had to return to the trader in order to obtain lead, to be melted and molded into shot, and gunpowder. Unable to repair firearms themselves, native people attempted to remain in the good graces of their European trade partners, who would provide blacksmiths to repair broken weapons. The trade in firearms instigated an arms race in the Southeast. Native warriors without guns found themselves at a disadvantage against any foes who had managed to acquire European weaponry.

Beginning in the 1670s and continuing into the early eighteenth century, southeastern coastal peoples such as the Westos and the Yamasees provided English traders with captives in exchange for firearms, powder, and shot. For the English, native captives who could be transported to the Caribbean and forced to work in the sugar fields were far more valuable than deerskins. Very few native captives remained in the Southeast. Those native slaves who were forced to work on plantations in the Southeast had ways to escape unavailable to enslaved Africans. For one thing, native slaves knew the landscape, and for another, they had the advantage of being able to flee to their former community, where they could count on help from their kinsmen.

Transported to Barbados and the Bahamas, most native captives from the Southeast, like most other slaves in the Caribbean, would have been worked to death in short order. Secure in the knowledge that slave ships from Africa always stopped in the Caribbean first (sugar planters also paid more for slaves than did their counterparts on the North American mainland), the very steep profit margin in sugar gave Caribbean planters little incentive to treat their laborers well or even to keep them alive.

However, rival English colonies, unable to crack the monopoly that the Carolina colony had on trade with the Westos, recruited other native people to attack, capture, and enslave them. In this endeavor, rival English traders recruited the Savannas, new arrivals to the region related to the Shawnees.

In time, English traders in the Carolinas – who boasted that Charles Town reached 1,000 miles into the continent – began trading with the Creek. Farther inland, and consisting of about 15,000 people, the Creek were encouraged by English traders to attack and capture their traditional native enemies, as well as Indians allied to the Spanish in Florida. The attacks by the Creek, and later the Yamasee – Carolina natives who became English allies – destroyed Spanish plans of defending Florida with Indian proxies. This would lead to problems in the future for the Carolinas, when the Spanish encouraged African slaves to run away to Florida. There, the Spanish set them up in so-called maroon communities, armed them, and employed them in raiding South Carolina, and later the Georgia colony.

The Yamasee War

Their success in obtaining large numbers of captives actually worked against the Yamasee in the long run. For the most part, native peoples who engaged in the slave wars were ill paid for their efforts. When native warriors could not pay in the form of captives for the powder, shot, firearms, and alcohol they had received as advance payment, English traders responded by seizing their wives and children and selling them into slavery to make good on the debts. When the Savannah fled northward to seek protection from their Shawnee relatives, leaders of the South Carolina colony and English traders paid another group, the Catawba, to pursue and capture them.

In the newly formed North Carolina colony, the Tuscarora people fought back, destroying many plantations and farms in 1711. Now North Carolina turned to South Carolina for military assistance, whose government called upon their Yamasee trade partners to augment their militia. Lacking other peoples to plunder and capture, the Yamasee assisted the two English colonies in defeating the Tuscarora. Nearly 400 Tuscarora were captured and sold into slavery. The Tuscarora War, as it came to be known, ended with the survivors who eluded the colonists and their Yamasee allies fleeing northward, where they joined their Iroquois relatives in what is now upstate New York, becoming the Sixth Nation of the Iroquois League.

Despite assisting the colonists in their war against the Tuscarora, the Yamasee, like other native peoples who participated in the slave trade, soon found themselves heavily in debt to English traders, who paid them very little for their Tuscarora captives. In addition, English traders demanded 100,000 deerskins as payment for the weapons they provided the Yamasee. When the Indians could not produce the deerskins – which would have required five years of hunting – English traders began seizing their wives and children and selling them into slavery, as they had done to satisfy other such debts.

In 1715, the Yamasee rebelled, attacking traders and plantations. The Yamasee also aligned themselves with other native peoples, such as the Catawba and the Creek, who also had grievances against the English traders. For the first time, the English in the Carolinas encountered united native peoples. Unfortunately for the Indians, the slave trade and the goods they acquired had made them dependent upon the English. Unable to acquire powder and shot, and lacking the ability and tools to repair their muskets, the Yamasee over time began to lose the war. Their role in the slave trade had also, not surprisingly, created native enemies for the Yamasee. The English now sought help from the Tuscarora, who led Iroquois warriors southward against the Yamasee. Both of the Carolina colonies also gained the help of the Cherokee, who had also become very dependent on English trade goods. The Yamasee lost the war and sustained many losses. The survivors fled to Florida, where the Spanish welcomed them as future allies against the English.

By this time the English began to realize that, while the native population of the Carolinas and Virginia had been severely reduced, it would not be in their interest to eradicate the Indians entirely. The Catawba, for instance, provided valuable services, not only as military allies in the future but as catchers of runaway slaves as the southern colonies shifted more and more toward using African slaves as their labor force. The English also recognized that they would need native peoples to fight proxy wars for them in the interior of the Southeast against Choctaws and other peoples who had allied themselves with the French.

Some native peoples, by virtue of their location and relative strength, maintained a balance of power in the interior, but still relied on European trade goods. The Cherokee, Creek, Choctaw, Chickasaw, and Catawba managed to make themselves valuable to their European allies as trade and military partners, ensuring their survival into the nineteenth century. English colonists in the South, after periods of war, peace, and then a resumption of war, learned to live with their native neighbors. They later appear to have unlearned their lessons when they instigated the trade in Native American slaves. But by exploiting divisions between native people, the English in the South also managed to sue them to secure their colonies from attack by the French and the Spanish.

The English experience would in some measure be repeated elsewhere. English colonies far to the North in New England would also engage in hostilities with native people, but would first (largely) have the comfort of a long period of peace. English actions in New England, and their acquisitiveness, as we will see, would eventually make peace impossible in the North as well.

5

Native Americans in New England

For nearly a century, the native peoples of what later became known as New England experienced sporadic encounters with European explorers and fishermen. Lacking a larger, unifying polity on the order of the Powhatan Confederacy in coastal Virginia, New England's native peoples lived in small, distinct communities. Nearly all of the regions' peoples spoke one dialect or another of the Algonquin language, and most of them could claim some sort of kinship to members of neighboring communities, bands, and tribes. To the south, the Mohegan, Pequot, Narragansett, Wampanoag, and Patuxet formed the principal tribes, while in northern New England, the Mi'kmaq and Abenaki were the largest and most important groups.

Like many peoples of the Northeastern Woodlands, southern New England natives pursued a seasonal round of subsistence. The late winter and early spring saw them harvesting and boiling maple sap for sugar. Later in the spring, as the days began to grow warmer, they planted their crops, principally maize, beans, and squash. They spent much of the summer along the rivers and the coast, where they fished and gathered shellfish. In the fall they returned to their fields and harvested their crops. While women performed nearly all of the agricultural labor, the men spent much of the autumn hunting in order to provide a winter store of meat. With the onset of winter, most native peoples of southern New England repaired to

"Times Are Altered with Us": American Indians from First Contact to the New Republic, First Edition. Roger M. Carpenter.

the deep woods, where they sometimes hunted, but for the most part attempted to stay inside – and warm.

Too far north to engage in agriculture on a regular basis, northern New England's native peoples depended far more on hunting than their neighbors to the south. The basic types of maize grown by native people in the Northeast, dent (so called because it forms a visible indentation on each grain when fully ripe) and flint maize, required 120 frost-free days in order to fully ripen and harden to the point where it could be stored over the winter, so that it could be pounded into meal or used as seed for next spring's planting. The short growing season made it difficult to raise maize successfully in northern New England. The native peoples of this region lived in smaller, more mobile communities than their counterparts to the south. Often little more than hunting bands that consisted primarily of clan members, tradition and practical concerns anchored these communities to small geographic areas, which prevented them from intruding into the hunting territory of other groups, and saw them largely avoid conflict. The anchor for each clan often consisted of a large, hollowed-out stump that served as a large, immovable, communal cooking vessel. Nearly every band had a sachem or sagamore (paramount chief) – who was usually, but not always, a male – who loosely governed it with the assistance of elders and prominent warriors. The sachem settled disputes within the community and handled all matters dealing with outsiders, such as trade, diplomacy, and war.

Like other peoples of the native Northeast, the natives of New England intensively managed the forested landscape, setting fire to the woods twice a year. This usually occurred in the early spring and late fall, while the woods were somewhat damp so that the fires – it was hoped – would not burn out of control. Burning the woods in this way removed impassable underbrush and prevented the accumulation of dead wood, which could become fuel for destructive wildfires. Besides making woodland travel and hunting easier, the practice contributed to the park-like openness of North America's forests, something that surprised and impressed Europeans. One Virginia colonist wrote that one could easily drive a carriage through the woods, while a French fur trader noted that one could easily ride a horse through the forest of what is now Maine. It seems not to have occurred to European explorers and colonists that the North American environment that they viewed as untamed wilderness had in fact resulted from human manipulation of the landscape.

Long before the landing of the Pilgrims in 1620, New England's native peoples had a good deal of experience with Europeans. Mi'kmaqs or Abenakis made contact with Italian explorer Giovanni Verrazzano nearly a century earlier when he sailed on behalf of the French. The Mi'kmaq also encountered Jacques Cartier a decade later near the mouth of the St Lawrence River. Seventy years later, the peoples of southern New England came into contact with Samuel de Champlain when he explored a portion of Cape Cod that the Pilgrims would later know as Plymouth Harbor. Champlain, as already noted, believed that any attempt to colonize the region would end in failure, since the large Indian population could easily overwhelm a nascent French colony. Unbeknownst to Champlain (or anybody else for that matter) this state of affairs would undergo a dramatic change within 15 years.

English Sassafras Hunters

Two years after Champlain's encounter with the natives of Cape Cod, an expedition led by English merchant Martin Pring landed at almost the same spot. Uninterested in exploration or the natives, Pring and his men busied themselves collecting large quantities of sassafras, a plant found only in the Americas. European medical thinking of the time held that the lands where diseases originated held their cures as well. European physicians thought sassafras might ease the symptoms of what the English called "the French poxe." Today referred to as syphilis, current research suggests that the disease probably did originate in the Americas. It did not make its first appearance in Europe until after Colón returned from his first voyage. Human remains in Europe that predate his voyage show no sign of the disease. Unfortunately for Europe's doctors and their patients, sassafras had no effect on the malady.

Pring and his men spent several months ashore in the vicinity of Plymouth Harbor, where they constructed a small palisade – English separatists would discover the remains of it over a decade and a half later – and for the most part, they enjoyed friendly relations with the local natives. In one notable instance, a member of Pring's party brought out a musical instrument somewhat similar to the modern guitar. When a young Englishman began playing the instrument, the Indians gathered around him and danced. Later, however, Pring and his men, for reasons that are not entirely clear, became suspicious of the natives and spent more time on guard in their palisade. When they did leave their small fort, they terrorized the Indians by allowing their two large mastiffs to run free. While native people in the Americas had dogs, they were mostly small animals, were not used in warfare, and were certainly nothing on the order of a mastiff.

John Smith Explores New England

John Smith, better known in American history for his exploits in Virginia, instigated the next notable European contact with New England's native peoples in 1614. Forced to leave the Virginia colony some years earlier after being seriously burned in a gunpowder accident, Smith returned to England to recuperate. By 1614, he had obviously recovered and spent much of the year exploring the coast of southern New England. In his book, *The Generall Historie of Virginia, New-England, and the Summer Isles* – in which Smith also gave the region its name – Smith took little notice of the native inhabitants. The commodities that the New England landscape could provide, such as fish, lumber, and furs, commanded his attention. Smith also made the claim – one that almost any New England farmer from the seventeenth century to the present would contest – that the soils of the region would be good for farming. Smith did take note of New England's native peoples when English sea captain Thomas Hunt lured approximately 20 Indians aboard his vessel on the pretext of trade. Instead of trade, Hunt seized the natives, clapped them in irons, and sailed off to Spain, hoping to sell his ill-gotten cargo into slavery. While John Smith had no great love of Indians, and did not oppose slavery, he recognized that Hunt's actions could result in hostilities with the natives, thereby damaging the fur trade. Hunt's actions, as we will see, would have far-reaching and unexpected consequences for future English colonists in the region.

Despite the more than 120 years that had elapsed since Cristóbal Colón's landfall in the Caribbean, Europeans still learned about the Americas in a piecemeal fashion. This reflected the pace of European overseas exploration, the vastness of the American continents, and the ability of explorers – those who could and did want to write – to get their narratives into print.

The Separatists

When John Smith's *History of New England* appeared, learned men, government officials, and curiosity seekers read it and poured over the map he drafted to accompany it. A group of English expatriates in the Dutch City of Leyden took particular interest in his book and examined the map very closely. This group of English refugees in the Netherlands – called Separatists, and later commonly referred to as Pilgrims in American history textbooks – represented the more radical elements of the Puritan movement. While most Puritans wished to reform the Anglican Church from within, the Separatists insisted that England had already provoked the wrath of God, and would soon be punished. Therefore, they deemed it best to leave the realm quickly, before the Almighty got around to wreaking havoc on it. In 1608, after several false starts, the Separatists fled England and settled in the Dutch city of Leyden. There they organized their church and began working in the city's textile industry. The religiously and socially tolerant Dutch did not interfere with the spiritual practices of the Separatists. But after a decade in the Netherlands, the Separatists became alarmed as they saw their children becoming, not surprisingly, culturally more Dutch than English. They did not regard a return to England as a realistic option, and so they began to think of relocating to North America.

One of their religious leaders had already approached a Dutch company, licensed by the government of the Netherlands to colonize North America, about the possibility of establishing a settlement there. This plan would have created a Dutch colony – populated with English colonists – at the mouth of the Hudson River. The Dutch government turned down this plan.

The Separatists later contracted with a London merchant concern that paid the costs of the voyage, provided the colony paid them back over the decade of the 1620s. Within Leyden's Separatist community, the prospect of removing to North America provoked a great deal of controversy. Those who objected to the plan pointed out that most narratives about the place emphasized that it was populated by barbarians who engaged in cannibalism.

The Separatists (Pilgrims) dropped anchor in Cape Cod in November 1620. Using their ship *The Mayflower* as a base, they sent several expeditions ashore in search of a suitable place to establish their colony. During their explorations of the Cape in November and

December of 1620, they saw very few Indians. Most of the Indians they did see kept their distance, and usually fled if the Englishmen attempted to approach or follow them. Finding deserted, disintegrating wigwams and unharvested maize rotting in the Indians' fields, the Separatists soon realized that something horrible had happened here. Clearly, the densely populated landscape that Samuel de Champlain had encountered 16 years earlier, and that John Smith had renamed New England just six years prior, had somehow been horribly transformed.

Finding native burial grounds, the Separatists exhumed an Indian's grave, and took the offerings of maize that had been given to the dead with them. The Separatists planned to use this maize as their seed for the spring planting, and justified this bit of grave robbing by promising to pay back the Indians when they met them.

Throughout the winter of 1620–1621, exactly half (51 of 102) of the Separatists perished. This high mortality rate probably resulted from their weakened condition after the long ocean voyage. Throughout the winter, the Separatists felt certain that they were being watched, even though they did not actually see any natives. Fearful that the Indians would take advantage of their diminished numbers, the English took care to bury their dead at night. Once they began their planting in the springtime, the surviving English would occasionally see an Indian in the distance. Whenever they tried to approach, however, the native person would always flee. On one occasion, some of the Separatists left their tools in a field; when they returned they discovered that the Indians had made off with them.

In March of 1621, a lone Indian man approached the settlement of Plymouth. Boldly walking into the middle of the Separatist's palisade, the man, whose name was Samoset, stunned the colonists by greeting them with the words "hello Englishmen." An Abenaki from northern New England, Samoset had a somewhat limited command of the English language. The little English he did know he probably learned through his interactions with traders and fishermen. In all likelihood, Samoset's presence in southern New England came about by his hitching a ride on an English fishing vessel. Understandably amazed that a person they regarded as a naked savage could speak to them in their own tongue, the Separatists kept Samoset in Plymouth throughout the day, and closely questioned him about the lands around Plymouth and its peoples, even though the language barrier limited the amount of information that they were able to extract.

As Samoset prepared to leave late in the day, he promised the Separatists that he would soon return with a person who could speak English much better than he could.

Tisquantum

True to his word, Samoset returned a few days later with a Patuxet person named Tisquantum, whom the Separatists referred to more famously as Squanto. Tisquantum had an unusual biography that contained gaps that could not be filled in. One of the Indians captured by Thomas Hunt in 1614, Tisquantum had been transported to Spain, where Hunt intended to sell his ill-gotten cargo into slavery, but Spanish port authorities stepped in, seized the Indians from Hunt, and sent them to live with friars in Catholic monasteries so that they could be instructed in Christianity. While the Spanish had no moral qualms regarding slavery (the Spanish, after all, practiced the institution in their Caribbean colonies), they did object to an Englishman profiting from it. Little is known about Tisquantum's life in Spain, and apparently he did not stay there very long. By 1617, through a set of circumstances that has never been adequately explained, he was living in London in the household of the Newfoundland Company's treasurer.

It is possible that Tisquantum, like other native peoples who had been transported to Europe against their will, attempted to make his way home by regaling his hosts with fanciful stories about mines and waterways that led to a western sea. Utilizing Tisquantum as a guide, the Newfoundland Company sponsored voyages by Captain Thomas Dermer to Cape Cod and Martha's Vineyard in 1619. During the voyage, Tisquantum, with Dermer's permission, left to find his own people; unbeknownst to him, however, epidemics of European disease had devastated the peoples of Cape Cod and much of southern New England, including the Patuxet.

Upon returning home in 1619, Tisquantum saw the results of what would greet the first Separatist expeditions a year later: devastating epidemics of European diseases had swept through the native populations of southern New England. While it is impossible to pinpoint one disease – and it could have been more than one – smallpox, given its virulence, lethality, and ability to travel, is the most likely culprit and may have unwittingly been borne ashore by English fishermen. Since John Cabot's discovery of the Grand Banks – and possibly earlier – English, French, Spanish, and Basque fishing vessels plied the cod-rich waters off Newfoundland and what became New England. Spanish and French fishermen had an advantage over their English competitors in that they could more easily procure large quantities of salt. Locales that lacked salt mines procured the mineral through the process of evaporation. England's wet foggy climate constrained its ability to produce large quantities of salt in this manner. While fishermen of other nations could preserve their catch by salting the fish aboard their ships, English fishermen often had to go ashore and set up drying stations in order to preserve their catch. And going ashore brought the crews of English fishing vessels into contact with native peoples. Fishermen supplemented their incomes by trading with natives, usually giving them cloth and metal goods in exchange for furs. They also unwittingly passed on to native people European diseases to which they had no natural resistance. Infected Indians spread the European pathogens when they returned to their villages.

Native methods of health care only helped spread the pestilence. Rather than isolating the sick individual, native healing practices called for others to gather round the sick person to care communally for him or her. Initial exposure to Old World pathogens meant that many individuals became sick at once, meaning that many of the functions necessary to sustain a native community also came to an abrupt halt. For example, the disease-stricken persons of a native community could not care for their maize fields simply because too many people had fallen ill, and the few who had not contracted the disease were preoccupied with attempting to care for those who had. Years after contact, native people related to a Puritan clergyman how sick individuals would crawl from their wigwams to get a drink of water and find themselves so weakened that they could not make it back and simply perished from exposure. Puritan clergymen celebrated these epidemics as signs of divine favor, arguing that God had helped clear the land of Indians so that Christians – specifically Puritan Christians – might settle them.

As a result of his time in London, Tisquantum had become very proficient in the English language and could easily communicate with the Separatists. Discovering all of his own people dead upon returning to Cape Cod, Tisquantum lived among the Wampanoag. With Tisquantum, and to a lesser extent Samoset, acting as interpreters, the Separatists were introduced to Massasoit, the leader of the Wampanoags, and signed a treaty with him. For his part, Massasoit may have been eager to secure an alliance with the English. Although they were few in number, they had metal goods and European weaponry. In all likelihood, Massasoit's primary concern would have been the neighboring Narragansett people, the primary rivals of the Wampanoag. During the recent epidemics that wreaked havoc on New England, the Wampanoag had experienced a population loss approaching 50 percent. The Narragansett, by contrast, remained largely unscathed by these outbreaks of European disease.

Tisquantum proved invaluable to the Separatists. Not only did he serve as an interpreter, but he also trained them in the planting and harvesting of maize and other native crops. The Separatists attempted to plant some European crops, but most of them, as their leader William Bradford noted, did not do very well. Tisquantum spent most of his time living among the Separatists, in part because he had managed to anger Massasoit. When he returned to Cape Cod, Tisquantum attempted to rebuild the Patuxet, scouring the region and visiting other tribes, seeking out fellow tribesmen who may have survived the epidemics that had devastated his people. Perhaps Massasoit saw this as a challenge, fearing that if Tisquantum reconstituted the Patuxet, and gained English backing, they could become the dominant power in the region. However, the Separatists, recognizing Tisquantum's value to them as an interpreter, protected him from Massasoit. Tisquantum did attempt to exert some influence over local natives, going so far as to tell them that the Separatists stored smallpox in their cellars and that, with the word from him, it would be loosened upon them. Bradford recognized that Tisquantum, as he put it, "played his own game." Nonetheless, when Tisquantum died in 1623, it was a great loss to the Plymouth colony.

Thomas Morton and "Merre-mount"

The Separatists made every effort to control the fur trade in southern New England. In the winter of 1623–1624, English adventurer Thomas Morton established a trading post within sight of Plymouth. Morton named the establishment, which was situated on a hill, "Merre-mount" and offended the Separatist's religious sensibilities by erecting a maypole to which had been fastened a set of moose antlers. Even worse, as far as the Plymouth colonists were concerned, were the wild rumors (that they probably concocted themselves) that in trading with the natives Morton exchanged alcohol and firearms for animal pelts. Other rumors, possibly true, claimed that Morton and his men engaged in intimate relations with native women, which only further served to stoke the ire of the Separatists. While Separatist leaders spilled a lot of ink over Morton's moral transgressions (both real and imagined), they really objected to the fact that Morton and his men had disrupted their monopoly on local fur trade. Sending their military leader Myles Standish and a few men to Merre-mount, the Separatists seized Morton, arrested him, and sent him back to England – which they did not have the authority to do.

The peace that Tisquantum and Samoset had helped broker between the Plymouth colony and Massasoit would hold for five decades, although there would be periods of tension along the way. In 1630, the Puritan Great Migration began, which led to the creation of the larger, more populous, and more powerful Massachusetts Bay colony. Lasting for a decade, the Great Migration resulted in an influx of thousands of English colonists. The new colonists, their livestock, and their desire for farms – in short their need for land – helped to create friction between native peoples and the English.

The Pequot War

An uneasy peace prevailed for much of the 1630s. However, in 1636–1637, the peace would end with the Pequot War. Like most conflicts, the Pequot War had more than one cause. The New England colonies seized upon the murder of two English traders as cause for the war. However, other causes existed. The English and the Dutch vied for control over the Indian trade in the lower Connecticut River Valley. The Dutch already had a presence in the region and had constructed a trading post that brought them into conflict with the New England colonies. The English, after a tense but bloodless standoff, forced the Dutch traders to leave the lower Connecticut River Valley. The murder of two English traders, John Stone in 1634, and John Oldham in 1636, became the excuse the New England colonies used to pursue hostilities against the Pequot. The Pequot claimed that Stone had kidnapped two of their tribesmen he hired as guides. Massachusetts demanded the Pequot pay compensation for the death of Stone in the form of wampum. The Pequot agreed to pay the indemnity, but never did. Oldham's vessel was discovered adrift by a fellow trader with several Indians on deck near Block Island, off the coast of Rhode Island. After a short fight,

Oldham's body was discovered and Massachusetts authorities accused a small group of native people, who paid tribute to the more numerous Narragansett, of being the culprits. The Narragansett intervened, arranging the return of goods taken from Oldham's vessel, but told the English that the Pequot were the guilty party. While the English publically insisted that the murder of the two traders was the flash point that ignited conflict, the primary reason for the Pequot War seems to have been a struggle for the control of the wampum trade.

Small beads made largely from the shells of whelks but also those of other mollusks, wampum or *sewan* could only be obtained and made by coastal native peoples. Usually found in the colors white and purple (with purple being more scarce, and hence, more valuable) many native people believed wampum possessed spiritual qualities. Lacking direct access to the shells used to make wampum, native peoples in the interior Eastern Woodlands often traded animal pelts in order to acquire it. Both the Dutch and the New English quickly realized that they could trade wampum (which they did not value) to native peoples for beaver pelts (which they did value). The Dutch, as a matter of fact, went so far as to provide metal tools to native people on Long Island and created a wampum factory.

In the wake of the deaths of Oldham and Stone, the New England colonies accused the Pequot of the killings, and demanded that they turn over large quantities of wampum, the murderers, and many of their children as hostages to insure their good behavior. Not surprisingly, the Pequot rebuffed these demands. After the Pequot refusal, the United Colonies of Massachusetts, Plymouth, and Connecticut outfitted an expedition to punish the Indians. Seeking to punish Oldham's murderers first, the troops landed initially on Block Island. The New England troops found few Indians and spent most of their time ransacking abandoned wigwams, structures that did not even belong to the Pequot. The New England troops and their leaders next went to Fort Saybrook in coastal Connecticut, where they did far more to irk the local commander than the local Indians. The troops challenged the Pequot to a battle. Thereafter the English stood in a field, waiting for the Indians to appear. Not until late in the day did they realize that the Pequot had chosen to decline the battle.

Unable to find Indians to kill, the New England troops burned a nearby Pequot village and then left the region. The actions of the troops angered the Fort Saybrook commander. In his view, the

Pequot had been needlessly provoked and he and his men would be left to deal with the consequences of any trouble the New Englanders stirred up. The Pequot justified the post commander's anger when, soon after the Connecticut troops left, the Indians subjected Fort Saybrook to a nine-month siege, killing several colonists and capturing others. Among the captives were two English girls from whom the Pequot attempted to extract the secret of making gunpowder. When it became apparent that the girls knew nothing about the manufacture of the propellant, the Pequot traded them to the Dutch, who eventually returned them to their families.

In May of 1637, the New England troops returned to the area, their numbers augmented by Narragansett and Mohegan allies. With their native allies acting as guides, the New England troops surrounded the Pequot fort on the Mystic River. Waiting until dark to launch their attack, the New Englanders attacked the circular palisade and attempted to force their way through openings at both ends of the fortification. Their attempts at entry were foiled, however, by brush and other obstacles the Pequot had placed in their way. By the time a few of the New England troops made it into the palisade, they had lost the element of surprise, and found themselves facing large numbers of armed and ready Pequot warriors. New England commanders John Mason and John Underhill quickly realized that within the confines of the palisade, the colonists' superior weaponry could not be brought to bear. Torching several wigwams, Underhill and Mason led their men outside of the Pequot fort and surrounded it. With the Narragansett and Mohegan allies forming a secondary line behind them, the English poured musket fire into the village, this as fire began to spread from one wigwam to another.

The Pequot in the Mystic River fort faced a terrible choice: they could either burn to death in their village, or they could run for it, hoping to make it through the English lines. And even if they made it past the English, they still faced capture at the hands of their Mohegan or Narragansett enemies. Only about five of the estimated 500 Pequots inside the Mystic River fort made it out alive. Stunned by the ferocity of the assault, the Narragansett and Mohegan allies of the English complained that their mode of warfare bordered on insanity: it killed too many men. The native warriors who accompanied the English hoped to accomplish the goal of most native war parties in the Northeast: they wanted to secure large numbers of captives. For their part, the English criticized the native way of war, arguing that it did not kill *enough* men.

The destruction of the Pequot's Mystic River fort did not end the Pequot War, but the tribe could not recover from the blow. Throughout the rest of the year, the New England colonies conducted mopping-up operations. Sassacus, the principal chief of the Pequot, fled with about 40 followers to the Mohawk, the easternmost of the Iroquois Five Nations, and sought their assistance. More concerned about maintaining their relatively new trading relationship with the English, the Mohawk killed Sassacus and presented his head to the English as a gift. As for the English, they executed most of the Pequot males whom they captured. The Narragansett and Mohegan took custody of most captured Pequot women and children and adopted them into their tribes. The New English found a more profitable use for other surviving Pequot, shipping and selling them to British sugar colonies in Barbados and Jamaica. In the aftermath of the war, the English declared the Pequot nation extinct.

Miantonomi and Uncas

Native American leaders did not agree as to what the English victory over the Pequot meant. While the Narragansett benefited from the influx of Pequot captives, one of their key leaders, Miantonomi, recognized that the arrival of increasing numbers of English colonists meant that the continued loss of land to the newcomers and the diminishment of game animals would soon extinguish their way of life. Realizing that the English viewed themselves as a common people, Miantonomi became one of the first Native American leaders to call for Indian unity against Europeans, arguing that native peoples, too, had to forge a common identity and stop thinking of themselves in terms of being members of distinct tribes and bands. Miantonomi proposed that the Indians of southern New England launch an all-out war against the English in order to drive them from their lands.

By contrast, the Mohegan sachem Uncas believed that his people's best chance of survival lay in allying themselves with the English. Uncas had forged such an alliance during the Pequot War and would come to the aid of the English again four decades later, during Metacom's Rebellion. As fate would have it, Miantonomi would meet his death at the hands of one of Unca's kinsmen. The conflict between the two came about when Mohegan warriors began attacking Narragansett hunters in their own territory. Obtaining permission from the New England colonies to prosecute a war against Uncas and the Mohegan, Miantonomi led a large force of warriors into the Mohegan country. In the skirmish that followed the meeting of the Mohegan and Narragansett warriors, Miantonomi, weighed down by chain mail armor that an English friend had given him, was taken prisoner. After his capture, Miantonomi and Uncas engaged in several long conversations. It has been speculated that they discussed an alliance between the two tribes that would be sealed through the intermarriage of some of their children or other kin.

Uncas, however, seems to have been far more concerned with proving his loyalty to the New England colonies. The Narragansett paid the ransom Uncas demanded in order to secure the return of Miantonomi. But unbeknownst to the Narragansett, Uncas colluded with officials from Connecticut and turned Miantonomi over to them. The English accused Miantonomi of conspiring against them, but the leaders of the United Colonies of New England questioned whether or not they had the legal authority to execute him. They hit upon an easy solution, however, that left their hands clean. They turned Miantonomi back over to Uncas, who saw to it that one of his clan members murdered him in the presence of English representatives.

John Eliot and the Praying Towns

The New England colonists exulted in the wake of their victory over the Pequot, and their clergy published sermons and tracts that interpreted their triumph as a sign of divine favor. Plymouth governor William Bradford portrayed the fight at the Pequot's Mystic River fort as one in which God intervened directly on behalf of the English:

> Those that scaped the fire were slaine with the sword; some hewed to peeces, others rune throw with their rapiers, so as they were quickly dispatchte, and very few escaped. It was conceived they thus destroyed about 400 at this time. It was a fearfull sight to see them thus frying in the fyer, and the streams of blood quenching the same, and horrible was the stinck and sente ther of; but the victory seemed a sweete sacrifice, and they gave the prays therof to God, who had wrought so wonderfuly for them, thus to inclose their enimise in their hands, and give them so speedy a victory over so proud and insulting an enimie.

Their co-religionists back in England, however, viewed the outcome of the conflict quite differently. Rather than praising the New England Puritans for their victory over the Indians, Puritans in old England criticized them for their savagery. One prominent Puritan clergyman pointed out the hypocrisy and un-Christian-like behavior of his New World brethren, noting that it would have been a far better thing for them to have attempted to save the souls of the Indians before killing them, so they could at least go to heaven. Other critics pointed out the hypocrisy of the Puritans, noting that the seal of the Massachusetts Bay Colony featured an Indian saying the words "come over and help us."

Stung by such criticisms, New England Puritans finally made attempts to convert native people to Christianity. John Eliot, the young minister for the Church in the town of Roxbury, led the first efforts. Eliot believed that simple conversion to Christianity would not be enough to save the Indians but that they would also need to surrender their culture and be transformed into Englishmen and women. In other words, Eliot and other Englishmen believed that Christianity and civilization – particularly English civilization – went hand in hand. Eliot regarded the presence of Indian converts' unconverted kinsmen as a key obstacle to lasting conversion. The presence of the unconverted, he reasoned, would tempt them to backslide. To solve this problem – or at least what he regarded as a problem – Eliot advocated the building of so-called Praying Towns, in which Indian converts would congregate, live apart from unconverted natives, and adopt English culture.

The move to a Praying Town signaled a significant cultural change for Indian converts. Men had to abandon hunting and fishing and take up the dawn-to-dusk agricultural labor in which English males engaged. Native women no longer worked in the fields to cultivate maize, beans, and squash, but now had to work *within* the household and learn tasks such as spinning cloth, much like their English counterparts. In addition to their traditional gendered roles, Indian men and women had to give up their native forms of dress. Women had to cover their hair, while native men had to cut theirs shorter. By coercing native people to remain in a fixed location, the English thought they would find it easier to control them. Nonetheless, Eliot's experiment with the Praying Towns did not find universal acceptance among the region's English colonists. Indeed, only Massachusetts allowed the construction of Praying Towns within its borders. In 1674, on the eve of Metacom's Rebellion (the English called the conflict King Philip's War), Massachusetts had 14 Praying Towns comprising about 1,600 inhabitants.

Perhaps most ambitiously, Eliot and other Praying Town missionaries set out to make native people into what one historian has called "Red Puritans." Being a good Puritan, however, required one to be able to relate his or her conversion experience – the exact moment when one realized that he or she had been chosen by God, anointed as one of the elect destined to go to heaven. Perhaps more daunting, at least from the perspective of the missionaries, was that a good Puritan did not need (although they had) intermediaries between themselves and the Almighty. In order to have a relationship with God, one must read the Bible and, therefore, be literate. Eliot set out to translate the Bible into the Algonquin language, using Latin letters. While a very impressive achievement on his part, the effectiveness of Eliot's efforts to promote literacy among the Algonquin people of New England has been questioned. Scholars have since wondered just how many Praying Town Indians actually became literate. For those who did, it had consequences that Eliot and other missionaries had not anticipated: rather than literate native people simply accepting the Christian message, some of the Praying Town Indians questioned it, often scribbling remarks or questions in the margins of their Bibles.

Most of the native people who moved to Praying Towns came from small, fragmented bands and tribes that had been decimated by warfare and outbreaks of European disease epidemics. Largely able to maintain their communities and culture, more powerful and populous groups such as the Wampanoag and the Narragansett showed little interest in the Praying Towns and conversion. Moreover, many of their leaders saw conversion to Christianity as a threat to their culture and their leadership.

Despite his outward success in establishing the Praying Towns, Eliot had his suspicions that not all of the natives who moved into these communities sincerely desired to become Christians. He suspected (probably correctly) that many native peoples viewed the Praying Towns as a means by which they made the hard choice of trading cultural extinction for physical survival. They also viewed Praying Towns as the only way in which they could maintain some vestige of their former territory. Perhaps nothing better illustrated this than the fact that the Algonquin name of the first Praying Town, *Natick*, translates into English as "my land." Eliot and other Puritan clergy also discovered, sometimes to their chagrin, that encouraging literacy and the reading of the Bible among Praying Town Indians often made them into sharp critics of English behavior. Praying Town Indians frequently noted that the behavior of English colonists often did not align with the dictates of the good book.

Many of the Puritan clergy – apart, perhaps, from Eliot himself – do not seem to have taken the task of converting native people seriously. In one instance, several Puritan clergymen traveled to a Praying Town so that native people could testify to them of their conversion experiences. The clergymen listened, but cut the meeting short, stating that it was too late and getting dark, and departed, choosing not to return. Such actions made it clear to native converts that many of the Puritans did not take them or their religious concerns seriously.

While Praying Town Indians may not have been completely accepted as Christians by their Puritan neighbors, they did find themselves integrated into the colonial economy. Praying Town Indians became part of the colonial labor force, often serving as field workers for their English neighbors. Women from Praying Towns often hired themselves out as housekeepers and to help spin cloth. Occasionally, Praying Town Indians worked in the less Puritan sphere of New England, signing on to serve aboard fishing vessels.

In the years since the Separatists and the Wampanoag leader Massasoit signed their initial treaty, matters between the two groups had remained largely peaceful, though with periodic tensions. The Wampanoag remained neutral during the Pequot War, and over the years Massasoit sold tracts of land to the Plymouth colonists, and later to colonists of the Massachusetts Bay as well. This resulted in incidents in which colonial authorities arrested native hunters for trespassing, tried them before colonial courts, found them guilty, and fined them. Not understanding the English concept of the private ownership of land, native people naturally resented this treatment. Most native people believed that land could not be owned and that the agreements they made with the English did not mean they surrendered the right to use the land and its resources.

Metacom's Rebellion

In 1660 Massasoit died and leadership of the Wampanoag people passed to his eldest son, Wamsutta, who the English called Alexander. Shortly after Wamsutta assumed leadership of the Wampanoag,

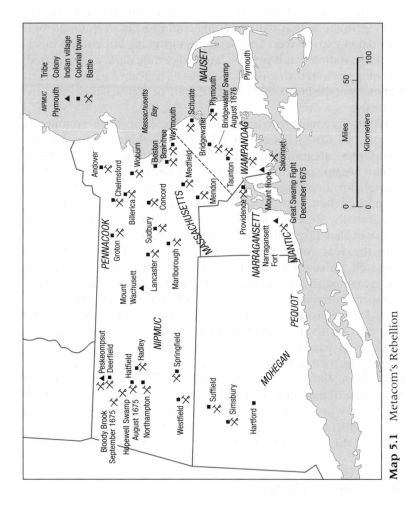

Map 5.1 Metacom's Rebellion

118

rumors began to circulate among the English that he was plotting to launch a war. Concerned about these allegations, the colonial authorities summoned Wamsutta to Plymouth, where they subjected him to intense questioning over a period of several days. When the governor of Plymouth finally released Wamsutta, he kept his son as a hostage to ensure his good behavior. While making his way from Plymouth to his home at Mount Hope, Wamsutta fell ill and died soon afterward. Many of the Wampanoag believed that the English had poisoned him. If the New Englanders did poison Wamsutta, thinking that removing him diminished the prospect of hostilities, they soon realized they had made a mistake.

Metacom, whom the English called Philip, succeeded his brother as the leader of the Wampanoag. It is difficult to ascertain what Wamsutta's attitude toward the English may have been, but Metacom's was less ambiguous. Despite his resentment of the English and their policies toward native peoples, Metacom did continue some of his father's practices in maintaining peace with the colonists by selling them land.

In the 15 years during which Metacom led the Wampanoag people, rumors persisted that he gathered arms and ammunition in preparation for a conflict with the colonists. However, the different New England colonies had competing economic interests. Metacom used this to his advantage, often playing one colony off against another. He also cannily dealt with the colonies by submitting to their demands – but not always in the way that they expected. When the Massachusetts Bay Colony ordered Metacom and his warriors to surrender their firearms, they did so. However, they surrendered only those weapons they had in their possession at that moment, and Metacom had taken the precaution of making sure that none of his men had brought a functioning musket with him. In other words, when Metacom "complied" with the order, he did so by surrendering only old and broken muskets.

The conflict known as Metacom's Rebellion (known to the colonists as King Philip's War) had its origins in a piece of espionage involving a native person. In his dealings with the English, Metacom realized the value of the written word. Although not literate himself, he realized that the English did everything by means of contracts, letters, and other written documents. This made Metacom somewhat dependent on the work of a Harvard College–trained Indian named John Sassamon, who served as his secretary. Sassamon had worked with John Eliot as an assistant minister in some of the

Praying Towns. Sassamon read the correspondence Metacom received from the governing officials of the New England colonies and drafted letters of response for him. Unbeknownst to Metacom, John Sassamon had another occupation: he was in the pay of Plymouth colony as a spy.

Shortly before Christmas of 1674 (which would have meant little to New England Puritans, as they did not celebrate the holiday) John Sassamon called upon the governor of Plymouth and informed him that Metacom and the Wampanoag had large stockpiles of weapons and would soon launch a war. Sassamon also related a piece of news that affected him personally: Metacom, he feared, suspected him of being a spy, and he was afraid for his life. The governor played down Sassamon's fears, arguing that Metacom could not possibly know he was a spy. He further pointed out that if Sassamon did not return to Mount Hope (Metacom's home) it would only fuel Metacom's suspicions.

Reluctantly, John Sassamon started out on the road from Plymouth to Mount Hope on Christmas Eve. No one saw Sassamon again until his corpse was dragged from beneath the ice of a frozen pond the following March. The Plymouth authorities summoned Metacom, questioned him, and learned nothing. Shortly after questioning him, however, an Indian convert came forward, claiming that he had witnessed John Sassamon's murder. According to the witness, two of Metacom's councilors and one other Indian had assaulted Sassamon, broken his neck, and shoved his corpse beneath the ice of the pond. Moving quickly, Plymouth issued a summons for the three Wampanoag and placed them on trial before a jury of 12 colonist and six Indians. The court ordered that Sassmon's body be disinterred as evidence. Seeking to establish spectral as well as physical proof of the defendants' guilt, during the trial the court ordered them to approach Sassamon's corpse, which according to the court records, began to bleed anew. Taking this as proof of the three Wampanoags' guilt, the 18-man jury unanimously convicted them and sentenced them to hang.

Angered by what they saw as a case of injustice, and of the colonists overstepping their authority, young Wampanoag warriors took it upon themselves to launch attacks on New England homesteads. Despite Metacom's preparations, and the suspicions of the New England colonists, neither side was prepared for the conflict. Realizing that the New England forces could trap him on Mount Hope simply by securing its narrow landed neck, Metacom led his followers off of the peninsula. In the early phases of the war, the shock of the Wampanoag attacks stunned the colonists, and they quickly realized that Metacom's Rebellion would not be a repeat of the Pequot War. In 1637, very few of the Pequot warriors had possessed firearms. In 1675, many of the Wampanoag – and other Indians who eventually became allies of either Metacom or the colonists – not only had flintlock muskets but were quite skilled in their use. And unlike the ill-trained New England militiamen that they faced, the Native American warriors had adapted European muskets for use in forest warfare. They shortened the barrels of their weapons to make them easier to maneuver in the thick underbrush, and whereas New England militiamen had been trained to fire in volleys, native warriors trained themselves to aim and to choose their targets. Unlike in the Pequot War, now the English quickly discovered that the Indians could match them on the battlefield – at least as long as they had access to powder, shot, and the means to repair their weapons.

In the first year of the war, Metacom and his followers assaulted over half of New England's 90 towns, completely destroying a dozen of them. New England's military forces proved ineffective when they first took the field in the summer and autumn of 1675. Metacom and his followers frequently ambushed New England militiamen as they floundered in unfamiliar forests and swamps. After attacking a homestead or village, Metacom and his followers typically melted into New England's vast swamps, which the colonists regarded as impenetrable strongholds.

Figure 5.1 Colonists clash with Indians during Metacom's Rebellion. Detail from *A Mapp of New England*, London, 1675. Map Reproduction Courtesy of the Norman B. Leventhal Map Center at the Boston Public Library.

The English did have their native allies, most notably the Mohegans under Uncas. They also had willing Native American volunteers, it turned out, in the Praying Towns. The English, however, doubted the loyalty of these willing volunteers. With the onset of hostilities, some Indians fled the Praying Towns and joined Metacom. Still, most Indian men of fighting age in the Praying Towns wished to join the English. Accusing many of the Praying Town Indians of assisting Metacom, many colonists attacked them as a sort of substitute for Metacom's elusive forces. Worried that Praying Town Indians may be informers and covert raiders, New England authorities took the step of removing Indians from the Praying Towns and imprisoning them on Deer Island in Boston Harbor. Left on the island without shelter, food, or the means to leave, many of the natives perished due to starvation and exposure. Others survived because slavers began visiting the island, seizing them and transporting them to British sugar islands in the Caribbean, where in all likelihood they would quickly be worked to death.

The New England colonies not only proved incompetent in the field in the first year of the war, but they also managed to turn neutral native peoples into allies of Metacom. New England diplomats managed to upset the Narragansett, who had already declared neutrality. The Narragansett, however, angered the English when they offered to feed and shelter the families of native men fighting with Metacom. The English regarded this as a form of aiding and abetting the enemy.

In December 1675, the United Colonies, with a force of over 1,000 men (including 150 native allies), attacked the Narragansett's fort, which was located on an island in Massachusetts' Great Swamp. For the attackers, the fort proved to be a formidable structure, consisting of not only a palisade but also a surrounding series of abattis (an obstacle made of pointed stakes or tree branches) that hindered their approach. Firing from pre-built platforms, the Narragansett forced the attackers back. Directed to a gap in the fort's defenses by an Indian captive, New England soldiers finally gained access to the fort. Meeting fierce resistance, the New Englanders set fire to the fort, destroying much of Narragansett's winter food supplies, which the New English had hoped to capture. Narragansett warriors sustained approximately 150 casualties in this battle, and during it and the conflagration that followed, between 300 and 1,000 Narragansett women and children perished. While disappointed that they could not capture the Narragansett food supplies that they desperately needed themselves, the New English congratulated themselves on their victory. It somehow did not occur to them that they had just transformed the previously neutral Narragansett into bitter enemies who would now willingly join Metacom's forces.

As early as February 1676, the Narragansett made their presence in the conflict known. They participated in an attack on Lancaster, Massachusetts, burning the village and slaughtering about 50 of the inhabitants. They also took captives, including most famously Mary Rowlandson, whose narrative of her experiences as a prisoner would become one of the earliest Indian captivity narratives to be published. Throughout February and March of 1676, Metacom and his followers destroyed all or part of the towns of Medfield, Weymouth, Groton, and Northampton, Massachusetts.

By May of 1676, however, the native war effort began to ebb, in large part because the Indians were almost too successful. While at war, Metacom and his followers could not plant corn, nor could they follow traditional food-gathering strategies or hunt. Instead, for much of the conflict the Indians counted on acquiring food during their raids on the English, seizing harvested grain and driving off their livestock. In one year of fighting, the Indians had turned back the line of English colonization by 20 miles, which represented half a century of work on the part of the colonists. What native people had created was a buffer zone between themselves and the colonists, consisting primarily of destroyed farms. English captive Mary Rowlandson provided an example of how desperately short of food the Indians were. She recorded one instance in which a group of Indians found an old deer leg bone in the woods. The starving Indians boiled the bone in water and drank the broth, making it serve as a meal for 10 to 15 people.

Another shortcoming in the Indians' long-term strategy also became apparent in the spring and summer of 1676. In the early phase of the conflict, native warriors demonstrated their superiority in the use of firearms and their ability to fight in the forests and swamps of New England. But whereas the colonists could obtain replacement weapons, have blacksmiths repair broken muskets, and assure themselves of a steady supply of gunpowder, the Indians could do none of these things.

By the summer of 1676, following the lead of their native allies, the English had learned how to fight in the forest. Indian fighters such as Benjamin Church taught his men how to move through the woods and how to select their targets and aim. Almost completely out of food, Metacom's warriors began to surrender to the English in large numbers. In July, English forces captured Metacom's wife and son. Along with hundreds of other native prisoners, Metacom's wife and son were shipped off to a life of slavery in the British West Indies. In August of that year, a native man serving with the English shot and killed Metacom. Allegedly, colonial authorities gave the Indian who shot Metacom his hand, which he kept in a bucket of whiskey and would show to curiosity seekers for a price. The English cut off Metacom's head and placed it on a tower in Plymouth as a warning to other native people who might think of resisting the English.

Metacom's Rebellion had several far-reaching effects. Much of southern New England's native population had been killed or sold into slavery. Many of the survivors of the conflict fled northward, where they became part of the Mi'kmaq and Abenaki peoples. In the future, they would assist the French in their wars against New England. The deadliest of the colonial wars in terms of per capita deaths, Metacom's Rebellion saw one out of every 16 English colonists perish, while an estimated 3,000 Native American warriors died. It also resulted in the discontinuation of the Praying Towns. The now elderly John Eliot suggested reconstituting the Praying Towns after the war, but New English colonists had largely lost interest in the conversion of native people, and no longer wanted them in their midst.

6

The Five Nations, the Dutch, and the Iroquois Wars

In many respects, New Netherland, the only Dutch colony in North America, came about almost as an afterthought. The Netherlands emerged as the economic powerhouse of Western Europe in the early seventeenth century by emphasizing commerce and investment. Eschewing the ruinous religious strife that wracked other European nations, the Dutch pursued a policy of toleration in spiritual matters, which coupled with their hands-off approach to private-sector business enabled to them to attract talented immigrants (and the capital that accompanied them) from all over the continent. When the French government began its persecution of the Huguenots (French Protestants) for example, many of them fled to the Netherlands. The policy of religious toleration also, as mentioned in Chapter 5, appealed to English Separatists, the most radical branch of the Puritan movement. During the first decade of the seventeenth century, many of them settled in the Dutch city of Leyden, where they found employment in the textile industry.

The Netherland's importance as a center of commerce and finance enabled it to participate in many overseas commercial ventures. The Dutch imported spices from far-off Java and Ceylon (now known as Sri Lanka), established sugar plantations in the Caribbean, and for a brief period occupied Brazil after

"Times Are Altered with Us": American Indians from First Contact to the New Republic, First Edition. Roger M. Carpenter.

expelling the Portuguese. Compared to other European nations, the Netherland's young people had an extraordinary number of opportunities available to them. A young man in the Netherlands, for example, could become a sailor or soldier for one of the private trading companies, or he could try his luck as a spice trader in the Far East, or in the transatlantic slave trade, which the Dutch dominated until the middle of the seventeenth century. The scale of the Netherland's commercial success throughout the globe made North America little more than an afterthought to them; with all the other opportunities available, young Dutch men and women had very little incentive to seek their fortunes in the wilds of North America.

Hudson's Voyage

Relative latecomers to North American exploration, the Dutch did not mount an expedition to the continent until 1609. English-born navigator Henry Hudson, sailing on behalf of the Dutch, explored the region around Long Island and Manhattan Island in his ship the *Half Moon*. Hoping to find a passage to the Far East, Hudson sailed 160 miles northward on the river that now bears his name. After 10 days, and upon reaching the site of present-day Albany, New York, he realized that the river did not offer a passageway to the west. Hudson could not have known that the river formed part of a mostly waterborne corridor, which extended northward, encompassing Lake Champlain and the Richelieu River. Observing that the Mohawk River branched off to the west, Hudson correctly surmised that it could provide an avenue to allow furs to be transported from the interior.

Hudson's interactions with the natives as he sailed upriver ran the gamut from hospitality to hostility. In one instance, some Indian chiefs visited Hudson aboard the *Half Moon* and he treated them to their first taste of alcohol. The Indians' reaction to the strange liquid was initially one of distrust, when the chiefs sniffed the offered glass of *aqua vitae* suspiciously. This quickly changed to distress, after one of the chiefs fell down after quickly quaffing the glass, and then to exhilaration, after the downed chief recovered, stated that he had never felt better, and asked for more. Some natives found the novel sensation that alcohol induced to be disturbing.

As they journeyed upriver, Hudson and his men traded with the natives, exchanging beads, knives, and hatchets for beaver and otter pelts. Much like Cartier 75 years earlier, Hudson also encountered native leaders who did their best – even though Hudson, like Cartier, could not understand them – to impress upon him that their domain encompassed all he saw about him. The friendly interactions with the natives paid important dividends to Hudson, as they provided him with information he needed to navigate the river, noting the location of submerged obstructions and its depth at different points.

But not all relations between Hudson and the natives were friendly. In one incident a native man stole aboard the *Half Moon*, filching a pillow and two shirts. As he fled, a sailor fatally shot him in the chest. Other natives in canoes waiting near the ship attempted to flee with the stolen items, but the Dutch pursued them. One of the natives attempted to board the Dutch pursuit boat, only to have his hands severed with a sword. Given the value of the items, the actions of Hudson and his men seem to be out of proportion to the offense. Not surprisingly, after these incidents relations with the natives quickly deteriorated. The next day, three canoes filled with native warriors approached the *Half Moon*. Once within range, they launched arrows at the Dutch sailors on deck, who responded by returning fire with muskets and a small cannon, killing several natives and forcing the others to retreat.

When he began his journey upriver in mid-August, Hudson could not have known that the Mohawk, the easternmost of the Five Nations Iroquois, had engaged in a losing altercation with French explorer Samuel de Champlain only six weeks earlier. It is possible that some Mohawks may have been among the natives who made contact with Hudson: more likely, they at least had heard about the vessel with strange men aboard it. Thanks to Champlain, the Iroquois had suddenly (and shockingly) been made aware of the advantages of European technology. The Mohawk realized they needed access to European goods to bring them to parity with the Wendat, whom the French referred to as Huron, and may have harbored hopes that this new group of Europeans would help them offset the advantage their rivals now enjoyed.

Figure 6.1 A native hunter prepares to club a beaver. In this case, the artist gave the native a beard. Note the size of the beaver in comparison to the hunter; that is an extraordinarily large animal. Detail from *France occidentale dans l'Amérique Septentrional ou le cours de la rivière de St. Laurens*, Paris, 1718. Courtesy of Darlington Library, University of Pittsburgh.

The Dutch West India Company

Moving slowly, the government of the Netherlands chartered the Dutch West India Company to develop and exploit the resources of North America. The Company established its first North American trading post, Fort Nassau, near the confluence of the Hudson and Mohawk Rivers in 1614. Initially, the Dutch situated the post too close to the rivers and it flooded every spring. A couple of years later, they relocated the post to the site of present-day Albany, renaming it Fort Orange.

The Dutch West India Company chose a good site for their trading post, as it provided easy access for native peoples to the north and west. Only years later did the Dutch recognize the need to guard the mouth of the Hudson River. Using only a few warships, a European rival could simply block the waterway's mouth and strangle the nascent colony.

Hoping to quell the potential threat, the Dutch took control of Manhattan Island and established New Amsterdam (the future New York City) as the administrative center of New Netherland in the 1620s. The famous story about the Dutch purchasing Manhattan Island for 24 dollars' worth of beads and useless trinkets is largely an exaggeration by a nineteenth-century American antiquarian. The Dutch did negotiate with a few native people who happened to be about, but in all likelihood these individuals were wandering peoples who did not live on Manhattan, but simply took the gifts the Dutch offered, not realizing that they had supposedly "sold" the island. In any case, it did not take the Dutch long to recognize what a bargain they had made. New Amsterdam's harbor may have been the finest port on the North American eastern seaboard.

Despite these seeming advantages, the Dutch West India Company experienced a great deal of difficulty in luring desperately needed colonists to North America. The success of the Netherlands' vast overseas empire actually worked against their North American colonization efforts. The Dutch West India Company discovered that young people in the Netherlands had little or no incentive to migrate to their New World colony. As mentioned, Dutch commercial success elsewhere around the globe presented them with many other choices, nearly all of them more attractive, lucrative, and probably less hazardous than anything that North America at the time could offer.

New Netherland's Two Indian Policies

While the Dutch West India Company realized great profits by engaging in the fur trade with native people, it also needed colonists to raise crops and livestock to feed its traders and employees in order to assure the survival of their enterprise. This resulted in New Netherland assuming an odd economic geography, and two distinct Indian policies. Along the southern portion of the Hudson River, Dutch farms sprang up in the vicinity of, and immediately to the north of, New Amsterdam. At Fort Orange, the Dutch had almost no – and did not want any – colonists, lest they create conflict with their Native American trading partners.

By serving as a funnel for the furs that native people brought in from the north and the west, Fort Orange also placed the Dutch in close proximity to their Mohican trading partners, and the Mohawk, who were the easternmost peoples of the Iroquois League. For the most part, the native peoples in the vicinity of New Amsterdam consisted of small groups of Algonquin peoples. Needing their land and recognizing their weakness, the Dutch often engaged in conflict with these peoples in an effort to drive them away from the region.

The Iroquois League became the primary trading partners of the Dutch. Consisting of five nations, they forged themselves into a formidable confederacy. By a happy accident (for them) of geography, the Iroquois sat athwart key trade routes to the north and west, as well as between the nascent French and Dutch colonies. Able to place hundreds of warriors in the field, and enjoying superior access to European goods that other tribes could not match thanks to their proximity to Fort Orange, the Iroquois would affect the direction of early American history to a greater extent than any other group of native peoples.

Their name for themselves, *Haudenosaunee*, meant the "lodge extended lengthwise" and alluded to the traditional Iroquois dwelling, the longhouse. The longhouse also served as a metaphor that explained the political geography of the Iroquois. The boundaries of the Iroquois League extended from the confluence of the Hudson and Mohawk Rivers in the east, where the Mohawk kept watch over the eastern door. Far to the west, in the vicinity of the Genesee River, the Seneca kept watch over the western door. In the center the Onondaga (located near what is now Syracuse, New York) kept the council fire. The Cayuga situated themselves between the Onondaga and the Seneca, while the Oneida sat between the Mohawk and Onondaga.

Together the Five Nations constituted the most powerful native polity in the Northeast. Since Samuel de Champlain's violent encounter with them in 1609, they had engaged in sporadic hostilities with the colony of New France and its native allies. The establishment of Fort Orange – and the Dutch quest for profit – assured the Iroquois of continued access to trade goods such as cloth, knives, and hatchets. The Iroquois began calling the Dutch *Kristoni,* which roughly translates as "metal worker," indicative of their value to the natives. The Dutch West India Company promulgated several laws and ordinances that forbade their traders and colonists from exchanging firearms for beaver pelts with the Indians, but they seem to have been largely ignored. As early as 1638 according to one source, the Mohawks possessed "firelocks, powder and lead in proportion," which gave them a marked advantage over their Algonquin and Wendat enemies.

While valuing native people as trading partners, the Dutch traders in North America generally held them at arm's length. Unlike their French counterparts, who made it a point to cultivate native friendship by observing their diplomatic forms and participating in their ceremonies, the Dutch often avoided these rituals – or as one trader derisively called them "the usual ceremonies" – that native people often regarded as essential, since they did not separate friendship from commerce.

Surprisingly, the Dutch, renowned and envied in Europe for their ability to forge commercial partnerships around the globe, knew shockingly little about the native peoples with whom they dealt. Dutch West India Company traders in the vicinity of Fort Orange knew who the Mohawks were and could often speak at least a smattering – usually just enough to conduct trade – of their language, but otherwise they appear to have been remarkably ignorant regarding the native peoples all around them. Dutch traders commonly referred to non-Mohawk Iroquoian speakers as "Senecas," or more ambiguously as the "far Indians," a catch-all term that indicates that they had little or no inkling as to the identity of these people. When one of the few Dutch missionaries to journey to New Netherland asked a veteran trader for guidance in learning Indian languages, he received the reply that he should not bother. The trader made the rather amazing claim that the Indians changed their language every few years, making it impossible for the Dutch to learn it.

Whereas other European powers made attempts of varying sincerity to convert native people to Christianity, the Dutch, interested primarily in commerce, sent only two missionaries to North America between 1609 and 1664. One of these men despaired of ever converting native people, concluding that they were as "stupid as garden poles," and regarded attempting to master native languages as a hopeless task. He argued that the best strategy to follow in converting native peoples would be to wait a few generations; presumably by that time the Indians would master the Dutch language. The other Dutch missionary noted that when he attempted to tell the Mohawk about Christianity, they pointed to the behavior of colonists and traders, and asked why they could not follow their own religion. For the entire history of New Netherland, Dutch missionaries recorded a grand total of only one native convert – a man who traded his Bible for brandy after only a few days.

The Mohawk–Mahican War

Access to Fort Orange became so valuable to native peoples that from 1624 to 1628 the Mohawk and Mahican fought a brief, bloody conflict over access to the fort and Dutch trade goods. In many respects, The Mohawk–Mahican War became the prototype for the far longer and bloodier Beaver Wars that the Iroquois League conducted against other native peoples in the Great lakes and Ohio country later in the seventeenth century.

Straddling the territories of the Mahicans and the Mohawk, Fort Orange and the traders stationed there found themselves as uneasy, and largely unwilling, witnesses to the conflict. Normally, the two native nations maintained an uneasy peace with one another, engaging in short, sporadic conflicts that typically revolved around the need to seize captives to replace their dead.

By planting Fort Orange on the eastern edge of Mohawk country, the Dutch unwittingly introduced a new twist into Native American conflicts. The post gave native people easier access to trade goods they desired, which both the Mohawk and the Mahican wished to acquire while denying them to their enemies. This seems to have been the thinking behind Mohawk attacks on the Mahican. If the Mohawk could displace the Mahican, and drive them away from the vicinity of Fort Orange, they would be weakened, and the Dutch would be forced to trade exclusively with the Mohawk.

While dependent on native people as trading partners, most of the Dutch in the vicinity of Fort Orange prudently retired to New Amsterdam, not wanting to be caught in the crossfire of a war between two Indian peoples. The traders who did remain seemed to have hoped that the Mahicans would win the war, but they largely stood by as the conflict raged about them, and were obviously more concerned about the impact of the wars on their profits than anything else.

At one point, the Dutch did get involved. Seven Dutchmen, led by a Captain from Fort Orange, actively sided with the Mahican, joining them on a war party against the Mohawk. Despite the presence of Dutch soldiers equipped with firearms, the Mohawks, armed only with bows and arrows, successfully ambushed them and their Mahican allies. Apparently, in the years since Champlain's encounter with them, the Mohawk had gotten over their fear of firearms – or perhaps had learned the limitations of European muskets. The Mohawk killed four of the Dutchmen, at least one of whom they "devoured, after having well roasted him."

Realizing the disastrous effect that this incident could have on trade, the Dutch West India Company moved swiftly to repair relations with the Mohawk. Within a few days, Dutch trader Pieter Barentsz visited the Mohawks and apologized. Peter Minuit, the new director of the Company's operations in North America, arrived from New Amsterdam, ascertained what had taken place, and also visited the Mohawk. Within a few days, he had appointed a new commander at Fort Orange, one who was "well acquainted with the language" of the Mohawks. For their part, the Mohawks expressed surprise that the Dutch had inserted themselves in the conflict. They apologized, stating that had the Dutchmen not interfered, "they would not have shot them." After this incident, the Dutch West India Company adopted a policy of non-interference with the Five Nations.

The conflict between the Mohawk and Mahican ended sometime in late 1628. After this time, most of the Mahicans fled to the east and south, and many of them relocated to the Connecticut River valley. Still others were captured and adopted by the Mohawk. The Mohawk–Mahican war differed from other intertribal conflicts in that it appears to have been the first time native people fought primarily for commercial motives, rather than over issues of honor or captives. Both sides attempted to secure their trade with the Dutch at Fort Orange at the expense of the other. It also appears to have served as a template for the later Iroquois wars against the Wendat and other native peoples to the west and north in their quest to gain primary control of the beaver trade.

Dutch and Algonquins at New Amsterdam

But if the Dutch took a hands-off policy in their dealings with native peoples in the vicinity of Fort Orange, they dealt with native peoples in the vicinity of New Amsterdam quite differently. Whereas the Dutch needed the Indians in the vicinity of Fort Orange as trading partners, they valued New Amsterdam for its strategic position at the mouth of the Hudson and for the lands immediately to the north of the city along the Hudson River, and those on the west bank of the river, where farmers raised food to feed the colony. The Dutch need for land on the southern extremity of the Hudson meant that the Indians who lived there had to be displaced. The fact that the Dutch engaged in agriculture on the lower Hudson also increased the opportunities for conflict as the colonists' cows and pigs – allowed to run free and forage in the forest rather than being fenced in – often invaded and destroyed the Indians' cornfields. In a familiar chain of events, the Indians retaliated, most often by killing and eating the offending livestock, which of course, enraged the farmers who owned the animals.

Several small conflicts, all of them aimed toward removing native people from the southern end of the Hudson River valley, took place between the Dutch- and Algonquin-speaking peoples of the region. One of these conflicts, Kieft's War (named after Governor Willem Kieft), resulted from his attempt to impose a tribute, to be paid in the form of pelts, maize, or wampum, on the "River Indians," a collective name the colonists applied to the small Algonquin bands who lived near Manhattan. Kieft justified the tax on the grounds that the Indians benefited from the presence of Dutch fortifications and Dutch soldiers. Kieft went further, claiming that Indians were subject to Dutch law, an argument that apparently did not impress the natives, who simply refused to pay. Kieft's real motive for the tax seems, however, to have been that he meant to provoke a conflict so as to have an excuse to remove the small Algonquin bands from the region and open more land to Dutch settlement.

In early 1643, hundreds of Tappan and Wecquaesgeek Indians fleeing attacks by the Mohawks, sought shelter at Pavonia near Manhattan. Seeking to make an example of the price of defying the Dutch, Kieft sent a force of approximately 80 troops to assault the encampment. Arriving during the hours of darkness, the Dutch set fire to the camp and killed over 100 Indians as they fled for their lives. But rather than end the threat of an Indian war, Kieft actually started another one that raged for two months. Other Algonquin peoples joined Tappan and Wecquaesgeek warriors in the attacks on Dutch farms and homesteads in the Hudson Valley, forcing most of the colonists to flee for the fortifications of New Amsterdam. Kieft managed to secure a peace in April of that year.

Kieft's peace turned out to be short lived, as incidents between the Dutch and the Algonquin peoples of the lower Hudson continued. By August 1643, Algonquin warriors began attacking Dutch trading vessels on the river. Having failed to end the conflicts with native peoples, Kieft employed John Underhill, the same military officer who had led New England troops in the massacre of the Pequot at their Mystic River fort in 1637. Employing 40 of his own men from New England to augment the Dutch militia, Underhill led attacks on surrounding native villages. In February 1644, Underhill and his men attacked a village occupied by about 500 Wecquaesgeek and Wappinger. Utilizing the same tactics that he used at the Mystic River fort, Underhill's men surrounded the village, set it ablaze, and shot down Indians as they fled the flames.

Convinced that he could eradicate the Algonquin presence on the lower Hudson, Kieft continued his wars against them. While he managed to kill large numbers of Indians, the resulting unrest prompted the Dutch West India Company to remove him from his post. Rather than helping the colony by opening more territory to Dutch settlement, Kieft's wars against the Indians actually appeared to have further stunted the already anemic rates of immigration to New Netherland. As late as 1645, only 300 colonists resided there. To remedy the situation, the Dutch West India Company appointed Peter Stuyvesant as the new governor. Stuyvesant ruled New Netherland as a virtual dictator until an English fleet sailed into New York Harbor in 1664 and compelled the Dutch to surrender the colony.

A decade after Kieft's departure, another Indian conflict, this one known as the Peach Tree War, began in 1655 when a Dutch colonist shot an Indian woman to death after discovering her picking fruit in his orchard. Unfortunately for the Dutch, the woman was part of a 2,000-strong force of Mahican, Esopus, and Hackensack Indians who planned to attack their traditional enemies on Long Island. The murder prompted them to turn their fury on the Dutch instead. With Stuyvesant and nearly all of New Netherland's 600 able-bodied men away conquering the colony of New Sweden, the virtually unopposed natives burned farms and orchards, seizing over 100 captives over a three-day period. When Stuyvesant returned, he negotiated with the natives, paying ransoms for the return of captured colonists.

Between 1659 and 1663, the Dutch fought a series of conflicts with the Esopus people. The first began in September 1659 when colonists attacked eight Esopus men, killing one of them, near the town of the same name. The Esopus responded by laying siege to the village for approximately three weeks. Governor Stuyvesant raised a force to lift the siege, but by the time he and his troops arrived, the Esopus had left. Stuyvesant renewed the conflict in March of the next year, but the war dragged on, stopping and starting, ending inconclusively at the end of 1663.

Iroquois Economic Crisis and the Weakening of the Wendat

Farther north at Fort Orange, relations between native people and the Dutch – with the exception of the brief dustup during the Mohawk–Mahican War – remained peaceful and prosperous. Throughout the 1620s and 1630s, the Mohawk and other Iroquois nations continued to funnel their furs to the Dutch trading post. Officially, the Dutch West India Company attempted to keep alcohol and firearms out of the hands of native people. Despite repeated official announcements and published ordinances that prohibited the trade of these items, Dutch traders habitually ignored these rules, and the Company made little or no effort to enforce them. The Dutch became the most reliable providers of firearms, gunpowder, and shot to the Iroquois, giving them a marked advantage over their native enemies.

In the early 1640s, however, the Iroquois experienced an economic crisis when it became apparent they had trapped out most of the fur-bearing animals in their territory. Dependent on the goods provided by the Dutch, the Iroquois faced disaster unless they could find a new source of furs. The Iroquois looked to the north, to peoples who shared a mythological origin with them, the Wendat.

While the Iroquois suffered through an economic crisis, the Wendat prospered. Their relationship with the French, and their location immediately to the east of Lake Huron, helped to make them the middlemen in the fur trade. Raising bumper crops of maize, the Wendat traded their surplus grain to native peoples farther north, such as the Nippising and Ottawa, in exchange for beaver pelts, which they then exchanged with their French trade partners for manufactured goods. However, the Wendat relationship with the French came with some drawbacks. In the early 1630s, a now elderly Samuel de Champlain, the governor of New France, insisted that the Wendat allow Jesuit missionaries into their communities as a condition for continued trade.

Known to the Indians as the Black Robes (because of the black habits they wore) the Jesuits' missionary efforts divided the Wendat people along religious lines. Settled in largely immobile agricultural villages, the Wendat – unlike more mobile hunting peoples such as the Montagnais and Mi'kmaq – would be easier to convert, the Jesuits believed. Unlike other European missionaries, the Jesuits took pains to ensure that catechumens (people receiving instruction in the Christian faith prior to baptism) understood the nature of the religion to which they were converting. After extensive instruction by a Jesuit, the potential convert often had to explain, in his or her own words, their understanding of the Catholic faith.

Traditionalist Wendat medicine men and shamans opposed the Jesuits, vying with them for control of native religious life. Native people believed these individuals possessed great spiritual power; likewise, the Jesuits argued that they also had great spiritual power, one granted to them by virtue of being the representatives of their god. But claiming to be a spiritually powerful being carried with it both advantages and disadvantages. The native peoples of the Northeast viewed spiritual power as double edged; it could be used for good or evil. Jesuits and medicine men often competed to demonstrate to native people who had the most effective cures for their ailments. If the patient improved or recovered, the medicine man or the Jesuit received credit or praise. If the patient continued to suffer or perished, a medicine man could expect commendation; Jesuits who failed to "cure" a patient may be threatened with death, but the need to maintain the economic lifeline to the French meant such threats were seldom carried out. Given the state of seventeenth-century medicine, the Jesuits could often offer comfort, but very seldom could they actually cure a sick person. The Jesuits usually gave ill natives lemons, raisins, cordials, or water sweetened with sugar (which the natives called "French snow"). None of these, of course, could cure ailments such as smallpox and other European diseases, but they did have a medicinal effect.

The unwitting importation of European pathogens often worked against the Jesuits. While Europeans had little understanding as to how disease spread, native people could not help but notice that the arrival of smallpox and the Jesuits seemed to be nearly contemporaneous with one another. Regarding the Jesuits as powerful spiritual beings, some native people, encouraged by medicine men and sha-mans, accused them of being sorcerers who purposely spread illness. It did not help that the Jesuits engaged in what native people considered strange behaviors. For example, they evidenced no interest in native women. In a society that had little privacy, the common European practice of locking their doors made the Jesuits seem suspicious, and some native people suspected they cast malevolent spells in secret.

In encouraging native people to think of them as powerful beings, the Jesuits utilized what could be considered "magic." One Jesuit, confronted by an audience of native hunters laughing at his attempts to speak their language, stunned them into silence when he produced a compass and told them that it enabled him to know the shape of the earth and where the sun went at night. Performing simple tricks such as picking up nails with a magnetized sword also impressed native people. The Jesuits augmented their status as spiritually powerful individuals by utilizing almanacs to seemingly predict lunar eclipses. They publicly challenged native medicine men to predict eclipses, something the Jesuits knew full well they could not do, giving their converts a demonstration of a superior spiritual power that they could point to in their disputations with traditionalists.

Other Jesuits astonished native people by demonstrating the power of writing. When a Frenchman damaged a canoe, he sent a note via an Indian runner to a trading post a short distance away. The Indians who accompanied him were impressed when another trader arrived a few hours later with a replacement canoe. The Jesuits explained that the written word gave the French the ability to make their will known from one end of the earth to the other. Native people expressed amazement, because writing seemed to be a form of magic that per-mitted one to read the thoughts of another at a distance. In one notable instance, Jesuits asked two Wendat converts to ferry supplies from one mission to another. During the voyage, the two men became hungry and devoured the communion wafers that formed part of their cargo. Upon arriving at their destination, a Jesuit checked the loading manifest, noted the missing communion wafers, and told the two astonished Indians that the piece of paper told him that they had eaten them. Literacy also enabled the Jesuits to deliver sermons that were identical.

Native people valued their own oral traditions, and prided them-selves on their accurate recall. Young people attempted to remember their people's stories and legends word for word. But they soon realized that the ability to record things in writing exceeded that of human recall. Native people expressed amazement when they heard a Jesuit sermon in Quebec, then traveled to Montreal, where they might hear another missionary give the same exact sermon with no deviation from what they had heard previously. When Jesuits informed Indians that the Bible contained the words of men who had been dead for a thousand years or more, it further solidified their reputation – while perhaps frightening some native people – as spiritually powerful individuals.

Like the New England Puritans they detested, the Jesuits created separate communities for their Wendat converts in an effort to remove them from the influence of their traditionalist brethren. But unlike the Puritans who created the Praying Towns, the Jesuits, realizing that their success (and that of the French colony as well) relied on maintaining native people's good will, wisely made no effort to force their converts to surrender their culture. "Civilizing" the Indians remained the ultimate objective of the Jesuits, but they saw the saving of their souls as their most immediate concern. Assimilation could come later.

In many respects, the Jesuits' conversion efforts appear to have been more effective than those of the English or the Spanish. Unlike New England's native peoples whose traditional world had largely been disrupted, or the Pueblos who faced forced conversion at the hands of the Franciscans, many of Canada's native peoples, despite epidemics of European diseases, remained receptive to the Jesuits' missionary efforts. While medicine men and shamans – the Jesuit's natural rivals – considered them to be overly aggressive, other natives saw them quite differently. Their willingness to learn native languages, and their attempts to explain, rather than dictate, their faith, and above all their physical courage when they went among hostile peoples, helped them win converts. To be sure, a good percentage of natives remained baffled by the Jesuits and Christianity and would never convert.

Unwittingly, the Jesuits set in motion a process that weakened the Wendat nation from within by splintering them along religious lines, and would also imperil French efforts to retain control of Canada. Converts enjoyed superior access to French goods, and as the Wendat weakened, many of them followed the Jesuits because they believed that their "magic" may provide them with some protection from the Iroquois. But the split the Jesuits created among the Wendat left them unable to resist Iroquois incursions in the 1640s and 1650s.

The Beaver Wars

The Iroquois economic crisis led to a series of conflicts that historians often call the "Beaver Wars," which lasted from the 1640s to the end of the seventeenth century. Punctuated by lulls, treaties, and truces, the Iroquois pursued the conflict with three primary objectives in mind. Looking northward, they sought to gain control of the Wendat fur-trading routes that linked them to native peoples of the Upper and Western Great Lakes. Once in command of the trade, the Iroquois planned to funnel beaver pelts to their Dutch partners at Fort Orange, thus ensuring their continued access to European goods. This would, in turn, help them achieve their second goal, the economic crippling of the New France colony. The third Iroquois objective was to extend the traditional "mourning war" practice. Clan matrons frequently instigated mourning wars, most often as a response to deaths due to combat with native enemies, or because of loss of clan members due to disease. When European disease epidemics – most notably smallpox – devastated the Iroquois in the 1630s, clan matrons demanded that their young men go to war in order to secure captives, some of whom would be adopted as replacements for the dead and keep the tribe viable.

At first the Iroquois attempted to avoid conflict with the Wendat by employing diplomacy in an effort to achieve their ends. In 1645, Iroquois representatives held a conference with the Wendat, offering them access to Dutch trade goods at Fort Orange. However, Christian converts among the Wendat deemed the price the Iroquois asked – the abandonment of their French allies and the Jesuits – for right of way through Five Nations country to the Dutch trading post as too high. This further contributed to an emerging split among the Wendat, as many traditionalists seem to have a least considered such an arrangement reasonable.

The Wendat rejection of the Iroquois peace overtures instigated the first phase of the Beaver Wars. Through 1646 and 1647, Iroquois warriors launched sporadic attacks against the Wendat, the key native trade partners of the French. Most of these attacks targeted Wendat fur-trading fleets as they made their way south on the Ottawa River. At other times, Iroquois and Wendat war parties encountered one another in the forest.

A new and troubling development for the Wendat occurred when the Iroquois launched attacks on a few of their villages in 1648.

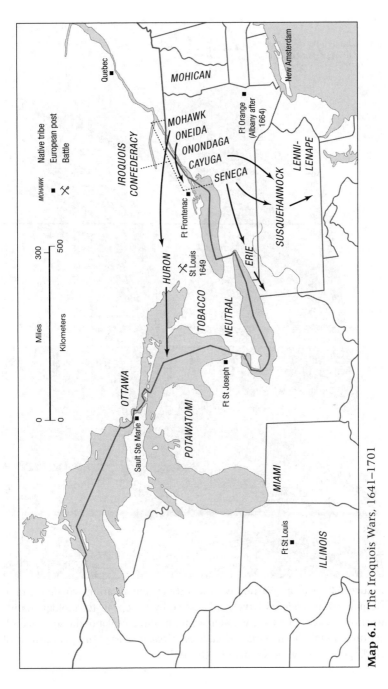

Map 6.1 The Iroquois Wars, 1641–1701

141

Figure 6.2 Huron Warrior with a musket and wearing wooden armor. Despite being rendered largely ineffective by European technology, native warriors occasionally wore wooden armor in battle well into the seventeenth century. Detail from *Partie orientale du Canada*, Paris, 1689. Courtesy of Darlington Library, University of Pittsburgh.

Previously, the Iroquois rarely attacked large villages. But in July of that year, a large Iroquois force lunged out of the maize fields that surrounded the village of Saint Joseph. Repelling the few warriors present in the village, the Iroquois fanned out into the forest, capturing roughly 700 women and children who made futile attempts to flee to other nearby Wendat communities.

But the heaviest blow to fall on the Wendat came in March 1649, when Iroquois assaults, aimed primarily at villages of converts, devastated their country. The scale and timing of the attacks made it clear that the Iroquois now practiced a new form of warfare. Prior to 1649, Iroquois military operations consisted mainly of surprise attacks, often carried out by small bands of warriors (usually 100 or fewer). These war parties struck, then quickly made off with captives or whatever loot they could carry, retreating to the safety of Iroquoia.

In the March 1649 campaign, 1,000 Iroquois launched an early morning attack on the village of St Ignace. Taking it by surprise, the Iroquois captured the village largely intact, seizing captives and foodstuffs. A few Wendat nevertheless escaped, fleeing to the nearby village of St Louys. Warned of the Iroquois presence, the warriors at St Louys braced themselves for an attack, while sending their women and children to the safety of the Jesuit mission at Saint Marie.

By mid-morning, the Jesuits and the Wendat refugees at the Ste Marie mission could see flames sprouting from St Louys. Having killed most of the village's outnumbered defenders, the Iroquois now paused, as if considering whether or not to assault Ste Marie. The Iroquois captured two Jesuit missionaries at St Ignace and tortured them to death. The deaths of the two Jesuits placed the divisions that they caused among the Wendat in a microcosm. On the one hand, the Jesuits reportedly comforted the converts who were tortured with them by reminding them they would soon be in heaven. The accounts of the Jesuits' deaths, however, also point out that Wendat traditionalists who had chosen to live with the Iroquois – and had joined their war parties – instigated and led the Iroquois in torturing and finally slaying the two Jesuits. In the Ste Marie mission, the Wendat converts and the Jesuits could see the flames rising from St Louys and readied themselves for the inevitable Iroquois assault.

The assault never came. On the third day – for reasons that neither the Jesuits nor the Wendat could fathom – the Iroquois, using their captives as pack animals, loaded them with loot, bound the elderly and feeble residents of St Ignace in their cabins, and torched the village as they retreated. The Wendat seem to have been in a state of shock. In the wake of the attack, they still had the numbers and perhaps the military capacity to pursue the Iroquois. But the divisions that the Jesuits created among them now ran too deep; traditionalist communities largely refused – or were slow – to come to the aid of their tribesmen who lived in Jesuit missions. A hastily assembled expedition did make a halfhearted attempt to pursue the Iroquois army, but they did not catch it, and the Jesuits suspected that the outgunned Wendat had little enthusiasm for combat.

The attacks stunned the Wendat because they differed from past Iroquois assaults in several respects. First, they occurred during a time of year when native peoples generally refrained from warfare. Native Americans (and many European armies of the time as well) often did not fight in the winter. For one thing, weapons frequently did not work in the cold. With metallurgy not quite being what it would be in future centuries, musket barrels were susceptible to "frost wedging," which could cause them to burst. Even with snowshoes, travel could be very difficult in a region crisscrossed with rivers, creeks, and streams. It was also unusual that the Iroquois ranged so far from their homes in March, when there was still snow on the ground in Ontario. A sudden March thaw could have easily transformed the landscape into mud and mire, rendering snowshoes useless, severely restricting their mobility, and making a rapid retreat impossible.

The Jesuits encouraged the Wendat to rebuild their mission communities. Wendat leaders refused, however, deciding that Huronia, now demonstrably vulnerable to the Iroquois, must be evacuated. The Jesuits attempted to convince their converts to resettle on Manitoulin Island in northern Lake Huron, but they refused, pointing out (correctly) that the growing season in that region was too short for growing a reliable crop of maize. Instead, most of the Wendat fled to Ganadoe (now Christian) Island, located in Georgian Bay, in the southeastern portion of Lake Huron. Wendat converts hoped to plant maize on Ganadoe, but they did not count on the difficulty of clearing the old-growth forests that covered the island. Unable to clear enough land, many of the Wendat perished of starvation in 1649–1650. The Jesuits recorded gruesome scenes as survivors found themselves reduced to cannibalism. Other converts went to Quebec, where they established a settlement under Jesuits guidance. Other surviving Wendat fled Ganadoe and dispersed throughout the Great Lakes region and the Ohio country. Some of them merged with other bands of Algonquin-speaking peoples, while those who settled in the Ohio country began to establish a separate cultural identity for themselves as Wayandot. Still others, however, opted not only for physical but cultural survival, going to live among the relatives who had been captured by the Iroquois. Many of these people ended up choosing to assimilate into one of the five Iroquois nations.

In the wake of their success in 1649, the Iroquois followed up with attacks on other native peoples throughout the 1650s. Some Wendat fled to the Eries and the Neutrals, who were linguistically and culturally very similar to themselves. The Iroquois assaulted the Eries and the Neutrals in the mid-1650s, killing most of them while incorporating the survivors.

The overarching Iroquois goal in these campaigns was to secure control of the fur-trading routes. The elimination of the Wendat, however, shifted the center of the trade westward, and Algonquin-speaking peoples in the northern Great Lakes region, such as the Ottawa and Nipissing, emerged as the new middlemen in the trade. The Five Nations easily had more firepower and could put more men in the field than either of these peoples. But the Ottawa and other small bands actually presented the Iroquois with difficulties they did not experience in their conflict with the Wendat. Unlike the Wendat, who settled in large, stationary villages, the Ottawa and Nipissing were largely nomadic hunters. They traveled in small bands, and when discovered could be overwhelmed by the Iroquois. One difficulty for the Iroquois, then, was finding them; another difficulty was that their experience with the Wendat taught the French that their native allies must be as well armed as the Iroquois. As a result, Iroquois warriors now found themselves going up against native peoples were just as well armed as they were.

The Iroquois, however, soon found themselves embroiled in another conflict, this time with the Iroquoian-speaking Susquehannocks. Numerous, backed by the colonies of Maryland and Delaware, and able to obtain powder and cannon from Swedish traders, the Susquehannocks proved to be formidable foes. Unable to fight the Susquehannocks and simultaneously continue their campaign in the Great Lakes region, the Iroquois made a temporary peace with their enemies to the north and west. They invited the Jesuits to establish a mission among the Onondaga. There the Jesuits discovered many of their former Wendat converts, most of whom were very happy to see the missionaries. They also noted the effects of the prolonged conflict on Iroquois demographics. The Jesuits noted that adoptees – Wendats and others – outnumbered native-born Iroquois. The Susquehannock threat came to an end, but for reasons that had little to do with the Iroquois. Attacked by Virginians in the opening phases of Bacon's Rebellion, the Susquehannock were dispersed, and the Seneca, the westernmost of the Five Nations, incorporated many of them.

Freed of the threat to their south, the Iroquois abrogated their agreements with New France and its native allies, and renewed their war with the peoples of the Ohio country and the Great Lakes. But over time, the ongoing conflict served to weaken the Five Nations. Their enemies acquired European weaponry, and Iroquois losses mounted.

Perhaps nothing pointed out the weakening of the Iroquois more than their inability to defend Iroquoia itself. In 1687, the French invaded the Seneca country. While the French and their native allies inflicted few casualties – the Seneca largely avoided open battle with the invaders – the attackers burned four towns, and most significantly destroyed more than a million bushels of maize, beans, and squash. Besides the hardship inflicted on the Seneca – and members of other Iroquois nations who dipped into their food stores to feed their brethren – they also learned that the English, who replaced the Dutch as their primary trade partners, made unreliable military allies. The Iroquois retaliated by attacking Montreal and French posts throughout the Great Lakes.

In 1670, the English established the Hudson's Bay Company, which shifted the focus of the fur trade northward, making it impossible for the Iroquois or their French enemies to gain anything approaching a monopoly on the fur trade. Weakened by half a century of warfare, the Iroquois looked for a way out of their predicament. They found it in a master stroke of diplomacy.

The Grand Settlement of 1701

In a series of treaties negotiated with the French at Montreal and the English colony of New York at Albany in 1700 and 1701, the Iroquois came up with a cunning diplomatic solution to their difficulties. In what came to be known as the Grand Settlement of 1701, the Five Nations began the new policy of what some historians have called "armed neutrality." Essentially, the Iroquois promised the French that they would remain neutral in future conflicts between them and the English in the colonies – under certain conditions. But at the same time, the Iroquois assured the English in New York that they would aid them in future conflicts against New France. This promise, however, came with a condition: the Iroquois wanted the English to secure for them the former Wendat hunting territory in Ontario. In 1701, this condition was impossible to fulfill, and the Iroquois knew it – as did the New York treaty representatives. In effect, since the colony could not fulfill this condition, the Iroquois for all practical purposes, would remain neutral.

For their part, while the French engaged in hostilities against the Iroquois for much of the 1690s (and most of the seventeenth century for that matter), they had no desire to destroy the League. The Iroquois formed a barrier between New France's native allies and trade partners, and the English trading post at Albany. The inefficiency of French manufacturers and higher shipping costs meant the goods they offered their Indian allies were more expensive and of lesser quality than English goods. While the French had no great love of the Iroquois, they realized that eliminating or weakening them to the extent that their Algonquin-speaking allies lost their fear of them would open the trading routes to Albany, and hence away from Montreal and Quebec. The French did not want their trading partners to discover that the English had better goods and better prices. In the late 1680s, for example, a native person who desired a musket, a pound of lead, and eight pounds of gunpowder could obtain them in Montreal in exchange for a dozen beaver pelts. In the same time frame, English traders in Albany offered the same goods – and in all likelihood the musket would have been of better quality – for only four beaver pelts. Thus while the Iroquois League may have been defeated, the French recognized that their destruction would not serve their long-term interests.

For the next half-century, the Iroquois would occasionally make noises about abandoning neutrality to ensure a steady flow of gifts from both the English and the French. On the part of the French, the thought that the Iroquois may abandon neutrality evoked dread. They would usually provide the Iroquois with presents to ensure they remained neutral. At the same time, when the League suggested that it may abandon neutrality, it raised the hopes of the English colonies, who often wanted the Iroquois to join them in their wars against the French. The English frequently lavished gifts on the Iroquois – only to be disappointed, when the League had a change of heart. This "play-off system," as it came to be known, would end only in the middle of the next century, toward the end of the French and Indian War, when the now Six Nations finally joined the English in a conflict.

7

Seeking a Middle Ground

For the first several decades of the seventeenth century, the native peoples of what later would be called the Middle Colonies had fewer and more mixed interactions with Europeans than did their neighbors in New England or the Chesapeake. The native people of Maryland shared some of the alternating shifts between peace, war, and at times quasi-war, which afflicted their brethren in Virginia. The Lenni-Lenape (also known as Delaware) who lived in what became eastern Pennsylvania and New Jersey, and the Susquehannock peoples of Maryland and Pennsylvania had intermittent contacts with European traders over three quarters of a century before the Dutch, Swedes, and English settled the region.

Native peoples in the region of the Delaware River Valley sometimes traded and fought with Swedish colonists. In the mid-seventeenth century, the Dutch seized New Sweden, bringing the Scandinavian nation's brief, underfunded experiment with North American colonization to an end. Early Lenni-Lenape contacts with Europeans included an encounter with the Dutch explorer Henry Hudson. More than a century after the event, a Lenni-Lenape person related a legend of the meeting with Hudson to a Moravian missionary, which offers a native perspective of the first meetings between native people and Europeans. Perhaps seeking to impress the Lenni-Lenape leaders, Hudson appeared to them wearing a red

"Times Are Altered with Us": American Indians from First Contact to the New Republic, First Edition. Roger M. Carpenter.
© 2015 John Wiley & Sons, Inc. Published 2015 by John Wiley & Sons, Inc.

velvet suit with gold trim. Inviting the Delaware chiefs aboard his ship, the *Half Moon*, Hudson offered them their first taste of alcohol (noted briefly in Chapter 6). Initially suspicious of the strange liquid Hudson offered them, each Delaware chief took a turn sniffing the proffered glass and, uncertain of its contents and not, apparently, liking its smell, passed it on to his neighbor. Finally, one of the chiefs gave an impromptu speech to the others, pointing out they should not be discourteous to Hudson – whom they suspected might be a representative of the Manitou – and that he would take it upon himself to uphold the honor of his country, even at the risk of his life. With that, the chief drained the glass. Within a few moments, he began to stagger and then passed out. The other chiefs, thinking that Hudson had poisoned their peer, became very much alarmed. Within a few moments, however, the inebriated Lenni-Lenape chief recovered and returned to his feet, claiming that he had never felt better and asked for some more of the strange liquid.

But the story did not end there, and indeed, it contained a lesson. Hudson distributed presents to the Lenni-Lenape, such as stockings and ax-heads. When Dutch traders visited the Indians some months later, they discovered that the Indians had transformed the stockings into tobacco pouches and that the ax-heads had become rather ponderous pendants. Supposedly, the Dutch demonstrated the "proper" usage of the items, and then requested that the Lenni-Lenape give them a small piece of land; just enough to be covered by a bull hide. Thinking that these few Europeans could not possibly need much land, the Indians agreed. The Lenni-Lenape looked on in dismay as the Dutch produced a bull hide and proceeded to cut it into one long, thin, continuous strip that encompassed a large amount of land. Obviously, the Lenni-Lenape thought, these newcomers possessed a great deal of cunning and bore watching.

The New Sweden colony established their primary post, Fort Christina (present-day Wilmington, Delaware) on the west bank of the Delaware River. The Swedes traded with both the Lenni-Lenape and the Susquehannock peoples. Like other European traders, the Swedish colonists traded metal goods and cloth with the natives, but in at least one instance they provided the Susquehanna with something really special in exchange: cannons. There is no record of the Susquehanna actually firing the weapons, but their mere presence caused a large Iroquois war party to abort an attack on a village that had them.

Unfortunately for the Lenni-Lenape and the Susquehannock, they faced twin threats as the seventeenth century turned into the eighteenth. Like other Native American peoples, they lacked immunity to European pathogens. Decimated by epidemics of smallpox and other Old World diseases, both peoples found themselves with diminished populations, rendering them less able to fend off the second threat, which did not come from Europeans but from the powerful Iroquois League. Because of their linguistic and cultural similarities to the Iroquois, the Susquehannock found themselves largely absorbed into the League in the early eighteenth century.

Trade with Europeans instigated the technological arms race among native peoples. In order to be militarily superior to their native enemies, Amerindians had to acquire European goods, such as steel knives, hatchets, and arrowheads. Native peoples closer to the coast had an advantage over peoples farther inland in that they made first contact with European traders and attempted to control the flow of goods to other peoples and to deny them to their enemies.

Pennsylvania

While sharing some slight characteristics with the profit-driven Chesapeake and the religiously motivated New England colonies, the Pennsylvania colony, established in the 1680s, differed from the others in significant respects that benefitted both native people and the colonists – at least at first. The initial wave of Pennsylvania colonists, like the Puritans before them, represented an English religious sect who had managed to irk not only the English government but much of the island nation's religious establishment at the same time. Viewed as religious radicals, the Society of Friends – called Quakers by their critics because they supposedly "quaked" when they prayed – did not always follow the social and political norms of England during the Restoration. Adhering to a philosophy of pacifism, many Englishmen regarded the Friends as treasonous because they refused military service on the basis of their religious beliefs.

William Penn, scion of a wealthy and important English family, converted to Quakerism as a young man. Whereas the vast majority of Quakers occupied themselves as middling farmers and shopkeepers, Penn stood out from them (and from most other Englishmen for that matter) in that he not only had immense wealth at his disposal, but access to those in power. Using these connections,

Penn persuaded the Duke of York (the future King James II) to bestow upon him the single largest land grant the Crown ever gave to an individual. The Delaware River provided the proposed capital city of Philadelphia with access to the Atlantic in the east, and the Forks of the Ohio River formed the colony's approximate border in the west. Brushing against Lake Erie and the New York colony to the north, Maryland formed Pennsylvania's (meaning Penn's Woods) southern border.

Unlike New England, Pennsylvania actually promoted religious toleration, eschewing an official church (although Quakers did dominate the colony politically in its early years) and welcoming Dutch and German immigrants – not just Englishmen – regardless of their denomination. The reasoning behind Pennsylvania's policy of religious toleration and the opening of immigration to peoples from all over northern Europe could not be found solely in Quaker principles. It also lay in William Penn's need to turn a quick profit. By opening Pennsylvania to a large number of potential settlers, he increased his chances of selling land in his colony at a relatively fast pace. Despite his already immense wealth, Penn managed to live even beyond his considerable means, and constantly needed to add to his fortune to support his lavish lifestyle.

Quaker notions of tolerance benefitted Pennsylvania not only in attracting colonists but in their dealings with the region's native peoples as well. Penn differed from the leaders of the other seventeenth-century English colonization ventures in that rather than attempting to intimidate or overawe the local Lenni-Lenape people, he chose to approach them respectfully. While other English colonies signed what they loosely termed treaties with native peoples – often without entirely explaining the contents of the documents – Penn attempted to ensure the accurate translation of treaty minutes, going so far as to learn the Algonquin dialect spoken by the Lenni-Lenape. He also, unlike other English colonizers, furnished native peoples with copies of the agreements and attempted to make sure that the Indians understood the parameters of the treaties. For their part, the Lenni-Lenape, after having been decimated by European disease epidemics, like other native peoples, found themselves with excess land to sell in exchange for much-needed European cloth and metal goods.

Conflicts often occurred in other English colonies because native people believed they had simply granted the English the right to use their land while retaining their rights to continue to use it as well.

The English, coming from a legal culture that regarded private land ownership as an exclusive right, saw things quite differently. In signing contracts with native people, and paying for the land with trade goods, the English believed they had extinguished Indian land title, and granted themselves exclusive rights to the use of the land.

These practices – and not making clear to native peoples the terms of the treaties – led to conflict. Pennsylvania differed from the other colonies in that Penn paid native peoples fairly for their lands, and thereafter permitted colonists to settle only on lands that had already been purchased. In this manner, Penn and other Quaker leaders did much to spare Pennsylvania the Indian conflicts that plagued the Chesapeake and New England colonies.

Penn's fairness in dealing with native people, and that of the Quakers generally, and their adherence to the tenets of nonviolence, resulted in Pennsylvania becoming a destination for native peoples who found themselves driven out of other English colonies. Large numbers of Susquehannocks, reeling from their conflicts with the Virginia colony and with the Iroquois Confederation, and Shawnees, who fled the Indian slave wars in the South, made their way to Pennsylvania, partially lured there by the knowledge they would receive fair treatment. In the 1690s, Penn returned to England, where the newly installed monarch revoked Pennsylvania's charter. Penn managed to regain the charter, and returned to Pennsylvania in 1699. But shortly thereafter he left his namesake colony, never to return. In the ensuing years, Penn would send written instructions to the colony's legislature, which they largely ignored. Nevertheless, Penn's legacy continued to influence relations between the colonists and the Indians. Pennsylvania representatives often invoked Penn's memory and reputation for treating native people fairly when conferring with Indians. Likewise, Delaware diplomats often mentioned "Miquon" (meaning "feather;" referring to the quill pen used to sign treaties; it could have also been a play on Penn's last name) in an effort to remind colonial representatives of their obligations. In a similar fashion, the Conestoga used the term "Onas" (which also meant "feather") as a way of reminding Pennsylvania's leaders of William Penn. In fact, Onas became a hereditary term, commonly used by Algonquin-speaking diplomats when referring to the governor of Pennsylvania or Penn's descendants.

For Pennsylvania's first seven decades, from the founding of the colony in the 1680s until the beginning of the French and Indian War in the 1750s, Penn's attempts to cultivate amiable relations with native peoples bore fruit. While colonies in the Chesapeake and New England suffered through savage conflicts with Native Americans, Pennsylvania – in spite of strains that occurred after Penn's death – remained relatively peaceful. The policy set in place by Penn – and continued by the Quaker majority in the legislature – resulted in Pennsylvania avoiding the outlays for raising and arming militias that plagued the finances of other colonies. As the native peoples who sold their lands to Penn and his successors moved west, they also benefitted the colony by providing a defensive screen against other native peoples on its western frontier.

Several factors contributed to the end of the amiable relationship between the Pennsylvania colony and its native peoples. In 1718, William Penn died in England. Despite his depleted estate, his sons, after a long legal wrangle with their father's widow, gained control of the colony. Like their father, the Penn heirs also wished to turn a profit quickly, and the easiest way to do so would be to sell more land to would-be colonists. However, they lacked their father's scruples in dealing with native people, from whom they needed to acquire the land.

The Walking Purchase

In the 1730s, shortly after gaining control of the colony, the Penn heirs, utilizing the expertise of James Logan – the colony's chief justice and de facto head of Indian affairs – sought to acquire more land from the Lenni-Lenape. Producing a purported deed from 1686, Logan told the Delaware leaders that their forefathers had signed agreement with William Penn granting the colony a tract of land to the west of Wrightstown, Pennsylvania, equal to the distance that a man could traverse in a day and a half. Logan made little progress with the Lenni-Lenape chiefs, who did not recall such an agreement or have a record of one. At best, the deed that Logan produced may have been a portion of a preliminary agreement between William Penn and older Delaware chiefs that had never been completed; there may have been talks and nothing more. At worst (and far more likely) is the possibility that James Logan and the Penn heirs fabricated the document in what ended as a successful attempt to defraud the Lenni-Lenape of their lands.

Under Logan's relentless badgering, the Delaware chiefs finally agreed to carry out the terms of the purported agreement by having three men walk the land to the west of present-day Wrightstown, Pennsylvania. Unbeknownst to the Lenni-Lenape leaders, Logan carefully chose and recruited the colonial equivalent of athletes to conduct the walk. He also hired axmen to cut trails through the forest to allow the walkers to cover more ground, and arranged for men on horseback to follow the walkers with food and water.

On the appointed day of the walk, Lenni-Lenape observers expressed surprise when the English walkers did not walk; they ran. The Lenni-Lenape protested to Logan that this violated the spirit of the purported agreement. They had thought the walkers would proceed at a normal pace, not run for hours on end. As one Delaware protesting to Logan put it, he thought the men would walk, pause to rest, and then walk some more. At the end of the 36-hour period, two of the English runners had fallen out due to exhaustion. One man, however, was still running, allowing Logan and the Penn heirs to claim more of the Lenni-Lenape's land.

In all, the walk resulted in the Penns acquiring over 1.2 million acres. Logan offered the Delaware a smidgen of the "Walking Purchase," as it came to be known, on which to live. The angry Lenni-Lenape leaders said no; this was their land. Then they did something that neither Logan nor the Penn heirs had anticipated. They flatly refused to leave their lands.

In any other colony, the refusal of native peoples to leave their lands – however the colonists gained them – would have resulted in bribes, coercion, threats, and, when those failed, war. But Pennsylvania differed greatly from the other colonies in British North America, and the refusal of the Lenni-Lenape to leave created a dilemma for Logan and the Penns. The Delaware had to surrender their lands in order for the Penn heirs to sell it to would-be colonists. Indeed, the Penns had already sold some of the land that the Delaware refused to vacate, creating the potential for conflict with the colony. Logan realized that only the threat of force – or force itself – could move the Delaware. In order to pressure the Lenni-Lenape, he would need a military force or a militia. But Logan also realized that he could not turn to the Pennsylvania legislature for assistance. The Quaker-dominated political body would have been appalled at the idea of raising an armed body of men, and they almost certainly would have balked at the idea of threatening the Lenni-Lenape. Indeed, the legislature adhered so firmly to Quaker principles that Pennsylvania did not even have a militia they could have called had they wanted to do so. Nor could Logan turn to another of the English colonies for assistance. There is a tendency to forget that the colonies constantly squabbled, regarding each other as competitors. It is possible that Logan may have been able to strike a deal with Maryland or New York to secure their assistance in forcibly removing the Lenni-Lenape, but they would have done so only for a price, and that price would have been very high.

The Iroquois Become Pennsylvania's Enforcers

At this point, the Iroquois League entered the picture. Since negotiating the Grand Settlement that placed them in a neutral position between New France and the English colonies in 1701, the Iroquois, through a combination of occasional mild threats and dexterous diplomacy, had managed to avoid being drawn into European conflicts. Pursuing a policy that some historians have dubbed "aggressive neutrality," the Six Nations played off the hopes and expectations of the English and the French for their own benefit. Over the first half of the eighteenth century, both powers sought either an Iroquois alliance or their continued neutrality at various times. The Iroquois learned that if they made the appropriate noises they could manipulate both European powers for their own ends.

Realizing great benefits from playing the English and the French off against one another, the Iroquois sought ways they could geographically expand their use of "aggressive neutrality." The most promising and obvious possibility by this time would be to play the English colonies off against one another; in a sense the Iroquois were waiting for the opportunity to present itself.

The League already had some limited experience in conducting diplomacy with English colonies beyond New York. In the 1630s, the Mohawk, the easternmost of the Five Nations, allied themselves with the New England Colonies during the Pequot War. Four decades later, during Metacom's Rebellion (King Philip's War), the Iroquois entered into an alliance with Massachusetts. Expanding their reach, the League regularly sent representatives to the colonies of Virginia and Maryland, and had established contacts with their new friends in Philadelphia by the early eighteenth century.

The Iroquois and the Delaware people found themselves locked into a complex relationship by the 1720s. By the turn of that century, the Lenni-Lenape appear to have been placed in a subordinate status vis-à-vis the Iroquois. Depending on the situation, the Iroquois referred to the Delaware as either "nephews" or "women." The relationship obviously encapsulated a complex and ever-changing status for the Lenni-Lenape – one that the Iroquois, as the stronger of the two, constantly redefined to their own advantage.

The Lenni-Lenape and the Iroquois disagreed as to how this state of affairs came about. The Iroquois offered a fairly straightforward narrative: they had simply conquered the Delaware and imposed a status of being metaphorical "women" upon them. The Lenni-Lenape account veered sharply from the Iroquois narrative, in that they claimed that they had won the war, and willingly became "women" as part of the peace process that ended the conflict. According to this account, the Iroquois had claimed that the Delaware would be honored by being "women," and that other Indian nations would heed the metaphorical woman of diplomacy when she spoke of peace. It is possible that this account is accurate. But the possibility also exists that the meaning of the term *women*, when applied to intertribal diplomacy, changed over time. In the early eighteenth century the Delaware invoked the status as a means of refusing to send their young men to participate in wars with the Iroquois. But in discussions with colonial representatives, the Iroquois used the status to heap scorn upon the Delaware. In any event, whatever meaning the Iroquois chose to assign the term is the one that prevailed.

Angered by the Walking Purchase, but wishing to avoid conflict, the Lenni-Lenape turned to their Iroquois "uncles" for assistance in fending off Pennsylvania's claim to their lands. Certainly, they reasoned, the English colonists would heed the powerful Iroquois League. Unfortunately for the Delaware, James Logan had already been in communication with the League, and had plied the Six Nations' leaders with generous gifts in exchange for their support. Moreover, the diplomatic situation had changed greatly since the end of the seventeenth century. Whereas the Six Nations once regarded the Delaware as a useful buffer between their lands in Iroquoia and Pennsylvania, they now deemed the Lenni-Lenape as politically expendable. The Iroquois also realized that by allowing the English to take lands belonging to the Delaware (and other native peoples for that matter) they could direct colonization away from their own territory. The old men in Onondaga – the seat of the Iroquois Confederacy – realized that they had more to gain by playing Pennsylvania off against the New York colony, and they sought closer diplomatic ties between themselves and Philadelphia.

The Lenni-Lenape now found themselves in the unenviable position of being inconvenient to both the Iroquois and Pennsylvania. The Iroquois recognized that the Delaware could perform – albeit unwillingly – one last, important service for the League. The Delaware now became useful in that by dispossessing them, the Six Nations would signal their loyalty to Brother Onas, the governor of Pennsylvania.

In a 1742 conference at Philadelphia, the Iroquois diplomat Canassatego stung Lenni-Lenape representatives when he invoked the gendered language of diplomacy, and altered the meaning of the term woman to belittle them:

> ...You ought to be taken by the hair of the head and shak'd severely... We have seen with our Eyes a Deed signed by nine of your Ancestors above fifty years ago for this very land... But how came you to sell land at all? We conquer'd you, we made Women of you, you know you are women, and can no more sell land than Women...we charge you to remove instantly. we don't give you liberty to think about it. You are Women; take the Advice of a Wise Man and remove imediately.

Canassatego gave the Delaware a string of wampum to help them remember his words – as if they would want to – and curtly ordered them out of the meeting: "We have...other Business to transact... therefore depart the Council and consider what has been said to you." Canassatego also gave the Lenni-Lenape a choice to move to either Shamokin or Wyoming, both located on the Susquehanna River, just to the west of the English settlements in Pennsylvania's Wyoming Valley. Not all of the Delaware moved, but most of them did. Unfortunately, as the Iroquois would later find out, the peoples they had divested of their lands did not follow their instructions precisely.

The Iroquois decision to help Pennsylvania divest the Delaware of their lands had two unintended consequences. A few Delaware ignored (and may well have been unaware of) the dictates of the Iroquois and remained in eastern Pennsylvania and New Jersey, where they managed to hide in plain sight. Others did take Canassatego's advice and went to Shamokin or Wyoming, but the majority of Delaware moved to the westernmost reaches of the Pennsylvania colony and beyond, into the Ohio River Valley, where they found themselves out of the effective reach of the Iroquois. But now they also found themselves far from English traders. While Logan and the Penn heirs took into consideration that they needed the Delaware's land to sell to new colonists, they did not take into consideration that a good number of Englishmen already living in Pennsylvania made their living by trading with Native Americans. With their customers and trade partners gone, many of these English traders followed the Lenni-Lenape into the Ohio River Valley region.

Today when one looks at a map of North America, the strategic importance of the Ohio River Valley to both the French and the English seems glaringly obvious. For the French, control of the Ohio could provide them with a bulwark to stymie English westward expansion, while shortening their lines of communication between their posts along the Mississippi River Valley and those in Canada. Likewise for the English, access to the Ohio country would give them a foothold and an entry point into the Trans-Appalachian West.

Into the Ohio Country

While it later became a critical battleground – and one of the main prizes – in the contest between France and Great Britain for control of North America, the Ohio River Valley – despite its obvious strategic importance – remained sparsely populated for the first part of the eighteenth century. In part, this came about as a result of the previous century's Beaver Wars, when many native people fled the region, as well as the eastern Great Lakes, in an effort to escape the Iroquois offensive. Now the population of the Ohio River Valley swelled, due to the influx not only of Lenni-Lenape who had been evicted from Pennsylvania, but also of Shawnee people who had also been pressured by the Iroquois to leave the colony.

The newly arrived native peoples of the Ohio River Valley did not find themselves lacking European trade goods for very long. In the quest for profits, English traders, largely from Pennsylvania, established posts in the Ohio country to be close to their customers. Yet another French–English conflict (King George's War) concluded in 1748. For most of the war, the French focused their efforts on the defense of their possessions and maritime Canada; the discovery that English traders operated freely in the Ohio country stunned them. The French quickly recognized the potential for disaster. For one thing, and as mentioned, English manufacturers produced trade goods superior in quality to those of the French. Indeed, the English had a huge advantage in the production of woolen duffel cloth, the single most traded item in European–native exchanges. Realizing that native people preferred English woolens to French-made ones, traders in Montreal and Quebec resorted to smuggling from the English post at Albany in order to satisfy the demands of their native trade partners.

Once they discovered English traders in the Ohio country, the French responded by moving to evict them from the region. In an effort to assert their claim to the Ohio, the French sent an expedition down the river, whose commander buried lead plates emblazoned with the arms of the king in the river bank. Here the French, who usually maintained good relations with native people, managed to offend them.

The Middle Ground

The Lenni-Lenape and other native peoples who moved into the Ohio Country found themselves at the southern portion of the region the French called the *Pays d'en haut* (upper country) that stretched, roughly, from the easternmost reaches of the Forks of the Ohio with the Mississippi forming its western boundary. Lake Superior and lands immediately to the north of it formed its northernmost points. The length of the Ohio River, roughly, formed its southernmost boundary.

The location of the *Pays d'en haut*, and the movement of native peoples into it, contributed to the formation of a "Middle Ground," a phrase created in the late twentieth century by historian Richard White. In the mid-eighteenth century, European colonists outnumbered aboriginal peoples in North America. This did not, however, automatically mean that Europeans controlled the continent. The English had the greatest number of colonists in North America, who occupied the region from the Atlantic seaboard in the east, to the foothills on the eastern slope of the Appalachians in the west. Scattered from the mouth of the Mississippi River in the south, throughout the Great Lakes region, and along the St Lawrence River, the slightly more than 50,000 French colonists, traders, and soldiers in North America found themselves greatly outnumbered by the 250,000 British colonists. French farmers densely settled the shores of the St Lawrence River near Quebec and Montreal. However, the remainder of the Frenchmen in North America formed a sort of loose periphery around an interior largely populated by native people.

Native people who had not fled west in the face of the Iroquois assaults of the mid- and later seventeenth century, settled in missions near the major French outposts of Quebec and Montreal. While Jesuit missionaries oversaw these missions, they also had to be cognizant of the secular concerns of the French colony. Greatly outnumbered by British colonists, the French colonial administration and the missionaries realized that the survival of New France depended on maintaining good relations with native people. While the Jesuit missionaries taught native people the fundamentals of Catholicism, they also learned, except in the most extreme cases, not to criticize the natives if they engaged in religious practices that blended European and aboriginal beliefs. The Jesuits also did not attempt to stop their charges from going on their winter hunts. On the one hand, they did not want them to leave the missions, fearing that they would backslide. On the other, they realized it was necessary in order for them to obtain meat and the furs that drove New France's economy.

West of the Appalachians, native people driven from their homes and hunting grounds by the Iroquois assaults coalesced in polyglot communities. Not all was well with these communities as many of these native peoples had longstanding disputes, and animosities divided them. They also fought each other for control of hunting grounds and for access to the trade goods that the occasional French trader might bring. To instill a sense of order in this shattered world, the French believed that they could exercise some influence.

In the Middle Ground thesis, neither native people nor the French could really claim to be in control the *Pays d'en haut*. In Richard White's formulation, native people and the Europeans who interacted with them realized that in order to live peacefully, both sides had to make accommodations for each other's culture, which often took the form of creative misunderstandings. In a way, the French took this idea (although they were unaware of it) a step further, appointing themselves as peacemakers.

The relationship between the native peoples of the Ohio Country and Great Lakes and the French provides an excellent example of these creative misunderstandings. Both the French and native people used familial terms in diplomacy in an effort to dictate the parameters of the relationship. For their part, the French insisted that native people refer to them as "father." In return, they referred to native people – who willingly accepted this – as "children."

Each side, however, had a very different conception of how the figurative parent-child relationship operated. The French approached it in a decidedly European manner. They expected the governor to command, much like a father in a French household, and that his native children would dutifully obey said commands of their parent. The natives, however, viewed the metaphorical familial relationship on their own terms. They expected the French to behave as the Native American father; shorn of the authority the European father possessed, but still obligated to provide his children, or sponsors, with protection and trade goods.

Since many of the peoples of the Ohio River Valley and the Great Lakes found themselves in conflict with one another over hunting territories and pre-existing animosities, they turned to the French to perform yet another parental role: that of mediator. By and large, native people accepted the French as mediators. In part, this may have reflected the outsized influence the French possessed as the only vendors of trade goods in the region.

But even if the French enjoyed a monopoly in trade, they realized that they could not take their native allies for granted. Indeed, the relationship depended much on each side realizing that they needed the other. The French, realizing the British colonists greatly out-numbered them, also needed the natives as military allies.

Relations with the natives, however, created a subset of French traders known as the *coureurs de bois* (translated as "runners of the woods"), who worked outside the framework of the colonial author-ities. Carrying trade goods with them into native communities, the *coureurs de bois* learned native languages and customs, and established firm relationships with native people in a dangerous world, all the while undercutting the large French trading concerns. No one seems to know how many young Frenchman adopted this lifestyle; one colonial official who attempted to count them simply gave up.

Native Americans as Military Proxies

The three major colonizing powers – England, France, and Spain – all utilized native peoples as military proxies from time to time. For most of the seventeenth and eighteenth centuries, the three powers did not maintain large numbers of troops in North America. Wars in the Americas were fought largely by local militias and by native allies. The English and the French discovered that during their first three conflicts in North America, they had a great deal of difficulty simply getting their forces into contact with one another so that they could engage in combat. Using Native Americans as proxies obviated this problem.

A new North American battleground for the European colonizing powers appeared in the American South in the late seventeenth and eighteenth centuries. When the French claimed Louisiana and began establishing trading posts at Biloxi and Mobile, they alarmed both the Spanish and the English. Drawing on their lessons from Canada, the French chose not to attempt to convert the natives of the vast Louisiana territory to Christianity. Realizing that the Jesuits had split their native allies, the French would not reprise the Huron experience in Louisiana.

Concerned with expanding trade in the South, the French looked with alarm upon the slave wars instigated by English traders. Fearing that constant conflict would destabilize the region and disrupt trade, the French befriended and armed natives who had fled the violence in the Carolinas. Quite simply the French hoped to use native people already hostile to the English (often with good reason) as buffers that would keep the Carolinian traders out of the region and away from their Louisiana outposts.

Just as they had done in the Ohio country and the Great Lakes region, in the South the French attempted to act as mediators between native people they hoped to enlist as their allies. Establishing a peace between two of the more powerful native groups in the Southeast, the Chickasaw and Choctaw, became one of the first orders of business for the new French colonial administrator in Louisiana, Pierre Le Moyne d'Iberville.

Culturally and linguistically similar, the Choctaw and Chickasaw had been at odds with one another since the mid-seventeenth century. At first, the numerically superior Choctaw usually prevailed in skirmishes with the Chickasaw. However, beginning in the 1690s, the balance began to tip toward the Chickasaw when they obtained muskets from Carolina traders. What the English traders wanted in return for their muskets were Choctaw slaves, who would be shipped to English sugar colonies in the Caribbean.

Wishing to end the conflict, and in the process stabilize the Southeast, D'Iberville bestowed copious amounts of powder, shot, cloth, and, most important, guns on the Choctaw and Chickasaw in return for their promise to pursue peace. An additional benefit would, of course, be that both tribes would funnel deer skins to the French outpost at Mobile. For a while, D'Iberville's initiative appeared to have worked.

Carolina traders, however, could not take the loss of one of their major trade partners so lightly. As in the Northeast, the English possessed the advantage of having more reliable supplies of superior quality trade goods to offer the natives.

While the French cultivated native alliances and friendship among large and powerful groups such as the Creek, Choctaw, and Chickasaw, they pursued a very different policy along the Gulf Coast and the lower Mississippi Delta, a region populated by numerous small tribes, whom the French referred to as the Petite Nations. The Petite Nations initially hoped that the French would prove to be a source of high-value trade goods; these hopes, once the French were established, were soon dashed. Generally speaking, when a member of the more powerful tribes murdered a Frenchman or otherwise offended the colonial administration, the colonial leadership would attempt to smooth over the matter, lest they offend their allies. Incidents involving the Petite Nations, however, usually provoked a swift and violent response. The murder of a French priest, for example, resulted in the destruction of a Chitimacha village, and the survivors were sold into slavery.

The French discovered that in Louisiana, however, they may have actually been more dependent on native people than they had been elsewhere. When the Natchez people revolted in 1729, the French colonial authorities quickly discovered just how dependent they were on the Choctaw to defend them. For a time, they controlled trade between the French and native peoples to the north of them. Diseases imported by Europeans decimated the Natchez, reducing them from a powerful nation of 60 villages to only six by 1715.

The last vestiges of the Mississippian culture, the Grand Village of the Natchez sat on a large bluff overlooking the Mississippi River. Unlike other locations along the Big Muddy, the Grand Village did not flood every spring. The lands of the Natchez were just as fertile as the lands along the river that were replenished with an annual deposit of silt. This combination of fertility and elevation made the lands of the Natchez attractive to French colonists.

In 1729, the newly appointed commandant of Fort Rosalie, Sieur de Chepart, acted on these desires and attempted to seize for himself the land upon which the Grand Village of Natchez sat. Planning to establish a tobacco plantation, he ordered the Natchez to vacate their Grand Village. This was apparently the last straw for the Natchez people. Stalling for time, the Natchez told De Chepart that they would move after their fall harvest. In exchange for extra time, they promised they would pay him tribute in the form of maize and game.

The Natchez, oddly enough, made few attempts to conceal their intentions. Villages erected poles painted red and festooned with arrows and hatchets. Warriors publicly declared their intent to die for their nation, while ingesting "black drink," a purgative made from boiled roots used to purify them before they went to war. Some French colonists warned De Chepart of Natchez preparations for war, but he disregarded the warnings.

At the end of November, the Natchez appeared at Fort Rosalie with corn and made a great show about going hunting, even going so far as to borrow muskets and ammunition from French colonists, promising them they would give them meat. With many of the French rendered defenseless, the Natchez fell upon them killing approximately 250 colonists, and carrying 50 women and children and approximately 300 Africans into captivity.

The assault shocked the French. Realizing the line of communication between New Orleans in the south and their Arkansas Post to the north had been severed, the colonial government moved quickly to assemble a military force. Having only a few troops in Louisiana, the French were forced to turn to their Choctaw allies to form the bulk of their army. Invading the heart of Natchez country, the combined Choctaw and French army discovered their foes had taken refuge in a strong fortress. Natchez leaders stalled for time, negotiating the release of French women and children, while many of their tribespeople snuck out of the fortress in small groups. Some fled east, hoping to find refuge with the Chickasaw.

Throughout the year of 1730, the Choctaw, Caddo, and other Indians allied to the French hunted down bands of fugitive Natchez. In most cases, the Choctaw massacred Natchez men while carrying their women and children off into captivity. As for most of the Africans, the native allies of the French return them in exchange for rewards, or in some cases it is suspected, simply kept them. Late in the year, a large group of Natchez were discovered hiding on an island in the Mississippi River. A bombardment by French ships killed most of them, with the rest being mopped up by French soldiers and Choctaws.

The Natchez war did have an effect beyond the battlefield; based on the statements of Natchez prisoners, the French were certain that the Chickasaw, and by extension their English allies, had encouraged Natchez resistance. Overlooking the rather obvious point that the actions of their own post commander provided the Natchez with sufficient cause to resist, the French launched a war against the Chickasaw that would last for much of the century, often using native warriors as proxies for their own troops.

In the interior of the Southeast, neither the English nor the French ruled. Rather, powerful native confederacies dominated. The Catawba, Cherokee, Creek, Chickasaw, and Choctaw confederacies exploited the European intrusion at the peripheries of the region. Survivors of smaller, weaker groups in the coastal areas that had suffered mightily from exposure to European diseases and violence at the hands of both the French and the English, fled inland and were incorporated by these larger and more powerful tribes. Many of the Natchez, for example, in fleeing east, sought refuge among the Chickasaw people.

Despite a vast wilderness that served as a buffer zone between their colonial possessions and the French, the Spanish still feared for the safety of their silver mines in Mexico. In response, they dispatched soldiers and missionaries to set up presidios and missions in present-day East Texas and western Louisiana. There, Franciscan missionaries attempted to convert the Caddo and Hasinai. The Franciscans, however, appear to have misread native peoples' intentions. The Caddo and Hasinai expected the Spanish to become a source of trade goods. They also thought that Spanish soldiers would provide them with protection from their foes.

The Spanish presence actually made relations with the Caddo and Hasinai worse. Unlike Jesuit missionaries, who made attempts to understand native religious practices in the hope that they would learn how to convert them to Christianity, the Franciscans, by and large, simply ridiculed native spiritual beliefs. The Spanish soldiers, rather than becoming Caddo and Hasinai allies, often violated native women. Perhaps the last straw came when an epidemic of European disease broke out among the natives. Suspecting (correctly) that the Spanish had carried the malady into their communities, the natives left them. By the early 1690s, the Spanish, too, had abandoned much of western Louisiana.

Just as in the North, the English and the French in the Southeast discovered that they did not possess enough troops to engage in battle, nor were they willing to send the few they had into what they regarded as a forbidding frontier interior. Instead, both sides sought native proxies, and with their treatment of native people, the English and the French each unwittingly provided the other with ready-made allies.

8

The Imperial Wars

One of the rationales that would-be colonists often gave for immigrating to North America was to escape the wars of Europe. However, as many of them learned, the wars that erupted in the mother countries had a tendency to follow them across the ocean. Between 1689 and 1763, England and France fought four conflicts that impinged on the Americas to varying degrees. Because these conflicts often spread to the Americas, it meant that in one way or another they involved native peoples. In all such wars, both powers did what they could to secure the alliance of Native Americans. The total number of French colonists, missionaries, and fur traders never reached 100,000, and often fell far short of that mark. By contrast, the number of British colonists reached 1.5 million by the middle of the eighteenth century. Whereas the French were parceled out amid a series of small forts, missions, and trading posts dotting a remarkably vast area that stretched from the Gulf of Mexico, all the way up the Mississippi, across the entire Great Lakes region, and terminated in the east at the mouth of the St Lawrence, the British by comparison, confined themselves to a comparatively compact region between the Atlantic Coast and the eastern slope of the Appalachian Mountains.

French colonization of the Americas remained slight for several reasons. French trading concerns, licensed by the Crown, bankrolled

"Times Are Altered with Us": American Indians from First Contact to the New Republic, First Edition. Roger M. Carpenter.

the earliest colonization ventures. These businessmen had little economic incentive to send large numbers of employees to the distant and dangerous North America. In addition, importing large numbers of colonists – as the English experience demonstrated – tended to crowd out wildlife. Since the primary business of the French trading concerns involved the acquisition, processing, shipping, and selling of animal furs, colonization would have conflicted with their business model. The French – as well as the English who engaged in the fur trade – found that by providing trade goods of sufficient quantity and quality, Native Americans could constitute a willing – but not always manageable – work force.

The Imperial Wars

Conflict in North America between Europeans – particularly the French and the English – was something of a sideshow to the colonizing powers, who sought to enlist Native Americans as allies. King William's War (known in Europe as the Nine Years' War) overlapped with the final phase of the Iroquois Beaver Wars in the late 1680s and much of the 1690s. Mohawks from Kanawake (across the St Lawrence from Quebec) who had converted to Catholicism and allied with the French were among the Indians who carried out a raid on Deerfield, Massachusetts, in 1704. Part of Queen Anne's War, the raid also harked back to Metacom's Rebellion, as native people who had been driven out of southern New England in that conflict joined the raiders.

Over a span of several decades, England and France waged four different conflicts with each other and with other European powers. The origins of these conflicts usually resided in, and their causes generally revolved around, matters such as which member of which royal family would sit on which throne. At first glance, the rationales for these wars had little or nothing to do with the lives of new world colonists. The causes of these conflicts would have been even more abstract to the native inhabitants of the Americas.

But that did not mean that the imperial wars did not affect both the native and the European inhabitants of the Americas. European colonists took up the cudgels either because of royal fiat, patriotism, or the need to defend themselves against another imperial power's colonists or their native allies. Native Americans also found themselves affected by these wars. They had aligned themselves with one

Figure 8.1 Canadian natives with French soldiers. Because few French immigrated to the Americas, they cultivated Native Americans as trade partners and military allies. Detail from *France occidentale dans l'Amérique Septentrional ou le cours de la rivière de St. Laurens*, Paris, 1718. Courtesy of Darlington Library, University of Pittsburgh.

European power or another, initially in order to secure access to European goods. But for many native peoples, trade relationships went beyond a mere commercial agreement. These relationships also implied friendship, and at times, kinship, meaning they obligated themselves to come to the aid of their European trade partners. Native peoples also had more practical reasons for assisting Europeans in these wars. Their dependency on European goods practically forced their hands. Particularly for native peoples in the East, the European quest for animal pelts had passed them by. As the beaver and other fur-bearing animals became scarce due to overhunting in the East, the focus of the trade shifted west. Many of the former native providers of furs – particularly those allied with the French, such as the Mi'kmaq and Abenaki of Northern Maine and Nova Scotia – were no longer valued as trading partners, but now assumed an important role as military allies, at least as long as any given war lasted.

Native peoples' reasoning for involving themselves in conflicts between European colonists would have been, understandably, multifaceted. Access to trade would have been an important factor, as would longstanding animosities between one native people and another. Another factor that cannot be overlooked would be native hostility towards European communities that had mistreated or waged war against them in the past. Peoples who had been driven from southern New England, for example, in the wake of Metacom's Rebellion, waged wars for years thereafter on the New England frontier.

There were to be sure, exceptions. As mentioned, the Iroquois League largely managed to avoid entanglement in most of the Imperial Wars by adhering to the Grand Settlement of 1701. Sitting on the sidelines, and taking advantage of their position athwart England's northernmost colonies and New France, the Iroquois made noises to the French about abandoning neutrality, and to the British about possible alliances, in order to extract concessions and gifts from both sides. The "play off" system, as it has been called, benefitted the League greatly in these years.

The Imperial Wars also saw a blending of a common cultural practice of the native people of the Northeast, the taking of captives, and a European objective, making a profit. Seizing captives, primarily young women and children, had long been a key part of Native American warfare in the Eastern Woodlands. Clans that suffered the loss of a member usually prevailed upon their young men to take up the hatchet and go on the warpath. One of the goals of sending young men to war was for them to return with captives who would replace the dead. Young women and children were specially favored as captives, since it was thought that they were unlikely to resist assimilation. Males on the other hand, particularly young men, were regarded as unsuitable since they would likely resist assimilation into a new society. Instead, captive males often faced death through torture. During the Imperial Wars, the native people still took captives, but now the motivations for doing so were not always traditional. Captives, both male and female, could now be ransomed to Europeans. In many cases, captives from the New England colonies would be purchased from the Indians by French colonists, who would in turn seek a ransom from the captive's relatives.

The first of the Imperial Wars was known in the Americas as King William's War (1689–1697) (English colonists preferred to name their wars after the reigning monarch). This conflict was fought primarily in northern New York and the St Lawrence River valley. While the imperial powers viewed this as a continuation of the conflict that they were fighting on the continent of Europe, English and French colonists saw it very differently, and saw trade with American Indians as very much a part of it.

Since seizing New York from the Dutch in 1664, the English had a marked advantage in both the price and the quality of their trade goods. The threat of English expansion – with the assistance of the Iroquois – to lands west of the Appalachians alarmed the French. While the French realized that the persistent conflict between themselves and the Iroquois League damaged their colonial enterprise, protecting their Indian trade meant that they had to keep English traders away from their native allies. To this end, the French saw it as imperative that they maintain hostilities with the Five Nations. In a perverse way, the continuation of war between New France and the League protected the French colony. As long as the Iroquois remained at war with the French, it would remain impossible for the native trade partners of the French to travel to Albany. The French realized that if their Native American trading partners discovered that they could obtain higher quality goods at better prices in Albany than in Quebec or Montreal, their colonial enterprise, built largely on the fur trade, would be doomed.

The Iroquois, however, also presented the French with a dilemma. The Iroquois posed a military threat to New France and its native allies. But at the same time, the French realized that it would not be in their best interest to eliminate the Iroquois. In a strange paradox, the French needed their Iroquois enemies to remain powerful enough that the route to Albany remained closed to their native trade partners. But they also needed to inflict damage on the Iroquois, since they provided a military shield that helped protect northern New York and the New England colonies.

In 1689, 1693, and 1696, French soldiers, along with their native allies, destroyed two Iroquois towns. From the French Point of view these tactics worked, as in their wake most of the Five Nations sued for peace. English officials protested that the French had no right to negotiate with the Iroquois, unless they first obtained permission from the English. The Iroquois responded that they were an independent entity, did not have to answer to the English, and could enter into negotiations with any other nation that they chose.

Iroquois motivations to engage in negotiations with the French sprang from several sources. One is that King William's War overlapped with the closing phases of the half-century-long Beaver Wars. The Five Nations, simply put, had reached the point of exhaustion.

They also had come to realize that while the English made excellent trade partners, they were less than reliable as military allies. For most of King William's War, the Iroquois did the bulk of the fighting in the region of northern New York. The Iroquois realized that brokering a peace was the best way to stop the French incursions into their territory. Their peoples having sustained large numbers of casualties, Five Nations diplomats sought a way out. Their solution was the aforementioned Grand Settlement of 1701, in which they pledged neutrality to the French, and told the English colony of New York they would remain their allies in any future conflict with Canada, provided that they fulfilled certain (unfulfillable) conditions. For the remaining Imperial Wars, the Iroquois generally remained on the sidelines, abandoning neutrality only when they realized that it no longer served their interest.

The next of the Imperial Wars, again named for the reigning English monarch, began in 1702 and became known as Queen Anne's War. This conflict saw an expansion of the battlefield. Whereas King William's War had been largely confined to the northern borderlands between New England, New York, and New France, this conflict affected English colonies in both the North and the South. The French had greatly strengthened their position with the establishment of posts on the Gulf Coast, along the length of the Mississippi River, and throughout the upper Great Lakes. While Queen Anne's War originated in Europe for many of the same old reasons – a controversy about who would sit on which throne – English, French, and Spanish colonists in the New World had their own reasons for fighting. Once again, the French were spooked by British expansion into the Trans-Appalachian West.

The Iroquois, recognizing that they had little to gain, refused to join either side, taking the stance of what came to be known as "aggressive neutrality." Wishing for the Iroquois to remain neutral, the French focused their attacks in the North on the colonies of New Hampshire, Massachusetts, and its northern province, Maine. While the New York colony could not induce the Iroquois to abandon neutrality, it did attempt to raise a force of colonials to invade Canada. The expedition failed miserably, as most of the vessels shipwrecked in the St Lawrence River. In their attempts to draw the Iroquois into the conflict, the New York colony arranged for Peter Schuyler to accompany five prominent Mohawk leaders to London, where they were well received and feted by Queen Anne. The reception did little or nothing, however, to move the Five Nations away from its neutral stance.

In the southern colonies, the Creek (Muskogee) and the Choctaw chose to side with the French. In the case of the Choctaw, they turned to the French for muskets, because their traditional enemies, the Chickasaw, acquired them from the English. As English traders from Virginia, North Carolina, and especially Charles Town, began to make their way inland, the French recognized them as a threat. In the region that is now western North Carolina, eastern Tennessee and northern Georgia, English traders established relationships with the powerful Cherokee nation. Farther south, the English made contact with the Chickasaw people, who not only helped them fight the French, but also helped them fend off Spanish incursions from their base in Florida.

The English alliance with the Chickasaw and the Cherokee, and the French alliance with the Choctaw and the Creek resulted in a war by proxy taking place in the interior of the Southeast. While the French and English supplied the respective sides, they did very little in the way of actual fighting.

Queen Anne's War came to an end in 1713. Like its predecessor, it ended with neither side able to claim victory. The extended peace that lasted until 1739 benefitted Europe, while a somewhat uneasy truce prevailed in the Americas. Despite the lull in hostilities, it appears that no one expected it to last. The Iroquois, despite their neutral stance, could not be sure that either side would respect their neutrality, and prevailed upon the English to build defensive posts in their territory. While the English took advantage of the Iroquois request to establish a key fur-trading post at Oswego on the eastern end of Lake Ontario, the French countered by constructing several posts, most notably at Crown Point near Lake Champlain, and by strengthening the post that guarded the portage at Niagara.

Throughout the 1720s and 1730s, the British negotiated with the Iroquois in an attempt to have them abandon neutrality. The League recognized, however, that their long-term interests were best served by maintaining trade relations with both the English and the French. They also recognized that entering into an alliance with the English could make Iroquoia a likely target of a French offensive should hostilities ensue. King George's War, the next imperial struggle to play out on the North American continent, grew out of the War of the Austrian Succession, which, like other European conflicts of the time, revolved around the question of whose posterior would rest on which throne.

Even prior to 1744, the English expressed unease about their northern frontier. The governor of New York sought reassurance from the Onondaga leader Canassatego, who replied that the League would remain firm with their English friends. But rumors that the League and some of their "props," such as the Lenni-Lenape and the Shawnee, would defect to the French troubled the English.

These concerns had a basis in fact, not because the Iroquois and other native peoples were actively planning to defect from their alliances with the English, but largely because of the actions of English colonists. In 1742, alarmed by rumors that the local Nanticokes had conspired with Indians from outside the colony to rise up and attack the local English residents, the governor of Maryland called out the militia. Thereafter an unwitting Iroquois war party heading south down the "Warrior's Path," on its way to launch attacks on their Cherokee and Catawba foes, came under attack by Virginia frontiersmen. In the melee that followed, eight colonists and four Iroquois perished. Now convinced that an Indian war was imminent, English colonists in Virginia, Maryland, Pennsylvania, and New York "forted up," and called on their colonial legislatures to raise troops for their defense. Fortunately for all concerned, the Pennsylvania colony dispatched Conrad Weiser, a veteran frontier diplomat familiar not only with native languages but with native diplomatic forms, to Onondaga to make peace.

The next year, however, just when the English colonies feared a renewed war with the French, three English fur traders were murdered in a dispute with Lenni-Lenape Indians. Settlers on the Pennsylvania frontier demanded that the Lenni-Lenape turn over the murderers. The Pennsylvania legislature again worried that the colony teetered on the brink of an Indian war. The combination of violence between native people and their supposed English allies, and conflicts between the English colonies themselves, led to the call for a conference that would convene in the frontier town of Lancaster, Pennsylvania, in 1744.

The Treaty of Lancaster

The participants in this conference could not have suspected that they would achieve anything noteworthy. As it was, the Lancaster Treaty had little or no effect on King George's War (1744–1748), which would finally, after its European preliminaries, break out on the frontier of the English colonies and result in somewhat successful assaults on New France. But the conference at Lancaster did achieve something historically important, just not in the way any of the participants expected.

The most important of the participants at Lancaster among the colonies would turn out to be Virginia, Maryland, and Pennsylvania. The Iroquois League would be the most prominent native entity involved in negotiations. The talks at Lancaster revolved around the Iroquois claim that lands in Maryland and Virginia, and portions of the Ohio country to the west, were theirs by right of conquest. Iroquois representatives argued that the League had long ago conquered the Lenni-Lenape and other coastal Algonquin groups. They also claimed to have defeated the Susquehannock, an Iroquoian-speaking people who had been formidable rivals to the League in the previous century. Colonial representatives appear to have been skeptical regarding the Iroquois claims. They were, however, also acutely aware that with a war with the French (who would be allied to the Spanish) looming on the horizon, they would need the Leagues' help, or at the very least its continued neutrality.

The Lancaster Treaty conference had two long-term outcomes. One is that the Iroquois managed to assert their land claims and convinced all three colonies – even if they were somewhat reluctant – to accept them. The other is that the Iroquois began a process that would sow seeds of distrust among other native peoples of the Eastern Woodlands. Claiming possession of the Forks of the Ohio by right of conquest, the Iroquois sold this junction of three critical rivers – the Ohio, the Monongahela, and the Alleghany – to the colony of Virginia. However, they also led the colony of Pennsylvania to believe that they had sold it to them as well. Not mentioned by the Iroquois (or the English for that matter) was the fact that the French also considered this as their territory. Thus began a process that would lead other native peoples to distrust the Iroquois League. The Iroquois created a strategy to direct colonial settlement away from their homeland in northern New York; they sold lands that belonged to other native peoples to the English. For the most part, as in the case of the Ohio country, the Iroquois' claim to these lands was questionable at best. Not that the English were greatly troubled by this, but the Virginia and Pennsylvania representatives may have been miffed when they discovered that the Iroquois had sold them the same plot of land, and left them to sort out to whom it actually belonged. The selling of land over which they had questionable ownership would become a pattern that the League would follow for the remainder of the eighteenth century.

For their part the colonies were unable to sway the Iroquois League from their neutral stance at Lancaster. Recognizing that the colonies were unorganized, and regarding them as unreliable allies, the Iroquois, with the exception of a few Mohawk led by old Chief Hendrick, sat out King George's War. The war also saw Sir William Johnson step into history. Arriving in New York during the 1730s, Johnson became an important figure on the Mohawk frontier. Marrying into a prominent Mohawk family, he learned their language and diplomatic forms, and became an important go-between for both the English and the Iroquois League. By the time the next conflict with France rolled around, Johnson's ability to influence the Iroquois began to pay major dividends for the English. During King George's War, New England's northern frontier, as well as that of New York, found itself under assault by French-allied Native Americans from Canada. In the South, the Cherokee remained firmly attached to their English allies, fighting the war, by proxy for the most part, in the interior of the American Southeast against the Muscogee (Creek) and Choctaw Allies of the French. For their part, the Chickasaw, important allies of the English, managed to sever a line of communications between French Louisiana and Canada.

Disputing the Ohio Country

But at the end of the conflict in 1748, none of these actions proved to be decisive. Much like the two previous Anglo-French conflicts in North America, this one ended largely in stalemate. There were, however, consequences for native people.

When the Iroquois assisted the Pennsylvania colony by forcibly removing the Lenni-Lenape in the early 1740s, they had ordered the displaced people to go west. Many of the Lenni-Lenape ended up going much farther west than the Iroquois had intended, beyond the Forks of the Ohio. One thing that the Pennsylvania government seems not to have counted on was that many of its own citizens made their living in the trade with the Indians. In short, English fur traders in the colony followed their customers out of Pennsylvania and into the Ohio country.

At the end of King George's War, the French were alarmed to discover the large number of English traders operating in the Ohio country. Once again, as they had at different times in different parts of Colonial America, native people in the region discovered that while the English did not treat them as well as the French, in that they did not bother to learn their languages or seem to care to learn much about their culture, they did have the advantage of being able to offer them better quality trade goods, much better than anything the French could provide, at better prices.

Considering the Ohio country as part of New France, the governor of Canada ordered the forcible removal of the interlopers. While some French-allied Indians participated in the destruction of English fur-trading posts, and the brutalization and banishment of the traders therein, other native peoples in the region opposed these actions. A French expedition traveled through the Ohio country in 1749 under the command of Captain Pierre-Joseph Céloron, attempting to intimidate native people and posting lead plates bearing the arms of the King of France along the Ohio River. This attempt to cow the native people of the region largely failed, except for one key factor.

Close behind the English traders that flooded into the region were English land speculators. One of the better-known English land speculation firms, the Ohio Company of Virginia (George Washington was later one of its investors), obtained a 200,000-acre grant from the crown in 1749. The tensions over the Ohio country meant that it would only be a matter of time before hostilities erupted.

The next Anglo-French conflict would differ from the previous three in several important respects. The new war would begin not in the Old World, but in the New. One can trace the origins of the conflict back not only to ongoing French and English animosity and disputes over territory, but to the Lancaster Treaty conference of 1744. The other key difference between this conflict and its predecessors is that its outcome would actually be decisive.

What was known in North America as the French and Indian War had its beginnings in 1754. Within two years, it would morph into a European war, where it became known as the Seven Years' War, which in turn would become a global conflict between England and France. Later in the war, Spain would enter the conflict on the side of the French.

In 1753, the governor of Virginia received word that the French were scouting the Forks of the Ohio, looking for a place to build a military post. Convinced that the region belonged to the Virginia colony as a consequence of the Lancaster Treaty, the governor appointed George Washington, a 22-year-old planter and surveyor, as an emissary to the French. Traveling west for several months, Washington reached the forks of the river, where he was cordially received by French officers. The officers wined and dined the young man and listened to the message that he conveyed from the governor of Virginia. Then they politely informed him that the Forks of the Ohio belonged to the French, and that the claims of the governor of Virginia, or any other English colony, carried no weight. After giving Washington some provisions for the return trip, they sent him on his way back to Virginia.

Surviving an assassination attempt by an Indian guide and nearly drowning on his return trip, Washington was given another mission by the governor of Virginia. He was to return to the Forks of the Ohio, this time as a lieutenant colonel of the Virginia militia with enough troops to dislodge the French if they would not take leave of the area voluntarily. Unbeknownst to the governor of Virginia and Washington, the Iroquois League had a representative in the area, Tanacharison, known to the English as the Half King. As representative of the League, the Half King functioned as a sort of overseer, monitoring the behavior of the Lenni-Lenape and Shawnee people whom the League had removed to this region. Tanacharison also favored the English over the French.

In May 1754, Washington and his detachment of Virginia militia found themselves lost and blundering through the forests of western Pennsylvania near their destination of the Forks of the Ohio. It is here that Tanacharison appeared at the head of a party of warriors and offered to lead Washington and his men to the French. As dawn broke, the combined force of Indian warriors and Virginia militia reached a clearing where a small party of French troops had set up camp. A few of the French soldiers were up and had started to cook breakfast, while others snoozed, catching a few more minutes of sleep. Washington quietly had his men surround the French, and then, on a signal, open fire. The fight was over in a matter of minutes, as the outnumbered and surprised French quickly surrendered. As Washington began to gather the prisoners, Tanacharison approached the wounded French commander, a young man about Washington's age named Jumonville. Addressing the badly wounded officer in French, Tanacharison told him "My Father, thou art not yet dead," while bringing his hatchet down and cleaving apart his skull. While Washington and the Virginia militia looked on in a mix of disbelief and horror, Tanacharison dipped his hands into Jumonville's gray matter, washing his hands with his brains, while his warriors began butchering the other wounded Frenchmen. Recovering from the shock and surprise, Washington ordered his men to protect the remaining French prisoners.

After examining Jumonville's person, Washington discovered papers that revealed he had been on a diplomatic mission. Knowing that the French would retaliate for the attack on Jumonville and his detachment, Washington constructed a hasty redoubt that he called Fort Necessity at Great Meadows. Taking one look at the flimsy structure that Washington and his men had erected, and its indefensible location, Tanacharison and his warriors departed. In early July 1754, the French, along with their native allies, attacked Fort Necessity. Washington had situated the fort in a valley surrounded by hills. Firing from the ring of forested hills, the Indian allies of the French subjected the fort to plunging fire throughout the day. When it started to rain, the French and their native allies had some cover from trees. Washington had constructed a trench just outside the flimsy walls of Fort Necessity from which his men fought. As the rain continued to fall, the trench began to fill with water. Unable to keep their powder dry, and taking a large number of casualties, Washington and his men were unable to fight back effectively and were forced to surrender. The French permitted Washington and his men to leave, with the proviso that they not return.

Upon his return to Virginia, Washington discovered that he had inadvertently lighted the powder keg that would explode into global conflict. Upon receiving dispatches from Virginia about what had transpired at Fort Necessity, Great Britain, even though it had not declared war on France, made plans to send a large force to North America. In the meantime, the English colonies, realizing that a renewed conflict with New France was upon them, again attempted to draw the Iroquois League away from neutrality and into an alliance. At Albany in 1754, representatives of seven of the colonies met with the Iroquois delegates. The appeals of the colonial leaders made little impression upon the Iroquois, who pointed out that the colonies were disunited, unorganized, and seemed to be unable to defend themselves. League representatives departed Albany laden with gifts, but without having given a commitment to the colonists. For the most part, the league would sit out the early portion of the coming conflict. The notable exception would be the Mohawk, who were influenced by Sir William Johnson, and engaged in the early phases of the conflict that took place in northern New York.

With the commencement of hostilities, both the French and the English began to recruit native allies. The French secured the allegiance of most of the native people of the Old Northwest (the present-day states of Wisconsin, Illinois, Indiana, Ohio, and Michigan), southern Canada, and the Great Lakes region. The English managed to recruit some allies in the South, most notably most – but not all – of the Cherokee, and a good number of the Chickasaw, whose reasons for joining the English had more to do with continued access to trade goods than with their antipathy toward the French. As they did in the previous conflict, the Chickasaw gained control of the Mississippi River, severing the line of communications between Canada and Louisiana.

Braddock's Defeat

The main British effort in 1755 was against the post the French had erected at the Forks of the Ohio, known as Fort Duquesne. A force of 2,000 British regulars led by General Edward Braddock, and augmented by Virginia militia led by Lieutenant Colonel George Washington, made the long march from eastern Pennsylvania to the Forks of the Ohio. From the point of view of England's few Native American allies, the campaign got off to an ill-fated start. When native leaders asked Braddock about Indian land tenure after the war, he replied that the land would belong to the English, and that the Indians could not keep any of it. During the long march, woodsmen preceded the army, hacking out a crude road through the wilderness for its wagons and artillery to traverse. The few native scouts Braddock employed noticed that he habitually disregarded their advice. As a result of both factors, long before Braddock's army reached Fort Duquesne, most of his native auxiliaries had deserted him.

For their part, the French had good intelligence and, given the size and relatively slow progress of Braddock's army, it would have been difficult for their scouts to miss them. When Braddock came within a few miles of Fort Duquesne, the French commander, realizing that the British force grossly outnumbered his garrison, made preparations to destroy and abandon the post. He ordered one of his junior commanders to lead a small force, consisting mainly of Indians, to engage Braddock's column, with the intent of delaying the English.

The delaying action became a rout. Once the combined French and native force began firing on the head of the column, the surprised British halted. Stretched out along a snakelike trail, British troops moving forward to reinforce the head of the column became mixed in with supply wagons and other units, throwing the British into confusion. The French and allied Indians spread through the forest on either side of the column, firing into the British, who formed ranks and fought in the open as if on a European battlefield. Taking command after General Braddock was killed, Washington organized the remnants of the British army into a quasi-organized retreat. The defeat of Braddock's army filled native people with confidence. In the aftermath of the battle, James Smith, who had been a woodcutter with Braddock's army, spent four years as a captive of Delaware people living in the Ohio country. Smith related that his hosts expressed great confidence that between the French and the Indians, they would be able to expel the British from all of North America, with the possible exception of New England.

Lake George

When the remnants of Braddock's army limped home to eastern Pennsylvania, the colonists panicked. They had placed their faith in the British army, and now, with French-allied Indians assaulting the Pennsylvania and New York frontiers, it seemed nothing could protect them. They did, however, have a stroke of luck. Three months after the French and Indians shattered Braddock's army, a combined British and Mohawk force led by Sir William Johnson turned back a French attempt to seize the recently completed Fort Edward on Lake George. During the battle, the senior French commander in North America, Baron Dieskau, was wounded and captured by the English. Johnson's protégé, Joseph Brant, took part in his first battle at Lake George. Despite the success, the battle resulted in personal tragedy for Johnson. His friend, old Chief Hendrick, was mortally wounded during an altercation known as the "Bloody Morning Scout."

Montcalm Takes Command

The capture of Baron Dieskau had an unforeseen benefit for the British, besides removing a capable commander from the battlefield. Dieskau, realizing France lacked the resources of the English in terms of manpower, carefully cultivated good relations with France's Native American allies. His replacement, the Marquis de Montcalm, would arrive in 1756. French emissaries spread the word to the native people of the Ohio country and the Great Lakes that their King had sent a great warrior who would lead them to victory over the English. Thousands of warriors from throughout the region flocked to join Montcalm's army as it assembled in Quebec. In fact there were a few warriors present (who may have been Ioways) with whom no one else could communicate.

For his part, Montcalm appreciated that native warriors augmented the strength of his army. He disliked, however, that they tended not to follow orders, and unlike soldiers in the French army, they could simply come and go as they pleased, meaning that he and his officers had very little control over them. He also disliked what he regarded as their overconsumption of French supplies of powder, shot, and food.

The first campaign that Montcalm mounted against the English took place in the summer of 1756, when he laid siege to the British post at Oswego. It was here that Montcalm got his first real taste of how differently French troops and Indian warriors behaved towards a defeated enemy. While French troops obviously followed Montcalm's orders to the letter, native warriors shocked him by killing British wounded and looting prisoners of personal possessions. The French did not compensate their native allies; the warriors compensated themselves through looting and by taking prisoners, many of whom they led off to Canada, from where they would try to ransom them back to their friends and families. This angered Montcalm not only because it violated precepts of European warfare, but because he needed the Indians' manpower to carry out the rest of his plans.

The next phase of Montcalm's offensive, while militarily successful, would result in the wholesale desertion of its Native American allies. Montcalm's plan was to proceed south along the Lake Champlain–Hudson River Valley corridor. By seizing control of these two major waterways, Montcalm hoped to sever New England from the rest of the English colonies. A major part of his plan involved gaining control of Lake George, and that would require the capture of Forts William Henry and Edward. While many British colonists fled to Albany, Montcalm launched his attack against Fort William Henry.

After putting up a stubborn defense, Fort William Henry surrendered. Montcalm permitted the garrison to surrender with the honors of war. After the post surrendered, the troops, camp followers, and civilians who worked at the fort, spent the night camped outside of its walls. Montcalm and the British commander, Colonel Monro, intended for the defeated garrison and its civilian auxiliaries to begin their march to Fort Edward the next morning. But Montcalm's Native American allies were angry that the surrender deprived them of the opportunity to seize loot and take prisoners. Perhaps fueled by alcohol, and perhaps encouraged by Canadian militia, many of the natives entered the British camp and proceeded to take personal possessions from the defeated British. Other natives began to seize individuals as personal prisoners. When some of the British resisted, the natives killed them. Alerted to what was going on, Montcalm and some of his officers rushed to the scene and tried to stop the natives. By and large, they were successful in extracting prisoners from the warriors. But Montcalm's actions in rescuing the English had a cost. Angered by his interference, many of his Indian allies went home, determined never again to fight on behalf of the French.

The Tide Turns against the French

There were, however, elements far beyond Montcalm's control that contributed to native dissatisfaction. Among the factors that worked against the French was increasing British naval power in the Atlantic. The longer the war lasted, the more strength the British navy gained, as it built more ships and pressed into service more sailors. Conversely, French naval power declined throughout the conflict, as they were usually on the losing end of confrontations at sea. Gaining control over the Atlantic shipping lanes, the British reduced the ability of the French to supply their North American garrisons, and in turn to supply their Native American allies with trade goods.

Another key factor beyond Montcalm's control came when William Pitt became Prime Minister of England. Unlike the leaders of previous governments, who may have been uncertain what British objectives should be in this global conflict, Pitt very clearly identified the English objective as driving the French out of North America. To this end, he went much further in securing the cooperation of English colonists and their legislatures.

The taking of Fort William Henry proved to be the high-water mark for Montcalm and the French in North America. For the rest of the war, the French, often short of supplies, found themselves on the defensive. In 1759, General James Wolfe seized Quebec, placing the English firmly in control of the St Lawrence River and cutting off French posts farther inland from any hope of resupply. The Battle of Quebec is remembered for several things, among them the deaths of both Montcalm and Wolfe. But for native people, it also had meaning in that it was the first battle – even though it was nearly the last of the war – in which the Iroquois League took part. Quebec would also have consequences for Native Americans in that General Wolfe's superior, Jeffery Amherst, would become the commander of his majesty's forces in North America, and as such, would have a hand in the implementation of post-war Indian policy.

Recognizing that the French were about to lose the war, the old men in Onondaga – the seat of the Iroquois League – realized that the playoff system that had worked so well for them since the Grand Settlement of 1701 would now have to end. The next best thing, they surmised, was to ally themselves with the winning side, and to be ready in the future to remind the British of their loyal service back in 1759 – and to neglect mentioning their studied neutrality in the previous years.

For all practical purposes, the English victory at Quebec ended the French and Indian War in North America; a significant number of French troops defended the large outpost at Montreal, but the starving and under-supplied garrison quickly surrendered to the English, after a short, sharp fight that satisfied European conceptions of "honor." In the Montreal campaign, General Amherst, thanks to Sir William Johnson, had the assistance of 700 Iroquois warriors who guided his troops through rapids and the waterways around the city. Despite their assistance, Amherst regarded the warriors as a nuisance and thought the price Johnson paid for their services (about £17,000, mostly in trade goods) had been exorbitant. Amherst's disdain of Indians – even those who allied to his army – would one day prove to be his undoing.

The Peace of Paris ended the global conflict between Great Britain and France, as well as France's ally, Spain, in 1763. While the peace treaty had global ramifications, its greatest implication regarded the changing of maps of North America. France lost all of its possessions in North America, yielding Canada and everything east of the Mississippi to Great Britain. Recognizing their limited ability to police all of France's former North American possessions, the British granted Louisiana to Spain, thinking that they could wrest it from them later, should the occasion arise.

The Cherokee War

For the latter part of the French and Indian War, most of the former native allies of the French – such as the Lenni-Lenape, Shawnee, Ottawa, Ojibwa, and Potawatomi to name a few – sat out the fighting. As British troops began arriving and taking control of French posts throughout the Great Lakes, Ohio country, and Mississippi River Valley, most Native Americans looked on with a sense of ambivalence. While the Iroquois viewed the defeat of the French with a sense of sadness, since it meant that the playoff system that they had used for so long had finally come to an end, other native peoples merely interpreted the change by noting that they now would have a new set of European trading partners.

Even before the fall of Quebec, however, tensions between native people and English colonists erupted into open conflict. In the South, the English suddenly found themselves at war with peoples who had been their most reliable allies against the French.

The Cherokee, one of the more numerous groups of native peoples east of the Mississippi River (approximately 12,000 persons in the 1750s) had proved to be invaluable allies to the British. Their ability to place thousands of warriors in the field against the French and their native allies, and to fight as proxies on the behalf of the English in the southeastern interior, prompted one English official to compare their military service to that of more than 1,000 British troops in terms of value.

But tensions between the English and the Cherokee began in earnest in the autumn of 1758. Cherokee warriors had served as auxiliaries to the army of General John Forbes, which had finally succeeded in taking Fort Duquesne. After the fall of the stubborn post at the Forks of the Ohio, Cherokee warriors on their way home to what is now western North and South Carolina, eastern Tennessee, and northern Georgia, came under attack by Virginia militia, who justified the assault by claiming that the Cherokee had stolen horses from colonists in the area. In all likelihood, the militiamen had other, less noble, motives. They made it a point to scalp the dead Cherokee and collect the bounties that the colony offered for Indian scalps.

In the late 1750s, once it became somewhat clear that the French were losing the war, English colonists on the frontiers of both of the Carolinas (North and South) made incursions westward into Cherokee country, where they exacerbated tensions with the natives by killing their deer, an important food source for the Cherokee and the root of the deerskin trade, a valuable economic resource.

Like many other English colonies, South Carolina offered bounties of up to £50 for the scalps of enemy Indians, that is those allied to the French. Reasoning that the officials who paid out the bounties could not tell one Indian scalp from another, South Carolinian frontiersman bushwhacked Cherokee hunters.

The Cherokee retaliated in 1759, killing about 30 colonists on the Carolina frontier. South Carolina governor William Henry Lyttelton prohibited traders from providing the Cherokee with arms and powder in the summer of 1759. Gathering a force of 1,300 militiamen, Lyttelton led the march into Cherokee country in October of that year. In an effort to forestall the conflict, a delegation of Cherokee leaders headed by Oconostota (meaning "Great Warrior") visited Charles Town, the colony's capital, hoping to negotiate with the governor. Lyttelton demanded that the Cherokee turn over the 24 warriors who had been accused of murder. The Cherokee representatives countered with an offer that the men accused of murdering English colonists would instead present the governor with the scalp of a French enemy, or that of a prisoner. At this point, Lyttelton broke off negotiations and seized the entire delegation as hostages, declaring that he would only be satisfied once the Cherokee warriors accused of murder were turned over to him. Moving his prisoners to Fort Prince George on South Carolina's northwestern frontier, the governor met in late December with the Cherokee peace chief Attakallakulla (known to the English as Little Carpenter), who promised that he would attempt to have the 24 warriors accused of murder turn themselves in. Attakallakulla managed to secure the release of Oconostota, but not the remaining Cherokee hostages.

In January, 1760, Cherokee warriors tried to force their way into Fort Prince George in an effort to free the hostages. Repulsed, the Cherokee laid siege to the post and launched attacks on settlements in the western portion of Virginia, both of the Carolinas, and Georgia. Later in the month, Oconostota invited the commander of Fort Prince George to a parley outside the post. It is not known what was said in the meeting, but the upshot of it was that the Cherokee killed the post commander. The garrison at Fort Prince George retaliated by slaughtering their remaining 22 hostages. The Cherokee responded by escalating the scale of the conflict dramatically. By the end of March, the Cherokee had rolled back the frontier 100 miles, and were launching attacks on forts only 100 miles from Charles Town.

South Carolina's bellicose stance masked the colony's military weakness. Throughout early 1760, the Cherokee launched assaults on the Carolina frontier with virtual impunity. Militarily outmatched, South Carolina's new governor, William Bull, requested help from General Jeffery Amherst, the commander of his majesty's forces in North America. Amherst dispatched a 1,600-man force to Charles Town in April. The British experienced success at first, lifting the Cherokee siege of Fort Prince George.

Going over to the offensive, in early June English troops destroyed the large Cherokee village of Keowee, in western South Carolina. Later that same month, English troops marched on another large Cherokee Town, this one on the North Carolina frontier. The English successfully rebuffed a Cherokee attack en route to the town, but in so doing they sustained significant losses, so many that they were forced to retire to Charles Town. While the English did not consider this a significant setback, the Cherokee viewed it as a grand victory. When news of this battle spread to Cherokee towns west of the Appalachians, known as the Overhill towns, more warriors flocked to join their brethren in the East to fight the English.

The Cherokee augmented their campaign against the English by laying siege to Fort Loudoun in eastern Tennessee. The fort was built near the Cherokee capital of Chota in 1756, a time not so far back during which relations between the Cherokee and the English were much better. The post had created a British presence in the Cherokee country, even though it was situated far from normal supply routes. Nonetheless, the Cherokee hoped to use the British presence to create a playoff system, similar to the one the Iroquois used in the years leading up to the French and Indian war.

While the English had considerable difficulty resupplying Fort Loudon due to its location, the Cherokee were favorably disposed to the post at first, since it served as a handy refuge for Cherokee women and children during attacks by native enemies. The issue of the lack of regular resupply of the post by the military did not present a major hardship for the soldiers garrisoned there, as they traded extensively with their Cherokee neighbors, who provided them with maize and other foodstuffs. Indeed, many soldiers at the post developed relationships with Cherokee women, who had planted corn fields around the fort and routinely tended the crop.

When Oconostota began his siege of Fort Loudoun in March 1760, the Cherokee women abruptly stopped delivering supplies and food to the post. Besieged for several months, fort commander

Captain Demere surrendered the post in early August, after the Cherokee granted the garrison safe passage. But on August 9, as the British column made its way eastward toward the South Carolina frontier, they came under attack by the Cherokee, who killed Demere and the other officers and seized the regular soldiers and militiamen as prisoners.

Stung by the fall of Fort Loudoun, General Amherst sent a 2,500-man force under the command of Lieutenant Colonel James Grant to Charles Town. In March of 1761, Grant's force arrived at Fort Prince George. There he conferred with Attakallakulla, perhaps the most pro-British of all the Cherokee chiefs, and the one who most frequently advocated peace. Attakallakulla made a peace offer, but Grant declined it, arguing that the British humiliation at Fort Loudoun had to be avenged. Now Grant led his force to the Cherokee middle towns. Despite falling into an ambush that resulted in a significant number of casualties, Grant and his men spent much of the summer going from one Cherokee town to another, destroying lodges. More significant, the British destroyed food stores and burned cornfields and peach orchards – the Indians could live without permanent villages but not without food stores. Lacking the gunpowder they needed to fend off Grant and his troops, the Cherokee could only look on helplessly after having fled into the forest. In all, the British destroyed 15 Cherokee towns, in the process burning 1,400 acres of maize.

Teetering on the brink of defeat, and lacking the means to resist the British effectively, the Cherokee reached out to the area's other native peoples for assistance. Unfortunately, the other tribes wished to maintain their existing alliances with the British. An element within the Muskogee (or Creek) nation was opposed the British, but they were too few to influence tribal policy. The Chickasaw had been Cherokee allies, but a number of them also had served as scouts for the British expedition against the Cherokee. Lacking powder and allies, Attakallakulla and other Cherokee leaders met with the British at Fort Prince George in September 1761 to negotiate a peace, but, given the ferocity of the campaign, the terms of the peace appear to have been quite moderate. The Cherokee returned captured British posts and prisoners. The worst part of the agreement for the Cherokee was that South Carolina's frontiers were extended about 25 miles westward, taking away even more of their territory.

Native peoples in the Ohio country and the Great Lakes region knew about the Cherokee wars with the British in both of the Carolinas and Virginia, and looked on in interest. They drew three lessons from the Cherokees' predicament: one, that they had to be wary of the British; two, that the Cherokees' dependency on European supplies of powder and other goods had impaired their ability to defend themselves and their country; and three, that native peoples had to find something that could unite them. The Cherokees' inability to receive assistance from other native peoples had doomed their efforts.

On the face of it, a Native American nativist movement that coincided with Amherst's attempts to restrict British expenditures unwittingly seemed to bolster his efforts. Ever since the eviction of the Lenni-Lenape from their homelands in Pennsylvania in the 1730s, a series of prophets had appeared among them. The majority of these prophets preached messages rejecting Christianity and the use of European goods. For some reason, however, most of these seers – some of whom were women – simply disappeared after a few years. Despite their professed hostility toward Christianity, some elements of the faith found their way into the teachings of these native prophets. Most notably, they began to profess that there were different destinations in the afterlife for good and bad people – a very Christian idea.

The most notable of the Lenni-Lenape prophets would be Neolin, whose message in some degree would inspire the Ottawa leader Pontiac. Like other prophets, Neolin advocated avoidance of Europeans and their goods. Unlike other prophets, his message appears to have been timely; he arrived on the scene just as the British began to take control of the former French posts west of the Appalachians, and just as they instigated a policy that attempted to do away with the giving of gifts to native people, and to decrease the amount of trade goods.

9

Pontiac's Rebellion

Neolin, the Delaware Prophet

When the Pennsylvania colony, with the connivance of the Iroquois League, evicted the Lenni-Lenape people in the 1740s, the resulting, and understandable, sense of dispossession and betrayal contributed to the rise of a number of religious prophets among the Delaware and other Algonquin-speaking peoples of the Ohio country. The Walking Purchase, one of the most notorious of all colonial land swindles, would now bear unintended consequences for the English.

In the wake of the loss of their Pennsylvania homelands, a succession of prophets, both male and female, appeared among the Ohio country Lenni-Lenape, preaching, gaining followers, and then disappearing over the course of two decades. The majority of these prophets argued that native people suffered because they had embraced – in varying degrees – Christianity and the consumption of alcohol.

The Lenni-Lenape prophets emphasized that a combination of two factors created native peoples' woes: Europeans, and the turning of their backs on the Master of Life. But few actually emphasized the degree to which native peoples had become dependent on European goods. Native peoples and the prophets who preached to them were no doubt aware of their reliance on European merchandise; many of the prophets in all likelihood used these items extensively themselves.

"Times Are Altered with Us": American Indians from First Contact to the New Republic, First Edition. Roger M. Carpenter.

This dependency probably muted the criticisms the prophets had of European trade goods; native peoples, like it or not, needed them. As one historian put it, native peoples' demand amounted to the greatest consumer revolution in history. And no wonder. European goods made native peoples' lives easier. Steel knives made it easier to dress game. Flint and steel could create fires much more quickly and easily than rubbing two sticks together.

In the early 1760s, a new prophet, Neolin appeared among the Lenni-Lenape. It is difficult to say why Neolin's message caught on and is remembered, whereas those of his many predecessors are largely forgotten. In many respects, the basic tenets of Neolin's message reflected the same principal concerns of other, earlier Lenni-Lenape prophets. Another aspect that helps ensure Neolin's continued mention in history is his association (how close exactly, we cannot say) with Pontiac and his rebellion. In other words, his association with Pontiac attracted the attention of European, and later American, historians. Unlike the messages of the other prophets, European witnesses (usually of the second or third hand variety) recorded Neolin's teachings.

In terms of being recorded for prosperity, Neolin also happened to come along at the right time and with a very pointed message. While most of the previous Lenni-Lenape prophets had avoided pointing out the obvious native dependency on European trade goods, Neolin did not. He began preaching this truth at the very moment when continued access to trade goods had actually been threatened, which may have heightened his listeners' receptivity to his message. Other factors also helped make Neolin more memorable than his immediate predecessors, including his compelling story of how he received his commission from the Master of Life himself.

Neolin related that he had a vision in which he went on a long journey. Arriving at a point where the road split three ways, he chose the widest road, only to be forced back by fire. Neolin then tried the narrowest of the three roads, only to encounter fire once again. Neolin took the third route, traveling along it until he reached a village where a beautiful woman greeted him. The woman commanded Neolin to strip naked and to climb up a nearby mountain, using only his left hand and left foot. After an exhausting climb to the peak, Neolin encountered the Master of Life. The Master of Life told Neolin that he had created the earth and that he had set aside different lands for different peoples. The Americas had been set aside for the use of Indians, whom he loved, and not for the use of

Europeans, whom he did not love. The Master of Life went on to inform Neolin that he must tell all Indians (whom the Master referred to as his children) to be obedient and not to engage in behaviors of which he disapproved. Native people must not drink alcohol, nor should they have more than one wife, nor chase the wives of others. He also told Neolin that native peoples must reject the trade goods of the whites. The Master of Life also claimed that native people's difficulties in finding sufficient game to feed themselves was his doing; he had called the animals back to the depths of the forest, where humans could not find them. Once the Indians rejected the Europeans and their goods, and again prayed to the Master of Life, he would allow the animals to return, and native life would be much as it had been prior to the arrival of the Europeans. The Master of Life showed Neolin the afterlives that awaited native people. Those who obeyed the Master of Life occupied an afterlife free from disease, the influence of alcohol, and the presence of Europeans. Another, much different vision showed native people filing into what Neolin described as a large oven. He saw drunkards consuming rum, only to have it turn into molten lead in their mouths. The Master of Life then commanded Neolin to return to his people, and to spread the word among them that he was angry with them and that they must change their ways. He had given them animals to hunt, corn to grow, and had made a world for them, but they had allowed Europeans to corrupt it.

Neolin's message differed from those of his predecessors in one key respect. The prophets who preceded Neolin adhered mainly to native conceptions of the afterlife, maintaining that it was a world somewhat like this one, but, in a vague sort of way, better. Neolin – perhaps subconsciously – introduced Christian elements into the concept of the native afterlife by emphasizing the notion that an individual's behavior on earth determined their eternal fate. He also presented the alternatives of separate spiritual domains: one much like the Christian hell, where the wicked would be punished for eternity, and a benign one for the good. In all likelihood, Neolin may have been influenced by Christian missionaries or by second-hand reports he had heard about their message. Historically, Neolin and his resulting message – although we have to question our sources, which come to us second- (or even) third-hand, and are in some cases self-serving – became something of a template for later Native American revitalization efforts, particularly those that attached themselves to resistance movements.

The French Leave

The last important battle in North America of the French and Indian War (known as the Seven Years' War in Europe, or as some historians term it to describe its global implications, the Great War for Empire) took place in the autumn of 1760, with the English seizure of the important French post at Quebec. Montreal's starving and ill-supplied garrison surrendered the next spring. English control of Quebec and the mouth of the St Lawrence River denied French posts farther inland resupply and reinforcement, effectively ending the conflict in the Great Lakes region and the Northeast. For all practical purposes, the conflict between England and France in North America had come to an end. But while the war ended for British and French colonists in North America, it did not end in Indian country, and it continued elsewhere around the globe. England would continue to fight France (whose ally Spain entered the conflict in 1762) until signing the Peace of Paris in early 1763.

The contents of the treaty proved surprising to native peoples who had become accustomed to the English and French being at odds with one another. The two great European powers in their midst had waged war sporadically for eight decades. From the Native American perspective, these contests could best be described as indecisive. The conclusion of each one rarely saw any territory change hands, and the two colonizing powers seemed to resume their tense standoff until the outbreak of the next war. But this time would be very different. At the conclusion of the French and Indian War, the French surrendered all of their territory in North America. French claims to all of the land between the Appalachians to the Mississippi, as well as all of their possessions in Canada, would be transferred to the English.

The departure of the French would have direct consequences for native people. Native American tribes, most of whom had allied themselves to the French, may have initially feared retribution from the English, even if most groups who sided with the French at the beginning of the conflict deserted them as the war wore on and the French could no longer provide them with trade goods (native warriors had also been irked when French commanders, such as the Marquis de Montcalm, prevented them from taking the loot or prisoners they had wished to seize in lieu of payment). Many Native American tribes had even changed sides in the hope that they might reap rewards from the British for their loyalty. For the Iroquois Six Nations, the absence of the French to serve as a counterweight to the British meant they could no longer employ the playoff system, which had worked so well for them for so long – since the beginning of the century – which they used to gain an advantage in trade and diplomacy.

The seeds for the conflict that became known as Pontiac's Rebellion (and there is a question as to whether it should be named after him or not, as we shall see) were sown before the end of the French and Indian War, when the Seneca, the westernmost members of the Iroquois League, attempted to initiate a war against the British in 1761. Following the British seizure of Quebec, General Jeffery Amherst assumed command of his majesty's forces in North America. Having favorites among his officers, Amherst sought to reward them and went about it by dispensing land grants to them. Unfortunately, Amherst selected lands that belonged to the Seneca, whom he did not bother to consult before handing out the land grants. Angered, the Seneca sent a war belt – a wampum belt painted red – to other tribes of the lower Great Lakes region (southern Michigan, northern Ohio, western New York and Pennsylvania). None of the other tribes – perhaps given the Iroquois League's practice of selling land out from underneath other native people in the past, as they did at the Treaty of Lancaster – accepted the war belt. In the meantime, Sir William Johnson, the Crown's man in Onondaga, found himself in the awkward position of having to raise a Mohawk force for a possible fight with the Seneca. Using his influence, Johnson managed to smooth everything over and convinced the Crown to revoke the land grants. Amherst may have been miffed at having had one of his decisions reversed, which might partially explain his unwillingness to heed Johnson's advice in the months to come.

In the meantime, English subjects on both sides of the Atlantic enthusiastically celebrated their victory in the Great War for Empire. On a global basis, the British Empire had greatly expanded. North American colonists, noting their membership in a far-flung empire, proudly referred to themselves as Englishmen. Many colonists now looked westward, thinking that, with the French and their Indian allies subdued, they finally would be able to take up lands west of the Appalachians. Even those colonists who had no plans to settle in the region themselves began to eye the lands west of the Appalachians, as wealthier colonists (such as George Washington, for example) invested in land companies that bought up vast amounts of acreage in the Ohio country in the hopes of selling it to settlers at a steep profit in the future.

The British Economize

With the war recently concluded, however, Great Britain's government discovered exactly how steep the financial cost of victory had been. When William Pitt assumed the post of Prime Minister in 1757, he did so with the thought that winning the war superseded all other concerns, the costs be damned. The British Empire now found itself greatly expanded, but also greatly in debt. With the war won, Crown and Parliament decided that while William Pitt had been a wonderful wartime Prime Minister, he now needed to be replaced by someone more concerned with balancing the books and putting the empire on a firm financial footing.

Now Great Britain faced a set of financial and logistical problems it had never before encountered. In the past, when the English terminated conflicts with their European foes, they quickly demobilized most of their army, rather than absorbing the expense of maintaining a large standing force. In a sense, the English had been almost too successful in the Great War for Empire. As a result of the conflict, the English overseas empire expanded at the expense of its French and Spanish rivals, and not just in North America. The British also gained territories in Africa and India. But North America presented them with the most vexing problem. Having acquired all the former French territory between the Appalachians and the Mississippi River, as well as Canada, the English had to maintain a sizable force in order to garrison and police the vast region. Maintaining all these posts would require a standing force of 7,500 troops, all of whom would have to be paid and supplied.

In order to economize, the British decided that they would not occupy all of the former French forts west of the Appalachians. Instead, they dispatched garrisons to the major forts, while letting minor posts fall into disrepair. Native people had disliked the trade system (enacted by both the English and the French) that required them to travel to a fort or trading post in order to exchange animal pelts for European manufactured goods. For them, the journeys to these posts could be long and exhausting. By abandoning many of these forts, the English effectively made it even more difficult for a great many native peoples to obtain desired goods.

Jeffery Amherst's Indian Policy

When the English first began occupying former French posts in 1760, native people wondered what it would mean for them. The French had provided them with gifts of powder, shot, and woolen cloth as a form of rent for the land on which the forts sat. In 1760, Sir William Johnson, the British Superintendent of Indian Affairs for the Northern Colonies, and trader George Croghan arrived in Detroit with the first British troops sent to occupy the post. Johnson and Croghan assured the local Ojibwa, Ottawa, Potawatomi, and Wyandot peoples that the disbursement of gifts would continue much as it had with the French. They also pointed out that trade would continue with a rate of exchange similar to that the French had tendered. Having far more experience in dealing with Native American people than most Englishmen, Johnson and Croghan both recognized that placating the Indians would be far cheaper and easier than running the risk of provoking a needless conflict. They reported as much to General Amherst.

Amherst, however, rejected the recommendations of Johnson and Croghan, while enthusiastically embracing Parliament's new emphasis on economy. Forced to maintain large numbers of troops on the continent, Amherst sought to cut expenditures in other ways. One of the easiest ways to do so – or at least it seemed so to him – would be to reduce the amount of trade goods dispensed to native people as gifts or, better yet, to simply eliminate such gifts altogether.

Important in native–European diplomacy, gifts would usually be bestowed upon chiefs even before negotiations began. Then large amounts of gifts would usually be given at the conclusion of the signing of a treaty, as both the English and the French understood that the bestowing of large amounts of gifts on favored native leaders worked to their own benefit. These native chiefs and shamans, in turn, would distribute the gifts to their loyal followers, thereby increasing their stature in their own communities. As mentioned, the French also bestowed annual gifts on native people as a sort of "rent" for the land on which their forts sat, the same practice that experienced English Indian agents Croghan and Johnson encouraged General Amherst to follow.

But in his drive to economize, Amherst ultimately decided to end the practice of gift giving. While he characterized many of the gifts as trinkets, to native people they were necessities. The bulk of the

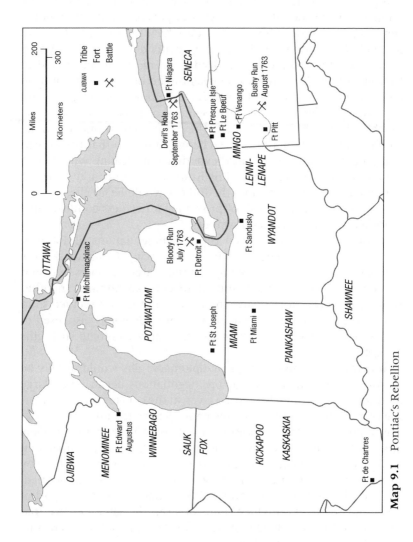

Map 9.1 Pontiac's Rebellion

gifts did not consist of mirrors, beads, paint, and other decorative items. Rather, native people had come to rely on gifts of blankets and woolen cloth – which they often transformed into clothing – as well as on supplies of powder and shot provided by the officers in the forts. They also relied on local commanders allowing them access to the posts' blacksmiths, who made necessary repairs on their firearms. As they needed to hunt and to defend themselves against their traditional native enemies, powder and shot could hardly be deemed unimportant, and certainly not a trifling matter or "trinket."

Drawing on his background as a British officer, Amherst seemed to believe that native people should be treated somewhat like British soldiers: they should be told what to do; and when they did not comply, they should be punished. Amherst also viewed the giving of gifts as an attempt to bribe native people in order to ensure their allegiance toward the Crown and their future good behavior.

Amherst's reasoning for suspending gifts went beyond mere economics, however; he also had concerns about English security in the region of the Great Lakes and the Ohio country. Some of the forts in this region had only skeleton garrisons. By limiting native supplies of ammunition, Amherst hoped to decrease the possibility of conflict, and to keep the Indians from killing a great many British soldiers and colonists, who now began to filter into the region. Native people, however, viewed Amherst's moves with alarm. Not having sufficient powder and shot would make it difficult for them to hunt and therefore to feed their families. Amherst's actions lent credence to rumors that the *habitants* (French colonists) – most of whom were unhappy about being on the losing side in the recent war – spread among Native Americans, convincing them that the British intended to launch a war of extermination, after first rendering them defenseless.

Pontiac

Although he could not have known it, Amherst unwittingly encouraged the native peoples of the Ohio country and Great Lakes region to heed the preaching of Neolin. At the same time, Neolin also encouraged native people to listen to the plans of a half-Ottawa, half-Anishinaabe chief named Pontiac, who also attracted the attention of the British.

In his forties when he strode onto the historical stage, Pontiac had obviously been a French partisan during the late conflict with England. It has been said, but of course cannot be proven, that Pontiac had been present at Braddock's defeat at Fort Duquesne. A key portion of Pontiac's message to native people emphasized that the French had been far more generous and respectful of native people and their customs than the British. Pontiac argued that if the native people successfully resisted the British, then the French King would send troops to help them regain his possessions in North America, trade would be restored, and things would be much as they had been before the war.

We cannot be certain if Pontiac and Neolin actually met. However, Pontiac had at least heard of Neolin's message and repeated a version of it in his speeches to his followers. While Pontiac seems to have agreed with the Delaware prophet's notions of eschewing contact with Europeans, he also tweaked the message a bit. Whereas Neolin wanted to return to a better, imagined pre-contact world, Pontiac actually wanted the restoration of trade with his preferred French allies and trading partners. Pontiac also made it seem as if the French were somehow different from other Europeans, a point that Neolin probably would not have agreed with. It appears that Pontiac utilized Neolin's religious message as a sort of glue to hold native people together in their antipathy toward the British. He would not be the last native leader to employ a spiritual message for secular ends.

Native people, drawing on their experience with both European powers, knew that French forts did not attract settlement, and that they seldom cleared the land around their posts, chasing off the game in the process. While the French took pains to maintain friendly relations with most native people, one Ottawa leader summed up the Franco-Indian relationship in more pragmatic terms. Neither as numerous nor as powerful as the British, he noted, the French could simply be driven away by native people if they wanted to be rid of them.

Pontiac's message also appealed to the peoples of the Ohio country, who were alarmed by the influx of English settlers now following the military road that General Braddock had constructed during his unsuccessful campaign against Fort Duquesne. Three years later, General John Forbes used that same, albeit greatly improved, road when he successfully seized the same post. The increasing British presence in the Ohio country unsettled Native Americans, as they watched more and more settlers arrive, clear their forests, and destroy their hunting grounds.

Pontiac is largely remembered because the war or rebellion (depending on the term one wishes to use) that broke out has his name attached to it. It may be that the British simply called it Pontiac's Rebellion for convenience's sake; it may have been easier to settle on one native leader as the culprit. Yet it may also be that the English did not want to accept that they faced a widespread revolt. We cannot be sure how much direction Pontiac gave the overall revolt. We can, however, be certain that he largely commanded – although it may be a misnomer to think of an Indian chieftain actually giving "commands" – the native forces that besieged Fort Detroit in the early spring and throughout the summer of 1763. Less certain, is how much influence he had over native people who attacked other British forts throughout the Great Lakes region and the Ohio country during the same spring and summer. One is tempted to think there was an overall plan to the rebellion, but it is difficult to see how Pontiac could have facilitated it. On the other hand, General Amherst's actions and his suspension of gifts had caused a great deal of ire among native people. In all likelihood, they required very little goading to go to war against the English; indeed, Amherst may have unwittingly sparked many local rebellions among native people.

The native people of the Ohio country and the Great Lakes region would have had some concerns before going to war with the British. They almost certainly would have been aware of the recent example of the Cherokee war. While they may not have been overly sympathetic to the distant Cherokee, they would have taken several lessons away from the conflict. They realized that, unless native people formed strong alliances, resisting the British would be futile. Both the Chickasaw and the Choctaw had rebuffed Cherokee pleas for assistance. The Muskogee (or Creek) chose to sit out the conflict, surmising that assisting the Cherokee did not serve their own interests. Native people probably took another lesson from the Cherokee war, one that might have given them pause. The Cherokee, much like Metacom's warriors nearly a century earlier, quickly discovered that the English could easily cut off their supply of powder and shot. The Virginia colony and both of the Carolinas exploited this advantage, depriving the Cherokee of powder and shot and access to blacksmiths who could fix their weapons.

However, native warriors also drew on other lessons from the Cherokee war that would serve them well during Pontiac's Rebellion. They noted that the successful capture of Fort Loudon took place because it had been isolated from supporting forts. Since there were few British posts in the region, this would not be a problem for the native peoples of the Great Lakes and Ohio country. But they also realized that they could not conduct a European-style siege. For one thing, they lacked the sort of weaponry, such as cannons, that could compromise a fort's defenses, nor did they have the equipment (or desire) to carry out complex trenching operations as European armies did.

The Siege of Detroit

Instead, native people resorted to stratagems such as trickery in their efforts to seize many of the larger British posts. Pontiac himself attempted to seize Fort Detroit by deception in early May 1763. Leading a small party of warriors to the post, Pontiac visited with the garrison commander, Major Henry Gladwin. Under the guise of conducting trade Pontiac's warriors reconnoitered the post, taking note of the location of the troops and the fort's defenses. When Pontiac took his leave of Gladwin, he informed him that he planned to visit again the next day with a larger contingent of warriors for a peace parley.

Using the information his warriors had gathered, Pontiac laid out a plan to seize Detroit on May 7. Pontiac informed his warriors that he would give a speech, in the course of which he would hold up a wampum belt. If he held the belt in such a way that the green side faced his warriors, that would be the signal to launch the attack. If, however, he held the side of the belt decorated with white wampum toward them, the warriors would know that Pontiac had decided to call off the attack. Confident that his warriors would easily overpower the surprised British garrison, Pontiac led them into the fort the next day. His confidence must have sunk after entering the fort, because it became readily apparent that the British had somehow learned of his plans. Major Gladwin had doubled the fort's guard detail, and the entire garrison had turned out on the parade ground, armed, and at the ready. Pontiac protested to Gladwin that his warriors had come in friendship, and demanded to know why the major had put on a hostile display. Gladwin replied that his troops were merely conducting routine training exercises to keep them in readiness. Recognizing that his plan had been compromised, Pontiac did not give a signal to attack, and left the post.

In the absence of facts, historians have offered much speculation as to who betrayed Pontiac's plans to Gladwin. No definitive source of Gladwin's information about the attack has ever been identified. Some sources indicate that one of the French *habitants* of the fort learned of Pontiac's intentions and alerted Gladwin. Others claim a woman from Pontiac's village warned the British, while still others go further, asserting that a native woman with whom Gladwin was carrying on an affair warned him of the plot.

Thwarted by Gladwin, Pontiac initiated the attack on Detroit the next day (May 8), falling first upon British colonists and traders outside the post. Approximately 500 French *habitants* lived along the Detroit River, outside the boundaries of the fort. Pontiac ordered that they not be harmed, and it appears that his warriors obeyed him on this point. Pontiac had the advantage in numbers, having about 460 warriors to Gladwin's 125 redcoats. In the first week of fighting, the Indians killed 20 of Gladwin's soldiers while capturing 15 others. These were losses that Gladwin could ill afford. Pontiac's warriors also attempted to control the narrow span of the Detroit River. Elsewhere west of the Appalachians, other native warriors assaulted and seized smaller British posts such as Forts St Joseph (southwestern Michigan), Venango, Le Boeuf (in western Pennsylvania, north of Fort Pitt), and Sandusky (northeastern Ohio). While most of the native people engaging in the war against the British were Algonquin speakers, a number of those who had cast their lot with Pontiac were Seneca, the westernmost of the Iroquois Six Nations, perhaps still smarting from Amherst's seizure of some of their lands.

The majority of the British posts west of the Appalachians had fairly miniscule garrisons, with many of them having fewer than 20 troops on hand. The Indians overpowered most of these forts quickly and easily. A number of the local commanders wisely chose the better part of valor, abandoning smaller, indefensible posts and marching their troops to one of the larger, more secure British posts in the region.

In New York City, where General Amherst had established his headquarters, reports of Indian attacks on British garrisons began to flow in. At first, Amherst simply refused to believe the reports, or thought they had been grossly exaggerated. And even when he did finally begin to take the dispatches from his fort commanders seriously, he still did not appreciate the scale and scope of the rebellion, and seemed to have the impression that he need send only a few troops west to quell the uprising. It cannot, however, be said that Amherst lacked intelligence about events in the west. Sir William Johnson had his own sources of information among native people, and he shared what he had learned with Amherst; Johnson however, could not always get Amherst to listen.

Michilimackinac

In the early eighteenth century, the French established Fort Michilimackinac on Mackinaw Island. Sitting in the narrow strait between Michigan's upper and lower peninsulas, the fort controlled the passages between Lakes Huron and Michigan. Long an important fur-trading post, the British had taken control of Michilimackinac, and thereby effective control of the upper Great Lakes, in 1761.

While Pontiac kept Detroit under siege, his warriors made it impossible for British vessels to traverse the narrow passage formed by the Detroit River and Lake St Clair, which connected Lakes Erie and Huron – the route that communications and supplies to Michilimackinac and other posts on the upper Great Lakes north of Detroit had to follow. This is why the garrison at Fort Michilimackinac, even as late as early June, had no idea that a general Indian war had broken out and that troops at many of the other British posts were fighting for their lives, when a contingent of Anishinaabegs – also known as Ojibwa – appeared.

Whereas Pontiac had attempted but failed to take Detroit by trickery, the Anishinaabegs at Fort Michilimackinac employed the same stratagem successfully. On a pleasant summer day in early June, a large number of Anishinaabeg men and women – sources do not say how many – appeared at the fort, claiming that they had come to trade. The men had brought with them their *lacrosse* sticks, and in a few moments had a lively game going. The 40-man English garrison relaxed outside the post with the gates wide open, watching the game and making wagers with one another as to who would win. Despite the warmth of the day, the Anishinaabeg women had blankets draped about them as they gathered near the fort's open gates and seemingly watched the game. Suddenly, one of the players "accidentally on purpose" launched the ball over the wall of the fort. The garrison looked on while the players charged through the gates after the ball. As the warriors passed the women, they handed them hatchets and short spears from underneath their blankets. The Anishinaabegs quickly took the fort, killing most of the British troops and traders, while reserving a few as prisoners.

Elsewhere, the Indians had a great deal of success as they captured nearly all of the British posts west of the Appalachians. They did not, however, take the three most important installations: Forts Pitt, Niagara, and, of course, Detroit. These three posts sat athwart important supply and communication routes. As long as they still held them, the British still had a chance to regain control of the situation. Located in western Pennsylvania, Fort Pitt, the largest of the three posts, sat athwart the Forks of the Ohio River. Fort Niagara controlled the portage around the falls that bore the same name. The British desperately needed to hang on to this post in order to reinforce and resupply Detroit. Detroit, the westernmost of the three, became the focal point of Pontiac's Rebellion. The installation controlled the Detroit River and would have allowed the British to supply garrisons elsewhere in the Great Lakes region.

Lacking the sort of equipment the European armies used in sieges – such as mortars and artillery – Pontiac and his followers could not hope simply to batter down the gates and palisades of Fort Detroit. Nor were they going to conduct a frontal assault; that would have been foolhardy. Native American warriors, and the societies they came from, saw no sense in taking excessive casualties. In fact, losing too many warriors in a clash often resulted in a war chief being removed from his position.

At one point, very early in the siege, Pontiac seems to have hoped that he could negotiate the surrender of the fort. He convinced some of the leading French *habitants* in the vicinity to approach Major Gladwin about the possibility of negotiating Detroit's surrender. Gladwin reluctantly agreed to an exchange of hostages, sending two of his officers with the *habitants* in exchange for two Potawatomi. Rather than negotiating, Pontiac, with the apparent cooperation of some of the *habitants*, seized the two British officers as prisoners. When Gladwin learned what Pontiac had done, he angrily demanded – but did not receive – the return of his officers. Two months later, one of the captive British officers escaped and made his way back to Detroit. Shortly afterward, a native warrior, upset at the death of one of his relatives in a clash with the British, slew the other officer. As for the Potawatomi hostages, there is no record as to what became of them, but we do know that Amherst directed Gladwin to kill all Indians within his power.

With the negotiation gambit having failed, Pontiac now hoped to starve the garrison into submission. In terms of directly engaging the British, the best Pontiac could hope for would be their infrequent forays outside of their palisade to engage the Indians. Not knowing when or if he could be reinforced and resupplied, Gladwin placed his men on half rations. He also had the responsibility of attempting to feed and shelter traders and a few of the French *habitants* who had fled to the fort for safety at the commencement of hostilities.

Native warriors experienced significant success once the war began, attacking small undermanned garrisons and taking other posts by surprise. After the initial outbreak of hostilities, native warriors settled into long, drawn-out sieges of the three major posts still in British hands. Only when the warriors could lure the British out of their forts, or if the troops sallied out on their own initiative, could the two sides directly engage one another. It did not happen that often, but when it did, the natives usually got the best of it.

Bloody Run

After the siege of Detroit had gone on for nearly three months, the first notable clash between British troops and Pontiac's followers occurred when Captain James Dalyell, the son of a baronet and Amherst's aide-de-camp, arrived at the post with approximately 250 men near the end of July. Although Major Gladwin commanded the post, and outranked Dalyell, the junior officer's status as one of Amherst's favorites may have inhibited him. Amherst had expressed his desire to Dalyell that the natives be "chastised." Despite receiving a briefing from Gladwin regarding the situation at the fort and its environs, Dalyell, rather than having his men augment Detroit's defenses, decided to conduct a nighttime raid against Pontiac's camp in the hope of breaking the siege. Unbeknownst to both Gladwin and Dalyell, the plan had already been compromised. While we cannot know for sure how Pontiac learned about Dalyell's plan, the prevailing theory is that French *habitants* in the fort communicated with their countrymen outside the post, who in turn relayed the information to the Ottawa leader.

Two hundred forty seven men quietly followed Dalyell out of the fort at about two o'clock in the morning. The captain pointed them in the direction of Pontiac's camp, about two and a half miles north of Detroit. A full moon lit up the night, making it easier for the newly arrived troops to navigate the unfamiliar landscape. They could not have known, however, that the moonlight also made it easier for the two large parties of warriors that lay in ambush to watch them. Once Pontiac's warriors launched their attack, the British found themselves trapped between the two ambushing parties and unable to retreat. Finally, led by Dalyell, the British broke out of the trap and began a steady retreat that dissolved into rout as order broke down in their ranks and most of the men fled for their lives. The survivors reached Detroit at about dawn, still pursued by Pontiac's men. Only then could the British pause and make an assessment as to how badly Dalyell's attempted raid had fared. Over half the men that set out just a few hours earlier had become either casualties or captives of the Indians. At least 20 soldiers who had set out on the mission, including Dalyell, lay dead, 35 of them were wounded, and approximately 100 had been captured. Pontiac's warriors cut out Dalyell's heart and cut off his head, displaying both body parts on a post in their camp. The battle became known as Bloody Run, since a stream on the battlefield was said to have turned red from the amount of British blood that flowed into it. As for the surviving men who made it back to Detroit, they now joined the besieged garrison.

The Devil's Hole

Fort Niagara, one of the other posts still withstanding Indian attacks, guarded the portage around the falls. The portage – known to the British as "the carrying place" – linked Fort Niagara with a smaller post nicknamed "Little Niagara." Without the two forts Detroit and other British posts to the west could not be resupplied or reinforced. The local Seneca recognized that they could not take the fort in a direct assault, but they saw the road linking Fort Niagara to the falls as a weak link in the British chain. In order to ferry supplies over the falls, the troops had to leave the protection of the forts. In September 1763, 25–30 British troops were wrestling oxen and carts along the portage trail when hundreds of Seneca warriors attacked. With both ends of the trail cut off, and a deep gorge behind them, the British had no choice but to stand and fight. Outnumbered and surprised, the British were cut to pieces in a matter of minutes. Hearing the gunfire, two companies of redcoats raced to the rescue, only to be severely repulsed by the Seneca, who inflicted more than 70 casualties on the would-be rescuers. The Seneca scalped the dead and hurled their corpses into the gorge, which the British christened "the Devil's Hole." Throughout the remainder of 1763, and into the next year, the Seneca periodically attacked the portage, forcing the Niagara garrison to commit large numbers of troops to guarding it while transporting supplies.

In the summer of 1763, the British did have some success against the Indians. For much of the season, Lenni-Lenape, Shawnee, and Wyandot warriors attacked colonists in the vicinity of Fort Pitt, but not the post itself. By June, most of the English in the vicinity had sought refuge in the fort. The problem for the Indians was that, while they controlled the countryside, they could not effectively besiege Pitt; it was a larger post than either Detroit or Niagara. The difficulty, of course, for the troops and civilians inside Fort Pitt was that they needed supplies and could not communicate with other posts.

Bushy Run

In late July, an expedition bearing supplies made its way from Fort Bedford in eastern Pennsylvania to Fort Pitt under the command of Colonel Henry Bouquet. The natives recognized that Bouquet's expedition amounted to a relief effort. For his part, Bouquet realized his men were not in the best shape. He had at his disposal two understrength companies that had recently arrived in North America from the Caribbean. Many of the troops still suffered from the effects of tropical diseases. Twenty-five miles out from Fort Pitt, Bouquet's men came under attack by a large force of Shawnee, Delaware, Wyandot, Ottawa, and Miami warriors at a spot known as Bushy Run. After a day-long battle that took a heavy toll on both sides, Bouquet laid plans for the next day. His men hastily constructed a defensive structure in which they placed their wounded. When the Indians resumed their attack the next morning, Bouquet's troops, following a prearranged signal, withdrew in the direction of the structure. Thinking that the British had broken and would begin to flee at any moment, the Indians rushed after them. They did not realize that Bouquet had positioned one of his companies on their flank. The sudden volley of musket fire, followed by a bayonet charge, shattered the Indian attack. Bouquet and his men made their way to Fort Pitt, but they had taken heavy casualties and had to abandon most of the supplies intended for the post on the battlefield. Nevertheless, from the British perspective, it was one of the few successes they had enjoyed that summer.

Figure 9.1 The Indians giving a talk to Colonel Bouquet in a conference at a council fire near his camp on the banks of the Muskingum River in North America, in October 1764. In this illustration, Colonel Bouquet negotiates with native leaders. Note that each culture has their own way of recording the proceedings. The Indian speaker has a wampum belt (used as a mnemonic device) while a scribe records the speech in writing. From *An historical account of the expedition against the Ohio Indians...*, Philadelphia, 1766. Courtesy of the Trustees of the Boston Public Library/Rare Books.

Bouquet is also somewhat notorious in Native American history in that he engaged in correspondence with Amherst discussing the possibility of purposely infecting the Indian population with small-pox. As it turned out, an officer at Fort Pitt had already had the same idea, giving handkerchiefs and blankets from a smallpox hospital to native visitors. Shortly thereafter, smallpox did break out among the natives besieging Fort Pitt.

The End of Pontiac's Rebellion

In the vicinity of Detroit, as the summer yielded to autumn, it became more difficult for Pontiac to maintain the siege. His warriors' supplies of powder and shot began to run low. The local French *habitants*, who had attempted to supply the Indians' needs – and one has to wonder how willingly some of them did this – also had run short of ammunition and provisions. Many of the warriors abandoned the siege because they needed to begin their winter hunts in order to feed their families. Successful British efforts in resupplying Detroit with vessels that managed to breach the native effort to block the river also discouraged Pontiac's followers. In October, Pontiac beseeched his warriors not to leave. Many of the Ojibwa, despite his pleas, departed anyway. At the end of October, Pontiac received unwanted news. A French officer arrived at Detroit and informed him that his government would adhere to the terms of the Treaty of Paris, which ended the war with the British, and that the French would not be returning, nor would they supply his efforts against the English. Defeated, Pontiac dictated a note to Major Gladwin, informing him that he would end the siege.

The Proclamation of 1763

At almost the same time that Pontiac gave up the siege of Detroit and realized that his cause was lost, the British government instituted a major change in their Indian policy. Still coping with the enormous debt from the Great War for Empire, the government decided that they did not need the additional costs associated with fighting Pontiac and his warriors. The government in London also planned to regulate the westward expansion of their North American colonies themselves, rather than leaving the matter to the individual provincial governments. In early October, King George III signed the Proclamation of 1763. In an effort to keep the Indians and the colonists away from each other – and avoid another war – the Proclamation drew a line along the crest of the Appalachians from Georgia all the way north to Lake Ontario. With the exception of British officials, soldiers, and licensed traders, all Englishmen were to remain east of the line of Proclamation, while the Indians were to stay west of it. Those colonists who crossed into Indian territory in an attempt to settle there would be escorted out by the army. One portion of the Proclamation created an Indian reserve to the west. In practical terms, however, the British army could not keep colonists out of the lands west of the Appalachian Mountains. The Proclamation Line stretched for thousands of miles, and there were simply not enough troops in North America to police it. The creation of the Proclamation Line angered a number of colonists, including notable individuals such as George Washington and Benjamin Franklin, who had invested in western land companies, but now could not expect to sell their lands to would-be settlers, since it would be illegal for them to travel there. The British never intended for the Proclamation of 1763 to be a permanent solution, nor did they intend for native people to have lands in the West reserved for them forever. However, the Crown never rescinded the Proclamation, and it remains the basis of most Indian land claims in Canada to this day.

The Paxton Boys

Pontiac's Rebellion had repercussions for native peoples not even remotely involved in the conflict. In December 1763, a band of frontiersmen from the community of Paxton, Pennsylvania, frustrated by their inability to capture and kill hostile Indians, decided to settle for an easy target. The men marched on the native community of Conestoga – people who had never been at war with the English – and slaughtered most of the inhabitants. The next day, when onlookers went through the embers of the burned village, they found a copy of a treaty the Conestoga had signed long ago with William Penn, which promised perpetual friendship between themselves and the English. Still, the Paxton Boys, as they called themselves, had not finished. Fourteen Conestoga survived their initial attack and fled to Lancaster, Pennsylvania, where the authorities, in an effort to protect them, placed the Indians in the town's jail. The Paxton Boys marched into Lancaster, broke into the jail, and murdered the surviving Conestoga. Two months later, the Paxton Boys, claiming the colony's governor had done little to protect them from Indian attacks, marched on Philadelphia. The city called out a militia – a very surprising development for the Quaker-dominated government – and the Paxton boys dispersed. None of them, however, ever faced prosecution for the crimes they had committed.

Pontiac's Fate

Late in the year 1763, General Amherst returned to England. His replacement, General Thomas Gage, sought out and heeded the advice of Indian Superintendent Sir William Johnson. The next summer, Johnson and Gage met with native warriors from different Ojibwa bands from the Great Lakes region and accepted their claims that they had not followed Pontiac in his rebellion. In July of 1766, Johnson and Pontiac finally met face to face at the British post of Oswego, located in New York on the southern shore of Lake Ontario. Pontiac, in a sort of roundabout way, claimed that he would be loyal to the English. Within two years of this meeting, Pontiac would be dead, murdered by a Peoria warrior while visiting a post near St Louis.

At first glance, it seems that Pontiac lost his war. The French did not return, and the British of course remained. Often forgotten in the summaries of Pontiac's Rebellion is the religious movement led by Neolin. It does appear to have simply evaporated, and often bears little mention. However, a message that mirrored Neolin's would reappear four decades later, in the teachings of Tenskwatawa (also known as the Shawnee Prophet). So, in some ways, Pontiac's Rebellion did establish something of a precedent for future native resistance movements, particularly those that had a spiritual component. Yet, in a way, Neolin also failed. His attempt to have native people returned to an imagined, somewhat better, past did not come about. In many ways, he and Pontiac were at odds as to what the rebellion was supposed to have accomplished. Neolin wanted the impossible: a return to a past that could never be retrieved. Pontiac, by contrast, wanted the return of the French and the restoration of trade, both of which Neolin would have opposed.

Flouting the Proclamation

As for the British, the Proclamation of 1763 did not prove to be a permanent solution, nor was it intended to be. Colonists repeatedly crossed the line and settled in Indian country, knowing there was little chance the British army would catch them. And even if they were caught, the troops would merely escort them east and let them go, the offenders in many cases simply returning to Indian country.

It also did not help that Royal officials flouted the intent of the Proclamation. In 1768, Sir William Johnson negotiated with the Iroquois representatives at Fort Stanwix, New York. Because it served their purposes, the English accepted Iroquois claims that they had defeated other Indian nations, and that therefore they owned their lands by right of conquest. Using this reasoning, Johnson and the Iroquois signed a treaty that moved the Proclamation Line of 1763 westward in New York and Pennsylvania. But the Iroquois also signed over to the English – for a price – much of present-day Kentucky and Tennessee, without consulting native peoples who lived there. This added to other native people's distrust of the Iroquois.

More than a decade after the King issued his Proclamation, Royal officials still encouraged settlement west of the line. In 1774, John Murray, the fourth earl of Dunmore and governor of Virginia, instigated a conflict with the Shawnee over land south of the Ohio River. In the Battle of Point Pleasant, Dunmore's 1,500-man militia threatened Shawnee villages, forcing the Indians to seek a truce. The resulting treaty forced the Shawnee to part with their Kentucky hunting grounds, and it opened the region to settlement.

In the decade after Pontiac's Rebellion, the influence of the native prophets seems to have waned, and trade to have been restored. Yet the promise of a lasting peace also proved to be an illusion. Native peoples still found themselves fighting with English colonists on the frontier. In a few years, many native peoples would shift alliances, and many groups would desperately seek neutrality.

10

The Great Plains and the Far West

Unlike their brethren in the east, the native peoples who lived west of the Mississippi River had fewer and less sustained contacts with Europeans in the seventeenth and eighteenth centuries. For the most part, throughout both centuries, Europeans pecked at the peripheries of the Far West. Even though California would become a Spanish colony as the seventeenth century came to an end, most native peoples living in what we now know as California had few interactions with Europeans prior to the eighteenth century. Spanish explorer Juan Cabrillo made peaceful contacts with the natives who lived along San Diego Bay when he landed there in 1542. Some of the natives that Cabrillo met indicated that they had encountered the Coronado expedition far to the east. Dismissing California as being too far from their valuable colony in Mexico, the Spanish did not follow up on Cabrillo's explorations. Four decades later, famed English mariner Sir Francis Drake went ashore near present-day San Francisco and exchanged gifts with the local natives. Drake's brief stop did not, however, result in a prolonged or recurring English presence on the west coast. Until the eighteenth century, distance and navigational difficulties limited European intrusions on any part of North America's Pacific Coast. But in the eighteenth century, the Russians, as part of their eastward expansion, would

"Times Are Altered with Us": American Indians from First Contact to the New Republic,
First Edition. Roger M. Carpenter.
© 2015 John Wiley & Sons, Inc. Published 2015 by John Wiley & Sons, Inc.

instigate a race for America's Pacific Coast, when they showed the world that the region had a rich supply of furs.

At the tail end of the sixteenth century, the Spanish Crown, badgered by the Franciscans, who demanded the natives of the region be Christianized, authorized the colonization of New Mexico. Nearly a century later, the French would begin colonizing the region near the mouth of the Mississippi. In the meantime, the native people who lived between these two colonial toeholds had what could be described as second-hand encounters with Europeans. Many Native Americans in the West never laid eyes on a European, but they heard about them, and encountered their trade goods (also frequently in second-hand form) and, unfortunately, their diseases. Most important, they encountered a European import that greatly altered the way the peoples of the Great Plains would live almost until the end of the nineteenth century.

No stereotype of the Native American has a stronger, more sustained hold on the popular imagination than that of the Plains Indian warrior, usually adorned in a large feathered headdress, and astride a horse. Other elements of the stereotype include large tepees and the hunting of bison from horseback. And for a while, this pervasive stereotype had a bit of truth to it. But this popular image of the Native American, propagated in numerous books and Hollywood films such as *Dances with Wolves* (1990), disguises the fact that this culture lasted for only about 200 years at most, beginning with the spread of horses on the Great Plains in the late seventeenth and early eighteenth centuries, and ending in the last decades of the nineteenth century, with the decimation of the bison. In a sense, the Plains horse culture was a hybrid that required Native Americans and the arrival of Europeans – and their importation of the horse – in order for it to come into existence.

The Plains

Largely a windswept sea of hardy grasses whose extensive root systems enabled them to thrive in a region that saw little rainfall, the Great Plains stretch from the margins of the subarctic regions of Saskatchewan and Manitoba in the north, to the semiarid lands where Texas and the Northern Mexican Desert meet. Bordered on the west by the foothills of the Rockies and almost brushing the Mississippi River to the east, nineteenth-century American farmers

Figure 10.1 Native Americans, a rather benign (and Europeanized) bison, and other "exotic" animals. In this illustration, the artist has given the two natives European features, and the bison looks also like a domesticated cow. Also note the opossum above the bison. Both the bison and the opossum were unknown in Europe and regarded as natural curiosities. European explorers often referred to Bison as "cows," so European artists, who had never seen one of the animals, quite naturally portrayed them as something similar to a cow. Detail from *Amplissimae regionis Mississipi…*, Nuremberg, 1730. Courtesy of Darlington Library, University of Pittsburgh.

would be stunned to learn just how hardy these grasses and their tramped-down root systems were, when they made their first – and usually failed – attempts to break the turf, or "bust the sod," of the Great Plains with their plows.

In the years prior to contact with Europeans, relatively few people lived on the Great Plains. The ancestors of native peoples often went there to hunt, but few lived there year-round. Semiarid, the region saw hot, unpleasant summers, and the flatness of the land, which offered few windbreaks unless one settled in one of the protected river valleys, only made worse the bitter cold of the winters. Generally speaking, two groups of native peoples populated the Great Plains in the pre-contact period. One consisted primarily of settled peoples who largely farmed, living in permanent villages in the river valleys that sheltered them from the winds of the plains. The spring floods deposited alluvial soils along the river banks, which the farmers, who lived in earthen lodges, transformed into fertile fields of maize, beans, and squash.

The other peoples of the plains consisted mainly of nomads who spent much of their summers following the bison herds and living in small skin tepees. Many of these nomads did not live on the plains year-round; most lived in other regions, such as the Eastern Woodlands or the Great Basin, to which they returned from their plains hunting grounds before the arrival of winter. From necessity, their teepees had to be small because pre-contact Native Americans had nothing on the order of European draft animals – such as the ox or the horse – that could be harnessed to move their possessions. Generally, native people packed their teepees – and everything else they owned – onto a *travois*, a device that consisted of two long pieces of wood of approximately the same length lashed together in a "V" shape. Two points dragged on the ground, while the crux of the V would be attached to a dog, or sometimes a human, as the nomads dragged their possessions from place to place.

The Bison

No animal affected the environment of the plains to a greater extent than the bison. Large and numerous, adult animals weighed in at about one ton. By studying the carrying capacity of the plains, modern scholars have estimated that bison probably numbered somewhere between 30 to 40 million at the time of contact. European explorers and later Americans – lacking incentive and having no desire to take on an impossible task – made no attempt to actually count the animals. Instead, overawed by the sight of the vast herds, they simply created fantastic estimates as to what the bison population might be. Nineteenth-century artist George Catlin set out to portray Plains Indian culture before it disappeared, and as a consequence included images of bison and bison herds in his many paintings. When portraying vast herds of bison, Catlin, like other artists, settled for the simple expediency of portraying the animals as an enormous black mass engulfing much of the landscape, stretching to the distant horizon. Doubters challenged the authenticity of these portrayals, but those who had been to the plains assured them that the paintings of Catlin and others accurately depicted the seeming numbers of bison. Because of their numbers, bison constantly migrated in search of fresh grazing grounds. In doing so, they unavoidably affected the environment. The enormous animals tamped down the turf of the plains making it a vast habitat fit only for the hardiest of grasses, and with the exception of the river valleys, did much to make the plains into a largely treeless region.

But while the bison undoubtedly did more than any other animal to shape the features of the Great Plains, the arrival of Europeans would, in time, result in their finding their once-immense region increasingly unable to support their numbers.

The Arrival of the Horse

For years, American history textbooks informed students that Hernán Cortés brought the first horses to North America. Readers of these texts also learned that Native Americans acquired their first horses by capturing mustangs, feral animals descended from the strays that escaped Cortés and his men after their conquest of the Mexica (Aztec) Empire. The truth is slightly less romantic. While it is true that the first horses to arrive on the American mainland landed with Cortés, the truth as to how native people acquired horses is, like most things that make their way into survey textbooks, far more complicated, and, in some ways, more interesting.

In 1598, the Spanish began their belated colonization of New Mexico, where the first groups of native people to acquire horses lived. But rather than the Indians having to capture escaped wild horses or stealing domesticated ones from the colonists, the Spanish actually gave them to the Indians, and even provided them with some rudimentary instruction in how to handle and care for the animals.

Coming from an Iberian culture that prized horsemanship, the Spanish could not help but be cognizant of the advantages that their mounts gave them over native people. When Cortés and his men conquered the Mexica Empire in 1519–1521, horses constituted one of their key military advantages over the native warriors they faced. The notion persists that Spanish firearms overawed the Mexica, but Cortés and his followers had a grand total of 16 arquebuses – an archaic form of musket – among them. While the smoke and fire of these weapons undoubtedly struck fear into the Mexica at first, their warriors quickly ascertained that firearms had certain limitations. Because the arquebuses were awkward to wield and took a good deal of time to load, the Spanish could not use them while mounted nor, given the state of gunpowder technology at the time, could they actually count on hitting what they aimed at. Indeed, *aimed* is a misnomer; many arquebuses of the time lacked a sighting device. The musketeer simply pointed his weapon at the target and hoped he would hit it – even if both the shooter and his target were stationary. What truly gave the Spanish an advantage was their armament of edged steel weapons, which they wielded easily and adroitly from horseback. The Spanish conquistador not only had battlefield mobility that native warriors could not hope to match, but he had a platform that enabled him to strike downward with devastating effect on his foes, while using the animal's power and weight to easily run down and trample his adversaries.

For much of the sixteenth century, the Spanish forbade their colonists from teaching Indians how to ride and care for horses. But as Spain expanded its colonial holdings northward into New Mexico as the sixteenth century turned into the seventeenth, its colonists found themselves increasingly forced to employ their native servants as herdsmen. Vast herds of cattle and horses formed the primary wealth of the prosperous colonists, who allowed these animals to wander freely over the open range. In order for their Native American servants to herd these great many animals effectively over the vast distances involved, the Spanish had little alternative but to teach them horsemanship. In a sense, economic necessity forced the Spanish to let the genie out of the bottle when they demystified the horse for native people. Thereafter native herdsmen did begin to steal horses from the Spanish *rancheros* (ranchers), using the stolen horses to teach other native peoples how to ride, and they did begin an illicit trade in the animals, setting in motion a process that greatly facilitated the spread of the horse throughout the Great Plains.

In particular, once the Pueblo servants of the Spanish learned how to ride horses, it did not take long before they stole or "lost" horses which somehow found their way to other Native Americans.

In the wake of the 1680 Pueblo Revolt, horses began to spread rapidly northward over the plains. By 1720, nearly all of the peoples on the southern plains possessed horses. By the middle of the century, horses had reached the northern plains, as European traders and trappers in what is now Saskatchewan and Manitoba witnessed Assiniboine and Cree peoples hunting bison from horseback.

Native peoples – according to stories collected by anthropologists – had long anticipated the arrival of the horse. In pre-contact times, the Cheyenne prophet Sweet Medicine foretold the arrival of the horse, and told his people not to fear the strange new animals. He told them that they would change conceptions of distance. Mountains on the far-off horizon, he told them, would be days, rather than weeks away.

The Plains before the Horse

One can appreciate the magnitude of the cultural impact that the arrival of the horse had on the peoples of the Great Plains only after examining how these Indians lived in the years before that time. In material terms, those settled groups who lived in the river valleys that intersected the Great Plains, such as the Mandans and Hadistas, had the upper hand. Constructing substantial earthen lodges, they lived next to the few permanent sources of water in the region. As farmers, they also had the advantage of having a stable food supply at their disposal. Like all peoples on the Great Plains, they also exploited the animal resources of the region, hunting antelope and deer, but especially bison. Those plains peoples who did not live in the river valleys eked out a far more tenuous existence. Like the peoples of the river valleys, they also hunted the bison, but because they did not grow crops, they depended almost exclusively on the hunt, necessitating that they continually follow the great herds for their subsistence.

While essential to the survival of the peoples who lived on the Great Plains, hunting bison on foot could easily – and often did – turn into a dangerous undertaking. To mitigate the hazards, Native Americans practiced several methods of hunting, but when dealing with very large and temperamental wild animals, the danger could not be completely eliminated. The most common method involved channeling herds into a buffalo pound – either a natural enclosure such as a box canyon or a man-made one such as a corral – where the animals could be killed with arrows, or possibly by dropping boulders on them. Another option, called the "buffalo jump," involved driving the animals off a cliff. Both of these methods involved nearly every member of the community – the young, the old, men, women, and children. To channel the animals in the desired direction, they surrounded the herd and, shouting and waving robes and blankets, attempted to frighten the buffalo to stampede over the edge of a sheer cliff. This method, however, had several drawbacks. A frightened bison – and these animals have very poor eyesight in the first place – may not see a human waving a blanket and may simply run over him or her – followed, in all likelihood, by several other animals. This grisly scenario played out frequently enough that archeologists excavating the sites of buffalo jumps in the twentieth century sometimes found damaged, trampled human remains. Using a "jump" to hunt buffalo also had a disadvantage in that native people could not pick off certain animals; in other words, they had little or no control as to the number of bison that they ended up killing in a single hunt. Archaeologists have discovered bison bones at jump sites that are free of knife marks, indicating that the animals were never butchered. In all likelihood, this indicates that native people sometimes killed more animals than they could dress and carry off with them to eat, or that perhaps, if a hunt took place on a hot day, some of the carcasses spoiled before they could be processed.

Native hunters had yet another, if far more dangerous, option available to them. Wolves often tracked bison herds, picking off old and weak animals as well as the very young. While wary of the wolves, bison had grown accustomed to their presence. Pre-contact native hunters attempted to take advantage of this fact by cloaking themselves in a wolf's skin. Sneaking into a herd on their hands and knees, the disguised hunters would attempt to pick off a few animals with bows and arrows at very close range. In the nineteenth century, American bison hunters on the Great Plains noted the animals behaved in one of two ways after being struck with an arrow. When the targeted animal collapsed, sometime the other beasts simply raised their heads, looked over at their wounded neighbor, and then went back to grazing, as if nothing had happened. Other times, however, their reaction went to the other extreme: they would become alarmed and start to stampede. For native hunters who had snuck into the middle of a herd of thousands of near-sighted and very large and powerful animals, a sudden stampede might well result in severe injury or death.

The Spread of Horses on the Plains

Other than native servants of the Spanish, the first native peoples to acquire the horse may have been the Jumano and Apache of New Mexico. In all likelihood, they may have traded for the animals at first, acquiring stolen animals from native servants who took them from their Spanish masters. Native servants likely showed them how to care for their new mounts as well. As early as the 1620s,

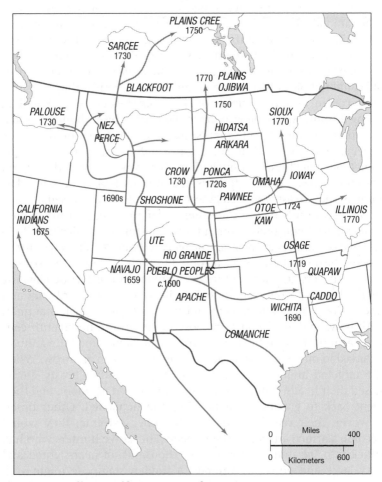

Map 10.1   Diffusion of horses across the West

native people raiding Spanish settlements made it a point to acquire horses. Having learned how to break horses from Spanish servants, Indians also began to acquire horses by capturing them from the small herds of mustangs that began to appear in the region in the early seventeenth century.

In the popular imagination, augmented by comments made by eighteenth- and nineteenth-century European and American observers, it is easy to think of Indians as "natural" horsemen. Some writings from this period give the impression that an Indian saw a horse, hopped on, and began riding. In truth, however, learning to handle horses effectively, like nearly every other skill, required great practice and experience. With the peoples of the Southwest being the first to acquire the horse, they naturally followed their nearest model – the Spanish – as an example of how to care for and manage the new animals. In many respects, the Apache and Jumano simply copied the Spaniards as best they could. European observers in the Southwest noted that the Apache fitted out their horses with leather armor, which seemed to follow the Spanish practice. In all likelihood, they gained their knowledge of how to care for the animals either by watching the Spanish, or by acquiring it second hand from the native servants who worked for the Spanish *rancheros* of New Mexico.

Thereafter horses apparently spread eastward and northward throughout the Great Plains and its margins fairly rapidly. In the early 1680s, the French explorer Robert La Salle, during his voyage southward down the Mississippi, heard that Kiowa had stolen horses from Mexico. Henri de Tonti, a survivor of La Salle's ill-fated expedition that shipwrecked on the coast of Texas, noted that the Caddo people of present-day east Texas and western Louisiana had approximately 30 horses. As early as the 1690s, other Frenchmen noted that the Choctaws of the lower Mississippi River Valley used horses to hunt deer. After the Apache and Jumano people acquired horses, the next southwestern native groups to get them probably were the Comanche and the Ute. For their part, the Comanche traded them northward to the Shoshone, who in turn traded them to the Crow, who may have traded them to peoples living in the Plateau region, such as the Nez Perce, who may have passed some animals on to the Blackfoot people. Other native peoples traveled to the Spanish trading post at Santa Fe, where they traded for horses. Another Frenchmen noted that the Wichita people, in what would be present day Kansas, had horses by 1719. By the 1750s, Hudson's

Bay Company traders in Saskatchewan were doing business with Cree people who had recently acquired their first mounts. By the mid-eighteenth century, the Lakota, Cheyenne, and nearly every other major tribe of Native American people on the Great Plains had horses.

In a sense, the acquisition of horses by native people set up a rich irony at the juxtaposition of history and American popular culture. In the late nineteenth century, and continuing through much of the twentieth, the stereotype of the Native American fostered by Wild West shows, penny dreadfuls (cheap pulp adventure magazines), movie westerns, and television, is that of the Plains Indian astride his horse.

The Cultural Impact of Horses and Muskets

The acquisition of the horse, and the arrival of European traders, had significant cultural impacts upon the native people of the plains. At first, the horse seemed to augment the advantages that the settled peoples of the river valleys had over the nomads. Because of their locations, they were easier for the French traders to find, and that is why they acquired cloth, metal tools, and firearms sooner than their plains rivals.

At this time, however, native people also acquired guns. Much ink has been spilled by historians and anthropologists regarding the native acquisition of guns. It has been pointed out that in many respects the muskets first traded to native people were impractical for use by buffalo hunters. Muskets had a slow rate of fire since they could not be reloaded quickly – especially by a shooter on horseback – and the report of the weapons tended to frighten away game. These are good points, and apparently native people recognized the limitations of the musket by not using it in bison hunting. Not so, however, in warfare.

In combat, native warriors used European weaponry to devastating physical – and to debilitating psychological – effect against their enemies. Musket balls created large gaping wounds and broke bones, causing deeper and more serious wounds than those caused by arrows. In addition, the noise and smoke generated by the new European-made weapon, for those unacquainted with it, would have been quite frightening.

In the 1980s, historian Francis Jennings placed the debate over Native American use of European firearms in its proper perspective.

Jennings acknowledged the shortcomings that others noted regarding muskets, such as their noise and slow rate of fire. He also noted that their acquisition made native peoples dependent on trade with Europeans for powder and shot, and on blacksmiths, who repaired their weapons. But Jennings concluded that arguments regarding the utility of muskets for natives were beside the point: while muskets did have their drawbacks, the historical record clearly shows that native warriors were insistent and vocal in their demand for them.

Smallpox in the West

It did not take long, however, for the advantages that the settled peoples in the river valleys enjoyed due to their having acquired guns first to disappear. While they acquired (from French traders) European goods sooner and on a more regular basis than did the nomads, engaging in trade, as well as living along the trade routes, meant that they came into contact with Old World diseases much sooner as well. And since the valley dwellers lived in concentrated, palisaded settlements, epidemics of European disease spread more rapidly among them than they did among peoples living farther out on the plains. The old pattern that had appeared on the Atlantic Coast now appeared again.

While the nomadic groups experienced disease epidemics later, they were by no means immune from the onset. In the 1770s and 1780s, a continent-wide smallpox pandemic ravaged native communities from the Pacific Northwest, throughout the Great Plains, and into the Eastern Woodlands. Canadian fur trader David Thompson offered a vivid description of the virulence of the pandemic when he described a 1782 Blackfoot raid on a Snake Indian encampment in what is probably present-day Montana. After their scouts had watched a Snake camp for a few days, having seen little activity, the Blackfoot decided to strike. As Thompson's native informant put it, "At the dawn of day, we attacked the Tents, and with our sharp flat daggers and knives, cut through the tents and entered for the fight; but our war whoop instantly stopt, our eyes were appalled with terror; there was no one to fight with but the dead and the dying, each a mass of corruption." Taking care not to touch or loot the stricken Snakes, the terrified Blackfoot warriors fled, only to see smallpox break out among their own number as soon as the very next day.

Witnesses and victims of local smallpox outbreaks in the 1770s and 1780s, whether European or Indian, had no way of knowing that they were a small part of a continent-wide pandemic whose victims included Europeans as well as native people. So severe was the outbreak of smallpox that it caused concern for both the British and the Continental armies then engaged in fighting the American Revolution. Both sides feared they could lose the conflict, but not because of enemy action. British and American commanders feared that smallpox would incapacitate so many of their troops that they would be unable to continue the war.

The Plains Migrations

The arrival of the horse, universally seen as a boon by native people, carried with it important ecological and human consequences. Because the horse made the meat and hides provided by the bison more accessible, it created a human population explosion on the Great Plains. By making bison hunting easier and safer (although it could never be completely safe), the availability of the horse encouraged Native American groups living in the Eastern Woodlands – or those who had lived on the margin between the Woodlands and Great Plains – and peoples who lived in the Plateau and Great Basin regions, to migrate to the plains. The Cree, for example, having obtained firearms from their Hudson's Bay Company trading partners, pushed west onto the northern plains region that brushed the subarctic. The Shoshoni, attracted by horses and the potential of a materially richer way of life, moved eastward from the Rocky Mountains. The Hidatsa, one of the nations that lived in permanent villages composed of earthen lodges, saw the arrival of the horse create a division in their community. Hidatsas who chose to become nomads coalesced into the Crow sometime in the late seventeenth or early eighteenth centuries.

The attractions of horses and bison led the Cheyenne – often thought of in the popular imagination as one of the most prototypical of the Plains Indians – to leave the Minnesota Woodlands in the mid-eighteenth century. The push factor took the form of a string of defeats at the hands of their better-armed Ojibwe enemies. After 1750, the Cheyenne settled on the upper Missouri River in present-day North and South Dakota, where they resumed life as settled farmers and competed for the region's resources with the Mandan,

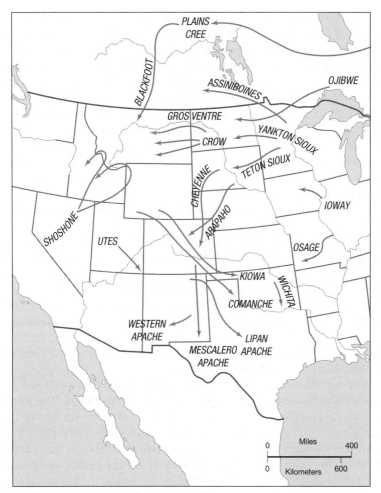

Map 10.2   Migrations to the Great Plains

who were irked by their presence. After 1780, the Ojibwe stepped up their attacks, nearly wiping out one of the Cheyenne villages. At almost the same time, an epidemic of European disease, probably smallpox, struck. The Cheyenne fled disease and defeat by migrating south, toward the high and southern plains, in present-day Kansas and Colorado, but they were also led by a series of pull factors. Chief among these was the new availability of the horse, which consequently made bison meat and hides easier to obtain.

The Dakota (Sioux), another of the prototypical Plains Indian group of the popular imagination, lived in the forests of present-day Minnesota. The Dakota people comprised numerous independent bands. The Dakota migration to the Great Plains began in the 1680s and continued in stages well into the nineteenth century. As in the case of the Cheyenne, a combination of push and pull factors influenced their actions. One of the pull factors was trade with the French, which led to some Dakota bands moving west to better hunting grounds for bison and beaver in the late seventeenth and early eighteenth centuries. It is at about this time that they began to acquire horses. The most notable push factor took the form of a string of defeats, again, at the hands of their better-armed Ojibwe enemies. American occupation of Minnesota in the early nineteenth century had the effect of terminating the centuries-long conflict between the two peoples. Not all the Dakota tribes moved west and adapted to life on the Great Plains in the eighteenth century; large contingents of Dakota would remain in Minnesota until finally pushed out by the Americans at the time of the Civil War.

The Comanche, often thought of as a southern plains people, left what is now present-day Wyoming in pursuit of horses and bison in the early eighteenth century. As they moved southward, they encountered and made enemies of the Apache and pushed them off of the plains into the desert Southwest.

The arrival of the horse created another ripple effect that accompanied the movement of peoples onto the Great Plains. The horse had made possible a culture based almost exclusively on harvesting the bison for their meat, hides, bones, and other body parts that could be transformed into a myriad of tools and artifacts that people used in their daily lives. The dependency on the bison, along with the influx of large numbers of native peoples onto the plains created conflict. As the Dakota and Cheyenne moved west, they clashed with the peoples of the river valleys, such as the Mandan, Pawnee, and Omaha.

War over the Buffalo

Peoples who had been long established on the Great Plains resented the intrusions posed by the newcomers, especially when these interlopers entered their hunting territories and killed what they considered to be "their" buffalo herds. As an important, and now contested, resource, bison herds became something that native people considered proprietary, and they warred with each other over the rights to hunting grounds. Horses not only made it easier to hunt bison, it turned out they also facilitated warfare between native peoples. At first, the settled peoples of the river valleys, being better mounted and having better access to European muskets, usually prevailed in combat with newcomers.

This new emphasis on warfare had far-reaching consequences for Plains Indian societies. Warfare became the surest way for young men to gain status (and in a few cases, young women who crossed the line between genders). A young man who went to war and returned with captives and horses, and who successfully "counted coup" on the enemy – that is, touched an enemy without harming him and escaped – became an admired member in his community. The prevalence of disease on the Great Plains led to a fatalistic acceptance of death, not just for warriors but for their families as well. Women who mourned a young native man who perished in battle counted him lucky in that he was spared the alternative of dying of smallpox.

The horse also affected the material culture of plains peoples in terms of mobility and wealth. Before the arrival of the horse, the dog was the largest draft animal available to the nomadic peoples of the plains; this had the effect of limiting their material possessions. The arrival of the horse changed that. Horses meant that the nomadic Plains people could have a great number of possessions, as they were now far easier to transport from place to place. For the first time, plains societies saw great disparities of wealth, as the number of horses that a man owned determined his status. Among many plains peoples, as well as Apaches in the Southwest, young men had to be able to present a sufficient number of horses as a gift to a potential bride's family to demonstrate their worthiness. Other measures of increased wealth became apparent. With horses, rather than dogs, to pull a travois, teepees now became larger. They also no longer simply provided shelter; they now became something of a status symbol and a way to display one's wealth and importance to one's community. They also became a medium used by warriors to boast of their accomplishments. One could ascertain the status of the owner of a tepee by looking at its size and the number and nature of the pictographs that adorned it. These often depicted his exploits in war, or on the hunt.

Women's Changing Roles and Status

Horses and the diseases that followed in the wake of European traders also helped to alter the gendered division of labor that had characterized many Native American communities. Prior to the arrival of the horse, men and women both contributed to the food supply. For the settled peoples of the river valleys, women performed the bulk of the agricultural labor, usually contributing to more than half of their community's subsistence. As a result, women in many of the pre-contact societies of the plains, as well as those of the Eastern Woodlands tribes that migrated into the region, often enjoyed a rough sort of equality with males. Because the horse prompted many native peoples to shift to bison hunting as almost their exclusive mode of subsistence, women's labor became less important in terms of community survival. Almost exclusively a male practice (although there were a very few females who hunted as well), the reliance on hunting meant that the status of women, and the value of their labor, declined. Women's responsibilities now centered on butchering the bison their husbands or other male kin killed, and preserving the animal's meat and hide. They also assumed responsibility for maintaining the camp, preparing for movements, and caring for children and the elderly.

European diseases, primarily smallpox, resulted in a greatly elevated mortality rate in plains communities in the eighteenth century. European pathogens did not discriminate in terms of gender or age – although the very old or very young were more susceptible. The intertribal wars over the bison hunting grounds, however, assured that the mortality rate among young men would be far higher. The combined results of the wars over the bison and the influx of European disease could be seen in the drastically altered demographics of Great Plains societies. Among males, few lived past the age of 40. Because women began to outnumber men by wide margins, many tribes increased, or began to practice for the first time, plural marriage, allowing men to take more than one wife. Among Dakota peoples, it became a common practice for a man to have more than one wife, provided he had the capability of supporting all of them. Dakota men often married sisters, on the supposition that they would get along with one another.

Yet the horse also brought advantages for native women. While they now had more in the way of personal property to pack for each move – and had to pack and move more often – the horse made such movements easier, since they could now ride instead of walk. Native people also seem to have had a more stable food supply thanks to the horse. In the early twentieth century, a Crow Indian woman related her grandmother's recollections of how the horse transformed life. Women could now ride, and moving was easier. Elderly people, who once might have been left behind to die, could now ride as well. She also recalled that there was plenty of food and that they never went hungry.

The Environmental Impact of the Horse

But the horse also led to a series of environmental impacts on the Great Plains. As more native people left the Great Basin, the Southwest, the Rockies, and the Eastern Woodlands for the Plains to follow the bison, they needed ever more horses. These horses in time became the bison's primary competitor for the key resource upon which both species depended: grass. Because owning a large number of horses became a mark of wealth, even a fairly small band of Plains Indians might possess hundreds, and in some cases more than a thousand horses. In large encampments with hundreds of warriors, the number of horses easily ran into the thousands. Campsites had to be moved frequently in order to ensure the animals had adequate forage. The need for adequate grazing grounds for their horses also provoked conflict on the plains. When the Comanche moved south, they attacked Apache bands that lived in the river valleys of northern and western Texas, partially to seize captives and to drive the Apache away, but also to gain control of the grasslands.

Lured to the plains by horses and bison, native groups were followed by European traders, who offered their wares in exchange for bison hides. With so many people now hunting them, both for their own subsistence and to satisfy the demands of distant markets, the number of bison began to decline. Visitors to the plains may not have noticed the decline, but the native peoples who subsisted on the bison certainly did. As herds diminished, native warfare for control of the hunting grounds intensified in frequency and level of violence.

The Russians

For thousands of years, the Aleut people lived along the northern Pacific Coast in what is today Alaska and on some islands in the Bering Strait. Over the centuries, they became masters of exploiting the harsh environment. The Aleut learned to hunt sea mammals and become expert fishermen and lived in dry, warm lodges, constructed mainly from earth and driftwood and thatched with grass. The Aleut developed a society with a clear pecking order. The chiefs stood at the top of the societal pyramid, while slaves, most of them war captives, occupied the bottom rung. The roles of men and women also sharply diverged. Males assumed responsibility for providing the bulk of the community's food by hunting and fishing, and for making useful implements, such as spears and darts used in hunting. Women, on the other hand, tended to the upkeep of homes and villages and the raising of children.

While other native peoples living elsewhere in North America contended with invasions by Western Europeans, the Aleut and other peoples of the Pacific Northwest dealt with a different sort of invader. Russian frontier history differs from that of Western European nations in its geographical context and direction. Westward expansion was not possible; but eastward expansion certainly was, and throughout

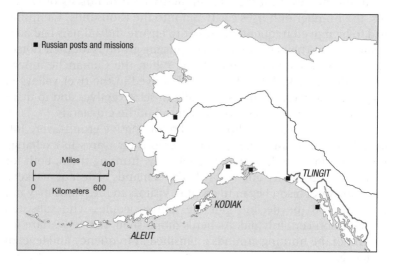

Map 10.3 Russian invasion of Alaska

the sixteenth and seventeenth centuries Russian fur traders made their way east, making contact with Siberia's tribal peoples. Rather than trade, Russian fur traders (known as *promyshlenniki*) possessing steel weapons and firearms, employed their technological advantages, and forced the tribesmen to pay tribute in the form of furs. The system worked well enough that the Russians would employ it later in North America.

Reaching North America, however, presented something of a challenge for the Russians. Despite the narrowness of the Bering Strait, the gap of sea that separates Alaska from Siberia (only some 50-odd miles), the difficulty of sailing and navigating in arctic waters delayed the Russian incursion into North America. Danish mariner Vitus Bering, sailing in the employ of the Czar, did not discover the strait that now bears his name until 1741.

Much like the English and the French more than a century earlier, the Russians believed that they could establish a unique relationship with native people, contrasting themselves with the Spaniards of the "Black Legend." The Russians also had extensive territorial dreams, believing that native people would prefer them to the Spanish, and therefore would help them, enabling Russian expeditions to move down the Pacific Coast and establish colonies as far south as Mexico. These suppositions, however, ignored the tendency of the *promyshlenniki* to mistreat native people; certainly, if they had forced the Siberians to hunt for them at gunpoint, they would have little compunction about forcing American natives to do the same.

The first Russian contacts with the natives of the Americas were less than promising. In July 1741, a 30-man Russian reconnaissance party came under attack by Tlingit warriors. Wiping out the Russian patrol and sinking their two small boats, the Tlingit compelled the rest of the expedition to return to Russia. One of the vessels ran aground on a small island in the Bering Sea. Over the winter, half of the crew perished. The survivors, however, managed to return to Russia the next summer, bringing with them over 900 otter pelts, which were highly valued by their Chinese trade partners. It did not take long, therefore, for the *promyshlenniki* to organize regular expeditions to the Aleutians.

Occupying small villages, the Aleut found themselves vulnerable to the *promyshlenniki*. Usually the *promyshlenniki* took villages by surprise, stunning the defenders with the noise and apparent deadliness of their muskets. The *promyshlenniki* made it a point to summarily execute Aleuts who offered sustained resistance, whether physically or verbally, in order to terrify the village's remaining population into compliance with their demands.

Drawing on their experience in Siberia, the *promyshlenniki* knew how to force Aleut hunters to do most of their work for them. Taking their wives and children hostage, the Russians assigned Aleut men large quotas of furs they had to pay as ransom. With the Aleut hunters away from their villages for months at a time in order to fill the quotas, the *promyshlenniki* used Aluet women as concubines. Within a short period of time, the *promyshlenniki* began to move south along Alaska's Pacific Coast in search of more sea otters, as they depleted the otter populations in the Aleutians.

The occasional resistance of native people was met with brutal force. In the mid-1760s, the Aluets rose up, burning four Russian ships and killing their crews. Two years later, in retaliation, a Russian expedition used ship-mounted cannon to bombard Aleut villages. Compelling the surrender of hundreds of Aleut hunters, the Russians slaughtered their war captives as an object lesson to other would-be rebels. Russian brutality and the introduction of disease resulted in the Aleut population declining by 90 percent in the first 60 years of contact.

Spanish Missions in California

The presence of the Russians on the Pacific Coast was enough to snap the Spanish out of their lethargy regarding California. After Juan Cabrillo's explorations of California 200 years earlier, Spain made no effort to follow up and colonize the region until the 1760s. Since the sixteenth century, Spain had shown little interest in Baja California, the region consisting largely of infertile desert occupied by small, scattered bands of Indians. Perhaps thinking that Alta California was too far away to be effectively governed, the authorities in Mexico City never mounted an effort to establish a colony there. But in the 1760s, learning that the Russians had moved into Alaska, and that British traders had been seen in the region, the Spanish decided the time had come to establish a presence in California. The exaggerated reports regarding the Russians and the British should not have worried the Spanish. Preoccupied with securing control of the eastern portion of North America and managing their increasingly unruly colonists, England had no designs on

California. While a few Hudson's Bay Company traders engaged in western exploration in this period, they were easily hundreds of miles from – and probably unaware of – California. Likewise, Spanish fears regarding Russian activity had little to do with reality; the nearest Russian traders would have easily been over 1,500 miles away, in Alaska.

Initial Spanish occupation of Alta California had little to do with its perceived actual value; it had more to do with creating a buffer between New Spain (with its capital at Mexico City) and the illusionary Russian invasion. At the time, Alta California contained the greatest number of native inhabitants in North America. Estimated to number approximately 300,000, the natives of the region practiced hunting and gathering, while eschewing agriculture. The rich, abundant environment provided sufficient animal, fish, and plant foods as to make agricultural labor unnecessary. Much like the native peoples of the Eastern Woodlands, the Indians of California also manipulated the environment for their own ends, setting fire to the woodlands periodically to clean out underbrush, and to encourage the growth of plants that attracted game animals. The Spanish did not know – and would not have appreciated had they known – that California also contained peoples who spoke over 90 different languages.

For the most part, the native peoples of California – and given the diversity of the region's many eco-niches and its peoples, it is difficult to generalize – practiced a seasonal round, spending their hunting seasons in one place, going to another to fish, and to yet another to gather edible plants. For the most part, California's natives lived in small, disparate bands. The Spanish rarely encountered native bands numbering over a thousand people.

The Spanish, however, lacked colonists for this new venture. Since the seventeenth century, Spanish colonization north of Mexico had declined significantly. The few northward colonization ventures that the government of New Spain undertook usually ended badly. Most Spanish colonists realized that most of the wealth of New Spain could be found in its center, that is, in Mexico. Unlike the earlier generation of conquistadors, New World Spaniards had lost their taste for further exploration of the Americas. And no wonder.

At the end of the sixteenth century, the Franciscan order invoked clauses of the Treaty of Tordesillas that required the signatories to participate in the conversion of non-Christians in order to encourage Spanish settlement of New Mexico. While the Franciscans went about their business of converting the Indians, New Mexico's colonists found that they largely struggled economically and, in 1680, found themselves at the mercy of the Pueblos when they revolted. In the early eighteenth century, after learning of the French presence in the lower Mississippi River Valley and the Gulf Coast, Spanish authorities encouraged the colonization of Texas in a bid to create a buffer between Mexico and French Louisiana.

Perhaps owing to the earlier experience in New Mexico, and to Texas's reputation for having an unfavorable environment for agriculture, and for containing a population of hostile natives, Spanish authorities had difficulties finding colonists willing to relocate to the far northern *frontera*. They once again turned to the Franciscans, who established missions among the Apache – who fled to the missions to escape the Comanche – and among the Caddo peoples along the Texas–Louisiana border. Unfortunately, the Franciscans had only marginal success in converting the natives of Texas to Christianity. They had a great deal of success, however, in offending them and in some cases causing powerful peoples – such as the Comanche and the Caddo – to turn on them, and to engage in hostilities with the soldiers who were supposed to be protecting the missionaries. It did not help matters when the soldiers sexually abused local native women.

Lacking colonists willing to settle Alta California, the Spanish again turned to the only group willing to take on the task: the Franciscans. In 1768, the Spanish began the process of establishing a chain of missions in coastal Alta California under the direction of Fray Junípero Serra. Given to self-mortification, Fray Serra represented an older strand of Franciscan thought.

Arriving in San Diego the next spring, Fray Serra led a group of approximately 100 priests, soldiers, and mariners in the building of the first mission in California. Realizing that they may need protection from the local natives – and the wherewithal to intimidate them – the Spanish also constructed a presidio (frontier fort) to house the soldiers. In the fall, the Spanish established their second mission, with accompanying presidio, hundreds of miles up the California coast at Monterey. Over time, the Spanish added three more coastal missions in between San Diego and Monterey, all connected by *El Camino Real* (The King's Road).

For the most part, the California natives did not resist the Spanish. Most of them lived in small, weak bands, and often found themselves overawed by Spanish horses and firearms. Since the Spanish could not convince many colonists to relocate voluntarily to California, the missionaries fell back on what had not worked with the Pueblo: they attempted to transform the Indians into Spaniards. In order to do this, the Franciscans first had to lure the Indians into the missions – and the fathers put on a good show. The ritual of the mass and the holding of Holy Day processions impressed native people, as did the religious artwork that adorned Catholic chapels. The apparent power of the Spanish, demonstrated by their mastery of livestock, the new crops they introduced, and the steel tools they brought with them, convinced many native people that the Spanish must have access to a different sort of magic. But while the missionaries attempted to convert the natives, the local Indians (not unlike the Pueblo) secretly practiced a form of religious syncretism, blending their traditional beliefs with those of the Spaniards.

The Spanish also sought to make it difficult, or near impossible, for the Indians to live outside the confines of the missions. The Europeans' livestock foraged on the open range, consuming native plants on which both the local Indians and the wildlife they hunted depended. When frustrated Indians killed the offending livestock, Spanish soldiers reacted by killing Indians. Like the English in New England, the Spanish did not understand the Indians' rationale behind the practice of periodically setting woods on fire. Fearful that the fires would rage out of control, the Spanish forbade the Indians from setting them. Just as the English had unwittingly imported invasive plants, so did the Spanish. Ironically, the Spanish suffered because they refused to let the Indians manage the environment. Without the periodic fires ignited by the natives, plants such as chaparral and greasewood grew out of control. Highly flammable and no longer periodically burned away, the dense, dry underbrush provided fuel for runaway wildfires that threatened Hispanic settlements. Likewise, California grizzly bears discovered that Spanish cattle herds made easy prey, and as a consequence, the populations of the fierce predators exploded, and the large animals soon menaced both Indian and colonist alike.

The English Arrive in the Pacific Northwest

The Pacific Northwest, stretching along a narrow coastal strip that ran from present-day Northern California to Southern Alaska, hosted a thriving native culture. Occupying an ecosystem that featured abundant woodland game and fish, as well as a large population of marine mammals, the native inhabitants never needed to develop agriculture. Living in the rainforests of the Pacific Northwest, the Haida, Tsimshan, Kwakiutl, Salish, Chinook, Tillamook, and other native groupings of the region lived in a world where their villages, headed by their local chief, served as the most important and visible political unit.

Largely freed from the threat of hunger by the abundant food resources of the environment, the peoples of the Pacific Northwest developed perhaps the richest material culture of all peoples north of the Rio Grande. Surrounded by enormous stands of timber, they built large plank houses, which they richly decorated with carvings. To European sensibilities, the most attractive feature of these societies was their material wealth; but their employment of wealth baffled Europeans. Rather than continue to accumulate goods, the wealthy opted to gain status within their communities by giving away nearly all of their possessions to their neighbors and the less fortunate, in a ceremony known as a potlatch. The man holding the potlatch would feast his neighbors, often to such an extent that he gave away all of the accumulate food in his household, and would give away his family's possessions, with the possible exception of their dwelling and the clothing on their backs. To Europeans, the potlatch may have seemed like a form of madness (and would still be viewed that way when the Canadian government attempted to suppress the practice in the early twentieth century) but to native people, it had its own logic. A man who generously gave away his possessions would not be without for very long. Since he had enriched his neighbors, it would not be long before one of them, seeking to increase his stature in the community, held a potlatch of his own – and probably remembered and rewarded the person who helped enrich him.

In 1778, famed English navigator James Cook explored the waters around Vancouver Island, establishing an English salient between Spanish and Russian claims on the Pacific Coast in the process. While Cook's voyages are largely remembered for their contributions to ethnology, science, and the expansion of geographical knowledge, his encounter with the native peoples of the Pacific Northwest drew the immediate interest of English traders, who traveled to the region in large numbers. Cook and his men acquired sea otter pelts, transported them to China, and realized an enormous windfall when Chinese merchants purchased them for anywhere between 100 and 120 percent more than Cook's sailors had paid the Indians in goods.

For the peoples of the Far West – particularly those of the Pacific Northwest – sustained encounters with European explorers, traders, missionaries, and colonists came late, especially when compared to peoples who lived in the Southwest and Eastern Woodlands. Regardless of the timing, these encounters proved to be no less devastating, as the native people who came into contact with Russian traders found themselves forced into virtual slavery, and as Europeans unwittingly passed Old World pathogens on to them.

11

Native Americans and the American Revolution

The unrest that developed between Great Britain and her American colonists over the decade following the end of the Great War for Empire could not have gone entirely unnoticed by native people. While many Indians probably had only a peripheral awareness as to the issues that provoked hostilities between the mother country and the colonists, others who lived close to colonial settlements, such as the Stockbridge Indians of Western Massachusetts, would have been wholly cognizant of the tensions between the King of England and their neighbors.

Even in the lands west of the Appalachians, Native Americans heard that difficulties existed between the Crown and its subjects in North America. For these peoples, the most obvious indicator of problems in the colonial relationship would have been the unwillingness of many colonists to obey the terms of the Proclamation of 1763. Native people understood that the King's Proclamation had created a reserve for them in the lands west of the Appalachians. Yet in the years since the Proclamation was issued, English colonists were still filtering into the west by way of the Ohio River Valley and through the Cumberland Gap, a route that had been discovered after the war by Daniel Boone of Virginia. While British troops occasionally rousted squatters, the trespassers far outnumbered the soldiers assigned to police the Proclamation Line, which stretched across the crest of the Appalachians, from New York to Georgia.

"Times Are Altered with Us": American Indians from First Contact to the New Republic, First Edition. Roger M. Carpenter.
© 2015 John Wiley & Sons, Inc. Published 2015 by John Wiley & Sons, Inc.

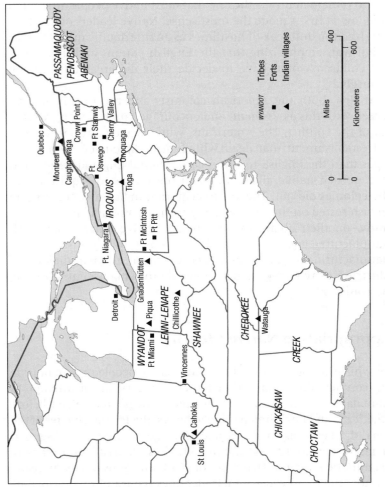

Map 11.1 Native Americans and the American Revolution

239

Nevertheless, news that American colonists had fired on British troops at Lexington and Concord still would have taken native people by surprise. In planning a course of action, Native American leaders realized they had three choices: to side with the English, to side with the Americans, or to remain neutral. The last choice, that to remain neutral – the one that most native people attempted to follow at first – made the most sense. Native leaders often characterized the outbreak of hostilities as an interfamily quarrel, or as a civil war, emphasizing that the English parents and their colonial children would have to decide their disagreements among themselves.

At first, both the American colonists and the British officials agreed with this assessment, and encouraged native people to stay out of the conflict. The Americans, while lacking any sort of central establishment that dealt with Indian diplomacy, were more eager than the English in this regard. Should England decide that they needed native allies, they had the means to acquire them. The colonies did not. The key to acquiring Indian alliances for the English rested on their pre-existing relationships, and most importantly, on their ability to furnish prospective native allies with manufactured goods. The American colonies, by contrast, lacked a manufacturing capacity, and focused most of their diplomatic efforts on convincing the native people to remain neutral during the conflict.

Appropriating Native Identity

Yet while the colonists sought to have native people remain outside the conflict, they appropriated their imagery in an attempt to intimidate (largely unsuccessfully) their English foes. Even before Americans and Englishmen came to blows, the Boston chapter of the Sons of Liberty appropriated native imagery when they disguised themselves as "Mohawks" and cast 342 chests of East India Company Tea into the harbor in December of 1773. The Sons of Liberty really did not attempt to conceal their identities – most of their acquaintances saw through their disguises quite easily – but the donning of native costume, it has been suggested, indicates that they saw themselves as being very much American rather than English. In a twist of irony, some Native American leaders who sided with the English during the conflict referred to the Americans as "Bostonians." The term was not meant as a compliment, and it is difficult to tease out the meanings the Sons of Liberty assigned to their costume, especially from a distance of two centuries. Yet the fact that they chose the garb of Native Americans does say something.

Other Americans also found the appropriation of native identity useful, including no less a personage than George Washington. As the commander of the Continental Army, the general once suggested that some units should outfit their riflemen in fringed leather hunting shirts with tomahawks tucked into their belts. Washington's rationale for this uniform was that he thought it may give Americans a psychological edge by striking fear into British troops. As Washington put it, many English soldiers seemed to believe that any man attired in hunting shirt must be an unerring shot. The tomahawk may have actually been useful, since Continental Army troops had little training or experience with the bayonet. In close combat, the Continental troops often came out a sad second best to the English. Not all Continental Army soldiers were expert marksman, but the English had unwittingly fostered this impression early in the war when British army recruiters had a captured Pennsylvania minuteman put on a marksmanship demonstration at a London park. Apparently the captured American put on a display that may have been a little too good; instead of convincing young Englishman to join the army, the Pennsylvanian's ability to hit small targets at long ranges convinced many would-be recruits they would be best off remaining in England.

Divisions among the Iroquois

The American Revolution caused historic splits among Native American nations, dividing them along lines of religion and political interest, and generationally. The most notable of these divisions occurred among the Iroquois Six Nations. Several factors contributed to the split even before the Revolution began. Perhaps the obvious event in the Iroquois division may have been the death of Sir William Johnson in July 1774. Johnson's death came as he exhorted the Iroquois not to ally themselves with the Shawnee and Delaware who were then fighting the Virginians in what came to be known as Dunmore's War. Guy Johnson, Sir William's nephew, succeeded him as the British Superintendent of Indian Affairs for the Northern Colonies. There was, however, a less visible but just as important struggle that would help determine the future of the League.

Several years before his death, Johnson permitted Presbyterian minister Samuel Kirkland to set up a mission among the Oneida and Tuscarora. Kirkland bypassed the easternmost of the Six Nations, the Mohawk, because many of them had already converted to the Anglican faith and made it clear they would not welcome a mission from another denomination. The northernmost Mohawk at Kahnawake had been converted to Catholicism by the Jesuits, and would have presented even more of a challenge for a Protestant missionary. Seeing Christianity as a positive, Johnson allowed Kirkland to establish his mission, and in a short time he had a good number of converts. Had the American Revolution not intervened, it is possible Johnson and Kirkland may have remained on good terms.

However, in the years leading up to the Revolution, Johnson began to have misgivings about Kirkland's activities among the Oneida and Tuscarora. Whereas political disagreements among the members of the Iroquois League had been a fairly normal occurrence, now they had religious disagreements as well. At the same time, the disagreements between Kirkland and the Anglican ministers who worked among the Iroquois became so severe that Iroquois parents complained to Johnson that the missionaries on either side of the dispute had permitted some of their children to die unbaptized. Kirkland refused to use the Anglican service and the Book of Common Prayer when he ministered to the Mohawk, who much preferred the relaxed Anglican notion of Christianity to Kirkland's brand of New Light Presbyterianism, Mohawk leaders complained to Sir William. Kirkland's sometime public disagreements with Anglican clergy who worked among the Indians tended to undermine the work of all missionaries. Witnessing the bickering, native converts began to wonder if the one true faith was actually two or more unstable religions.

The end of the Great War for Empire had serious consequences for the Iroquois and other native peoples in terms of diplomacy. With the French gone, the playoff system that many of them had relied on in their dealings with Europeans was no longer operable. While many native people first sought to remain neutral, many of them eventually sided with Great Britain. While British representatives encouraged native people to remain neutral at first, it would not be long before Native Americans would be drawn into the conflict.

Neutrality

Native leaders who were approached by the British to join them in an alliance against the rebellious colonists often demurred in the early phases of the conflict. British diplomats extolled the strength of his majesty's forces against those raised by the Americans. The natural counterargument that native leaders offered was usually along the lines that the English did not need their help; if the British were really as powerful as they claimed, they should be able to defeat the Americans with little or no assistance. Other native leaders were far more blunt, pointing out to both English and American representatives who sought their assistance that they must take native people for fools if they thought they would involve themselves in a fight that was none of their affair. It did not help the cause of American diplomats that in the years since the end of the Great War for Empire, representatives from the various colonies had developed a reputation among native people by participating in some of the more spectacular land swindles of the era.

Colonial governments in the southern colonies frequently undercut the efforts of British Superintendent of Indian Affairs for the Southern Colonies John Stuart. Georgia, for example, by playing the Cherokee and the Creek off against one another, acquired six million acres of land in a 1773 treaty. Unscrupulous land speculators convinced Cherokees to sign away lands (that did not actually belong to them) in the Ohio country. In exchange for signing over more than 25,000 square miles, unscrupulous Cherokees received a cabin full of trade goods. It did not help matters when Sir William Johnson, often well thought of by most native people, helped negotiate the 1768 Treaty of Fort Stanwix, in which the Six Nations signed over nearly all of present-day Kentucky and Tennessee to the English. This agreement outraged the Cherokee and Shawnee, many of whom actually lived in the region. Like earlier Iroquois land sales to the colonists, this one involved exchange of lands that the League did not actually own.

Before his death, Sir William Johnson encouraged the Iroquois to remain unified and on the side of the King. Johnson also came to regret having allowed Kirkland into the Iroquois villages, and now sought to blunt his influence. Kirkland, a native of Massachusetts, sided with the colonists who opposed the Crown, and many of his congregants chose to follow him.

The Continental Congress, perhaps aware of the disadvantages it faced in gaining Native American allies, also attempted to convince native people to remain neutral. While native leaders initially heeded the request of Congress, more than likely they remained suspicious of the Americans. The Americans could not provide native people with the trade goods upon which they had become dependent. But the key drawback the Americans faced in attempting to convince native people to remain neutral – or to join them as their allies – was the behavior of their own citizens. As mentioned, unscrupulous land speculators swindled native people out of vast amounts of territory, and colonists consistently violated the Proclamation Line of 1763. At least a few native people were somewhat aware of the large land companies that had been created, such as the Ohio Company, for the sole purpose of acquiring vast amounts of Indian territory and then selling it to would-be settlers. Native Americans and their leaders clearly recognized that, if the Americans prevailed in their war with Great Britain, they would lose their lands. Whereas the British government had a track record (albeit, a very short and imperfect one) of protecting Native American land claims, the colonists made it very clear that they intended to dispossess native people of their lands.

Joseph Brant

Despite the efforts of Iroquois leaders, the divisions within the League were already too deep. Besides the animosity between Kirkland and Anglican missionaries, other factors included the influence of the late Sir William Johnson's protégé, Joseph Brant. Sir William Johnson took an interest in Joseph, the younger brother of his favorite mistress Molly Brant, when he was still a boy. Looking after the youth's education, Sir William sent him to Eleazar Wheelock's Indian Charity School in Lebanon, Connecticut. Before the onset of the Revolution, Brant traveled to England with Sir William's successor, Guy Johnson. Brant made quite an impression on London society. He often appeared in public in traditional Mohawk dress, attending the theater and enjoying the city's nightlife with his friends, which included the Prince of Wales. London magazines published articles about him, noting his urbane manner and that he had translated portions of the Holy Bible into the Mohawk language. They also sought interviews with Brant, wishing to hear his views of the Iroquois alliance with England, and wanted to hear his opinions of the growing unrest among the colonists in British North America. He also sat for a portrait by noted artist George Romney.

Brant and Guy Johnson returned to North America at the end of July 1776, when their ship put in at Staten Island. They had arrived just as the British were landing the largest overseas invasion force they had ever assembled up to that time. Brant and Johnson remained in New York during the battle for the city and its environs. Brant reportedly took part in the battle of Brooklyn Heights, in which the British routed the newly formed Continental Army. Washington's army did have luck on their side, however; under cover of darkness and fog, most of his troops managed to escape by boat that same night. Brant and Johnson wished to return to Iroquois country but British commander General Howe balked at first, deeming it too dangerous. Brant persisted, however, and finally set out with a Mohawk Valley Loyalist who traveled with him. Donning disguises, and traveling by night and hiding during the day, Brant and his companion made it to Iroquois country that fall.

Brant returned just as the Iroquois and other native peoples had begun to reconsider if they could realistically stay out of the now-raging conflict between the British and the colonists. Brant related to his people the details of his trip to England, and emphasized why native people should side with the Crown. Many of the reasons that Brant cited were already well known to his audience. Foremost was the aggressiveness of American colonists in obtaining land. Second was native dependence on European trade goods. The Americans simply did not have a manufacturing capacity to provide them; the English, on the other hand, were the sons of the greatest manufacturing nation in the world and should have little problem continuing to fulfill native people's material needs.

Another key factor that swung the Iroquois into the conflict was a smallpox epidemic – part of the continent-wide pandemic that ravaged North America in the decades of the 1770s and 1780s – that struck the Onondaga. The timing of the smallpox epidemic that struck the Onondaga had consequences for the Iroquois League. Unable to meet with other nations of the League, and unable to follow the traditional practice of "condoling" other nations for the loss of chiefs and other important personages, the decision was made to extinguish the Confederacy's council fire for the first time since its formation more than three centuries earlier. Each of the Six

Iroquois Nations was now free to make their own decisions regarding war, neutrality, and alliances.

While the Iroquois League divided for the first time in perhaps 300 years, native people in the Ohio country also struggled in determining what their response should be to the unrest between the British and the American colonists. Like Joseph Brant, many of them almost instinctively recognized that the Crown was the only entity that restrained the colonists from taking their lands.

Many of the Shawnees entered the conflict on the side of the English, and attacked the frontiers of Virginia. For many of the Shawnee, these acts were in retaliation for Lord Dunmore's War of only two years earlier. The Shawnee choice to attack colonists who opposed the King reveals much of the irony of the American Revolution. Lord Dunmore, the governor of Virginia, had been appointed by the King, and sought to rally Virginia Loyalists to oppose the Revolutionaries. While Dunmore led Virginia's attack against the Shawnee at Point Pleasant, he now needed the very Indians he fought two years earlier as allies.

In this early phase of the war, the Continental Congress attempted to ignore Shawnee attacks in the hope they would stop, as they sought to avoid fighting an Indian war in the Ohio country to the west while simultaneously fighting the British army in the east. Cornstalk, a war chief who led the Shawnee at Point Pleasant, and negotiated a peace when he saw that victory could not be achieved, also advocated peace and encouraged his young warriors to remain in their villages. However, as the Moravian missionary David Zeisberger noted, as the conflict continued, the warriors ceased to listen to the old leaders. The same problem would vex not only the Shawnee, but also the Cherokee, as the American Revolution caused generational strife within Native American communities.

The main reason for the generational split within the Shawnee and Cherokee nations could be tied to recent land cessions, in which older men, wishing to avoid or stave off conflict, signed over large tracts of land to the colonists. Resentful that their peoples' lands had been yielded to the colonists, and encouraged by British Indian agents who often promised material support, the younger warriors began to ignore the advice of the old men.

While the older leaders certainly recognized the Americans were more likely to take their lands – Cornstalk certainly thought so – they also had difficulty seeing advantages for their communities if either side won. Considered in this context, it is easy to see why they continued to consider neutrality the only viable option. But the longer the conflict lasted, the more neutrality became a narrower ground on which to stand. Tragically, Cornstalk, an advocate for peace, would be murdered by American militiamen, driving even more Shawnee onto the side of the British.

While American frontiersmen and young Shawnee, Lenni-Lenape, and Mingo warriors imperiled an unstable peace in the west, the Six Nations divided into rival armed camps. Many Oneida and Tuscarora chose to side with the Americans. As for the charismatic Joseph Brant, he traveled to Montreal, where he joined a British expedition that hoped, with the help of the troops then garrisoned at New York City, to end the Revolution in 1777.

Oriskany

Brant arrived in Montreal at the confluence of two events, one fortunate for the British, and the other unfortunate. The good fortune lay in the fact that General John Burgoyne had arrived from England and begun putting together his plan that called for a three-pronged British attack that would target Albany. Burgoyne planned to move south with a large force down the Lake Champlain and Hudson River Valley corridor, while a force commanded by William Howe moved north along the Hudson. Brant and Lieutenant Colonel Barry St Leger would lead the third prong, which would seize the post at Oswego and Fort Stanwix. Brant and St Leger would then move down the Mohawk River to Albany where, according to Burgoyne's plan, British forces would link up and sever New England, considered the hotbed of the Revolution, from the rest of the colonies. The unfortunate part was that both Burgoyne and Brant arrived in Montreal just as smallpox – once again, part of a larger continent-wide pandemic – struck the community. Smallpox delayed Burgoyne's efforts to train and organize his army.

Brant arrived at Oswego in June at the head of 300 warriors. Linking up with St Leger, they advanced toward Fort Stanwix. Certain that they would easily capture the fort, British officers invited Seneca warriors to look on during the assault. Things did not, however, go quite the way St Leger planned. Most of the intelligence that St Leger had acquired about Fort Stanwix turned out to be faulty. The post had better artillery and was better garrisoned than he had been led to believe. Realizing that his 1,400-man force – nearly half of which were Native Americans – could not reduce Stanwix, St Leger settled in for a siege of the post.

In early August, a relief force of approximately 700 New York militiamen – augmented by 60 Oneida warriors – advanced toward Stanwix in the hope of raising the siege. St Leger could only detach approximately 450–500 men to meet the threat. Divisions appeared among the Iroquois allied to the British. The Mohawks led by Brant made ready to go with British regulars and Tory Rangers to ambush the Americans at a spot a mile west of the village of Oriskany. But the Seneca warriors held back, suggesting instead that a parley be arranged with the Americans in the hope that a battle could be avoided. A sharp response from Brant, questioning the Seneca's courage, ended their hesitancy.

The Battle of Oriskany marked the beginning of an Iroquois civil war as Mohawks and Senecas fought Oneidas in a day-long battle. Many of the Indians who participated in the battle lacked firearms, and were armed only with spears and hatchets. The Seneca leader Blacksnake later recalled how streams of blood flowed downhill from the battlefield. After a day of intense combat, Brant and other Iroquois leaders loyal to the British wished to continue the battle into the next day. St Leger, however, declined their advice; his mission was to bring the siege of Fort Stanwix to a successful conclusion.

Oriskany had two effects, one short term, the other long term. In the short term, the arrival of an American relief at Fort Stanwix two weeks after the battle forced St Leger to abandon the siege. This meant that one of the three prongs of Burgoyne's plan had failed. Apparently unbeknownst to Burgoyne – and St Leger for that matter – the other prong had also failed. Indeed, the movement of General Howe northward along the Hudson River never took place. When Burgoyne submitted his plan to London, Howe also submitted a proposed operation that would see his army attack the seat of the Continental Congress in Philadelphia. Both plans had been approved; while Burgoyne moved southward to seize Albany, General Howe and his army sailed for Philadelphia. It was the classic case of the right hand not knowing what the left hand was doing. In October 1777, Burgoyne, unable to reach Albany, but also unable to retreat to Montreal, surrendered his army in what proved to be the turning point of the war.

The Iroquois warriors who fought on the British side at Oriskany carried the brunt of the battle. The Mohawk and Seneca discovered that during the battle American militia had destroyed their camps and carried off many of their possessions. The Indians – particularly the Seneca – felt embittered in the aftermath of the difficult battle, particularly since the British led them to believe that they would not be doing the bulk of the fighting. Far more serious, however, was the fact that Iroquois were now killing Iroquois in combat. The rupture of the League was now complete.

Most native peoples, despite their desire to remain neutral, were finding it increasingly difficult to do so. While for many native groups dependency on European trade goods was an overriding factor in determining their allegiance, they found themselves pressured by both the British and the Americans to take sides. Those peoples that did attempt to continue to remain neutral discovered that one side or the other would still treat them as enemies.

American Allies

The Stockbridge people of Western Massachusetts – from the Praying Town of the same name – had a long history of interactions with the white community around them and chose to side with the Americans. Stockbridge, for all practical purposes, had become a mixed native and white community, one that provided the Americans with myriad of military and diplomatic services. In early 1775, even before shots rang out at Lexington and Concord, 35 Stockbridge men joined the local Committee of Safety and served as minutemen, and others signed up to join the provisional army that besieged the British in Boston later that year.

The Americans employed Stockbridge Indians as emissaries to other native peoples. Ethan Allen of Vermont chose three Stockbridge men to carry a message advocating neutrality to Native Americans in the vicinity of Montreal. It turned out that the Stockbridge representatives enjoyed a form of diplomatic immunity. When the three men were captured by the British, the commander at Montreal ordered that they be hanged, but he released them when the local Mohawks at Caughnawaga protested and demanded that the trio be permitted to deliver their message. Later in the war, Indian allies of General Burgoyne successfully lobbied him for the release of Stockbridge warriors who had been taken prisoner as part of Fort Ticonderoga's garrison.

In the fall of 1776, two Stockbridge diplomats working on behalf of the Continental Congress attended a conference at Fort Pitt.

Bearing a tomahawk and a war belt, the two encouraged the neutral Lenni-Lenape (Delaware) and Shawnee to enter the war on the side of the Americans. Interestingly, the Stockbridge representatives used the same arguments as Americans who opposed the King, citing alleged British abuses. At this fairly early date, neither the Shawnee nor the Lenni-Lenape of the region saw an advantage to entering the war; indeed, they made a counteroffer to the Stockbridge representatives, asking if they would like to abandon the violence-wracked east and relocate to the Ohio country.

Stockbridge Indians served in Washington's army during the New York City campaign, where he saw to it they were issued blue and red caps so that other American troops could distinguish them from "enemy Indians." A Hessian officer described the distinctive dress and armament of Stockbridge soldiers he faced on the battlefield. They went into battle with a hat made of basswood cord, wearing long, course linen shirts that almost reached their knees. Each one carried a short hatchet, which they could throw "very skillfully," as well as a rifle or musket, a bow, and a quiver that contained 20 arrows. The Stockbridge contingent of the Continental Army was shot to pieces in the Battle of White Plains outside New York City in 1778. Many of the survivors returned home to Massachusetts, and Stockbridge widows petitioned the state for relief, since they now had no means of support. Massachusetts had little to offer in the way of support, other than some blankets. With the exception of a few Stockbridge men who later served in the Sullivan Campaign against the Iroquois, this was the end of their service in the Continental Army.

The Ohio country presented a quandary for both American and British diplomats. Nearly every Indian nation in the region had pro-British and pro-American factions, as well as a significant portion of people who favored neutrality. Frontier diplomats such as the American George Morgan at Fort Pitt and the British commander Henry Hamilton at Fort Detroit vied for the allegiance of native peoples. However, while Morgan and Hamilton could perhaps convince a native leader to sign a treaty, there was no guarantee that individuals in a given native community would adhere to it. Some Native American groups such as the Wyandot and the Mingo were overwhelmingly on the side the British. Serving not only as British military allies, they also went on the offensive diplomatically, seeking to pressure the Shawnee and the Delaware, both of whom had dissolved into factions favoring one side or the other, into siding with England.

Some Lenni-Lenape (Delaware) leaders viewed the Revolution as an opportunity that their people should exploit in order to escape Iroquois domination. Earlier in the century, the Iroquois had intervened in a land dispute between the Lenni-Lenape and Pennsylvania, and assisted the colony in evicting the Delaware from their lands in the wake of the notorious Walking Purchase. After the Lenni-Lenape removed to the Ohio country, the League claimed suzerainty over them and the other Algonquin peoples of the region. The Iroquois exploited their supposed domination of these peoples and their lands in their diplomatic relations with the British. For their part, the British, who claimed the Iroquois as their subjects, made the argument to other European powers that the Iroquois League's land claims were simply an extension of their own.

Lenni-Lenape chiefs such as George White Eyes had long sought accommodation with Europeans. White Eyes, for example, had once run a trading post and a tavern; certainly not the usual present-day picture of a Native American leader. During Pontiac's Rebellion, he recognized that the upheaval that participating in the conflict would likely have would have detrimental effects for his people (and probably his business as well) and sought to encourage young men to ignore Pontiac and Neolin.

In an effort to have his people escape Iroquois domination, White Eyes signed a treaty of peace and friendship with the nascent United States in 1778. The treaty contained rather extensive provisions that allowed American troops free passage through Delaware territory and specified that the Lenni-Lenape would supply the American army with foodstuffs. The Americans agreed to build a fort in Delaware territory that would be used to protect the tribe from retaliation, most likely from the Wyandot and the Mingo. George Morgan later claimed that the treaty conference with the Delaware had been "villainously conducted." In all likelihood White Eyes and his fellow chiefs may not have known the details of each of the provisions. For his part, White Eyes arrived at the conference with a unique proposition: that the Delaware become the fourteenth state.

White Eyes served the Americans as a guide in a campaign against Fort Detroit in 1778. Later that year, the Delaware learned that White Eyes had succumbed to smallpox during the campaign: this turned out to be a lie. White Eyes, George Morgan noted six years later, had been murdered by American militiamen.

The Death of Cornstalk

The murder of White Eyes and the Delaware alliance point to the two most serious problems the Americans had in gaining and retaining the alliance of Native Americans west of the Appalachians. American settlers and militia commonly attacked Indians, often without provocation, and made little or no attempt to distinguish friend from foe. The Shawnee leader Cornstalk, unlike White Eyes, urged his people remain neutral, rather than become a belligerent in the conflict. Prior to the Revolution, Cornstalk led Shawnee warriors against Virginians in the battle of Point Pleasant, and he played a key role in negotiating the peace afterwards. With the beginning of the Revolution, Cornstalk once again encouraged his Shawnee people to remain neutral. In October 1777, Cornstalk and two other Shawnee leaders, named Red Hawk and Petalla, paid a diplomatic visit to Colonel Charles Stuart at Fort Randolph, in northern Virginia. Cornstalk informed Colonel Stuart that while he still preferred neutrality, British blandishments and American depredations against his people were driving many of them in to the British camp. In an effort to force the Shawnee to remain neutral, the post commander seized the three Shawnee leaders as hostages. A month later, concerned about his father, Cornstalk's son visited the post to find out why he had not returned. At that same time, American militia brought the body of a young man who had been killed and scalped to the post. Despite the efforts of their officers to stop them, the enraged militia – eager to kill any Indian they could find – burst into the room where Cornstalk and the other Shawnee were being held. All four men – including Cornstalk's son, were murdered. Such actions by American militia and settlers did much to drive native people away from neutrality and into the arms of the British.

Another factor, and seemingly a constant one, that damaged American diplomatic efforts was their inability to provide native people with promised trade goods. The Delaware who chose to side with the Americans, for example, complained bitterly that they could not even give them "a single blanket." In response, other native peoples mocked the Delaware, pointing out their folly in siding with the Americans. By the end of the war, the ineffectiveness of the Continental Congress in giving their native allies promised supplies, and their failure to restrain settlers and American militia, resulted in many former allies becoming their enemies.

A Generational Divide

To the south, native people witnessed ruptures of a different sort within their communities. Unlike the divisions that formed among the Six Nations, or the political divisions that bedeviled the Lenni-Lenape and the Shawnee, the Cherokee split along generational lines. At the end of the Cherokee war in 1761, older Cherokee leaders found themselves forced to cede vast tracts of land to the colonies of Virginia, North Carolina, and South Carolina. In the years between the end of the Great War for Empire and the American Revolution, unscrupulous colonial traders continued to extract land from the Cherokee.

In early 1776, Ottawa, Mohawk, and Shawnee representatives visited the Cherokee Capital of Chota, which sat near the Little Tennessee River. As Henry Stuart, the British Deputy Superintendent of Indian Affairs, looked on, the delegation presented the Cherokee with a large red war belt. This diplomatic mission sought to enlist Cherokee warriors on the side of Great Britain. Many of the arguments that they presented, mainly revolving around American hunger for native lands, would have been already familiar to the Cherokee and other Native Americans by that time.

For the most part, the older Cherokee leaders remained mute. Some among them, such as Oconostota and Little Carpenter, had already signed away thousands of square miles of Cherokee land the year before at Sycamore Shoals in exchange for trade goods. At first, the younger Cherokee men hung back. During the conference, however, word arrived of an altercation between Cherokee warriors and Carolinians. The mood of the young men quickly changed, and most of them made ready to go to war.

The older generation of Cherokee leaders grossly misread the temperament of the younger generation of warriors. The prominent young warrior Tsiyu Gansini, or "Dragging Canoe," the son of Little Carpenter, opposed his father and sought to make alliances with other native peoples to the north and south in an effort to stymie American westward expansion. Dragging Canoe became a prominent war leader, founding the Chickamauga War Society, naming it after the village from which most of its members came. In fact, many Cherokees viewed the conflict with the Americans as a war that involved the Chickamauga War Society, and not the Cherokee nation per se. Unsurprisingly, Virginians and Carolinians on the frontier never made the same fine distinction.

Older Cherokees remembered well the devastation of the 1759–1761 war with the British, when they had learned first-hand just how vulnerable their towns were to attack. Cherokee women also opposed the war. Even younger women, who had imperfect or no memories of the previous conflict, lobbied in tribal councils and in meetings with the British diplomats to keep the Cherokee out of the war. Since the women were responsible – and in a sense "owned" – the cornfields that fed their communities, they were very conscious of just how vulnerable their nation was.

The Chickamauga who followed Dragging Canoe launched attacks on the Georgia, Carolina, and Virginia frontiers beginning in 1776. But the American settlers, just as the old men and Cherokee women had feared, retaliated by burning their towns and cornfields and destroying their food stores. The following year, 1777, it became clear just how divided the Cherokee were as the old men made a separate peace with the Americans. The treaty that ended the Revolution in 1783 mattered little to the Chickamauga – they, like other Native Americans, were not party to the agreement – and their assaults on the frontier continued into the mid-1780s.

"Monster Brant"

Joseph Brant remained active in the north, becoming known to the Americans as "Monster Brant." Many of these accusations stemmed from what became known as the Wyoming (Pennsylvania) Massacre in July 1778. In this event, a force of Iroquois and Tory Rangers led by John Butler and the Seneca chief Cornplanter routed a force of patriot militia in a 45-minute battle in which more than 300 Americans were killed, and only 20 were taken prisoner. Butler later reported that his Rangers and the Indians took over 220 scalps. The Americans claimed the British and the Indians tortured most of the survivors to death, and most of the rumors blamed Joseph Brant for the atrocities – even though he had not in fact been present.

A few months later, American forces retaliated, attacking and destroying Brant's home at Onaquaqa. The raiders also destroyed apple orchards and cornfields, and in retaliation for the atrocities at Wyoming, they bayoneted Indian children they discovered hiding in the cornfields.

At the time of the Wyoming Massacre, Brant was in the Delaware Valley in Eastern Pennsylvania, in joint command of a mixed force of Mohawk, Seneca, Tory Rangers, and a few British regulars. He shared command with Walter Butler, the son of John Butler who was leading the Tory Rangers at Wyoming. Butler, who was exercising his first command, had disagreements with Brant, who thought he alone should be in charge. The Mohawk under Brant heard reports of what had happened at Onaquaqa, and the Seneca were angered after learning that many of their towns along the Susquehanna River had been attacked by Patriot militia.

Butler planned to capture an American post near the settlement of Cherry Valley. The Americans there were not on their guard, and Butler took the settlement by surprise; however, he had no control over the Seneca warriors, who were bent on exacting revenge. Although Brant attempted to stop the carnage that followed the taking of the settlement, he could not do so. Before the killing spree ended, the Seneca had taken the lives of nearly 50 Americans, most of them women and children. They also took approximately 70 captives before withdrawing. The attack on Cherry Valley contributed, if unfairly, to the legend of "Monster Brant." The massacres at Wyoming and Cherry Valley also affected the outcome of the war in significant ways for native peoples. The outcry on the frontier over the massacres at Wyoming and Cherry Valley prompted General Washington to order an expedition led by General John Sullivan designed to take the Iroquois out of the war.

The Sullivan Campaign

Taking several months to acquire supplies, Sullivan's campaign began in June 1779, when he proceeded from Easton, Pennsylvania, to Lake Ostego in central New York. There he assembled an army totaling over 3,000 men, with over 250 packhorses and bateaux – an inland water vessel that eighteenth-century armies used to move cargo – carrying its supplies. Sullivan's campaign continued into October of that year. Despite the extensiveness of the campaign, Sullivan's army actually did very little fighting. For the most part, the Iroquois attempted to avoid direct confrontation with the Continentals. Sullivan's troops spent most of their time destroying Iroquois food stores, cutting down orchards, and burning cornfields. Only at Newtown, toward the end of August, did Sullivan and his men encounter significant resistance. Against the advice of Joseph Brant and John Butler, the leaders of the community decided to make a stand against Sullivan's army. The result was a disaster for the Iroquois. Despite being augmented by a few Tories and a handful of British regulars, the Iroquois were still outnumbered by Sullivan by almost three to one, and he also had artillery.

By destroying Iroquois villages and depriving the native peoples of the means to feed themselves, Sullivan managed to transform the Six Nations from an asset into a liability for the British. While Sullivan actually killed comparatively few Indians, the refugee survivors of his campaign made their way to the British post at Niagara, where they drew on the King's supplies.

The Revolutionary War, for most of its participants, ended in October of 1781 with the defeat of the British army under Lord Cornwallis at Yorktown. The official treaty ending the conflict, however, dragged on in negotiation and would not be promulgated for another two years. During this time, conflicts on the frontier between American settlers and militia and native people continued, largely unabated.

Atrocity at Gnadenhütten

One of the most notorious incidents during these two years seemingly in limbo occurred at Gnadenhütten (meaning "tents of grace") near the present-day Ohio village of the same name. Gnadenhütten had originally been founded by Moravian missionaries to serve as a community for Lenni-Lenape and Shawnee converts. Throughout the Revolution, the British often accused Moravian missionaries of spying for the Americans. In the fall of 1781, Indians allied to the British forced the Gnadenhütten converts to relocate to the British post at Sandusky. The converts had to leave much of their stored food behind, but in February 1782 they returned to Gnadenhütten to recover their food, and to prepare their fields for spring planting. In the first week of March, however, American militiamen invaded the village and accused the Indian converts of having offered aid and comfort to the enemy. Holding a vote, the militiamen decided to put the Indians to death. They confined the Gnadenhütten residents to their cabins, where many of them spent the night praying and preparing themselves for their fate. The next morning, the militiamen took the Indians out of their cabins and, in groups of four, murdered them with hatchets and mallets and burned the village.

Moravian missionary David Zeisberger learned of the massacre from two young men who escaped, one of whom after having been scalped and left for dead:

> The militia, some 200 in number, as we hear, came first to Gnadenhutten… Our Indians were mostly on the plantations and saw the militia come, but no one thought of fleeing, for they suspected no ill. The militia came to them and bade them come into town, telling them no harm should befall them. They trusted and went, but were all bound, the men being put into one house, the women into another. The Mohican, Abraham… when he saw that his end was near, made an open confession before his brethren, and said: "Dear brethren… we shall all very soon come to the Saviour, for as it seems they have so resolved about us. You know I am a bad man, that I have much troubled the Saviour and the brethren, and have not behaved as becomes a believer, yet to him I belong, bad as I am; he will forgive us all and not reject me; to the end I shall hold fast to him and not leave him." Then they began to sing hymns and spoke words of encouragement and consolation one to another until they were all slain, and … Abraham was the first to be led out, but the others were killed in the house. The sisters also afterwards met the same fate, who also sang hymns together. Christina, the Mohican, who well understood German and English, fell upon her knees before the captain, begging for life, but got for answer that he could not help her. Two well grown boys, who saw the whole thing and escaped, gave this information. One of these lay under the heaps of slain and was scalped, but finally came to himself and found opportunity to escape…

This atrocity would not go unanswered. In June 1782, Colonel William Crawford, an associate of George Washington, led an expedition of 500 volunteers against Native American communities in the Sandusky region. Coming under attack by a combined force of Native Americans and Tory Rangers, Crawford's force dissolved into an unorganized retreat. Separated from the bulk of his army, Crawford and about 20 of his men were cornered by Native Americans and compelled to surrender. During the Revolution, British-allied Indians usually turned American prisoners, particularly officers, over to the English, who often paid a reward for them. But since the incident at Gnadenhütten, the Lenni-Lenape in the Ohio country – many of whom had relatives who were murdered there – resolved that the American prisoners would not be permitted to live. Several men who surrendered with Crawford were executed outright. Even though Crawford had had nothing to do with the events at Gnadenhütten, the Indians recognized that many of the men who made up his force had been participants. It was decided that Crawford would be tortured to death. He was taken to his place of execution, where he was stripped and beaten. Warriors fired gun powder into his body, and a large fire was built near him to slowly roast him. While over 100 Delaware looked on, and participated, Crawford was burned, forced to walk on hot coals, and had his ears cut off. After almost two hours, Crawford was scalped – reportedly by a former Moravian convert – and his body was burned.

While many of the Lenni-Lenape and Shawnee of the Ohio country looked upon Crawford's execution as justice for what had occurred at Gnadenhütten, Americans, not surprisingly, viewed it quite differently. The two incidents hardened the ill feelings between the two peoples in the period after the Revolution. Native people wondered if they could – or should even try – to fit into the new Republic. Many Americans wondered how native people could be part of the new nation. Indeed, many Americans would have liked to see a United States without Indians.

12

Coping with the New Republic

In October 1783, the United States and Great Britain agreed to the terms of the Treaty of Paris, ending the American Revolution. Thousands of Indians had participated in the conflict. Native warriors had fought for both the defeated British and the victorious Americans in the Revolution. Native diplomats had also contributed, serving as go-betweens for both the British and the Americans. Yet despite their participation in the conflict, the deaths of thousands of their people, and the dislocation the war caused in Indian country, the pact did not mention Native Americans. In fact, Mohawk leader Joseph Brant had to demand that Quebec governor Frederick Haldimand tell him the terms of the treaty. Unlike other native allies of the British, Brant – possibly because of his celebrity in England – did receive some compensation. The Crown gave him a large land grant along the Grand River in Ontario. The region became a reserve for Mohawk refugees in the years after the Revolution, and became known as "Brant's Grant."

The Conquest Policy

In its initial dealings with Native Americans, the nascent United States adopted what came to be known as the "conquest policy." In the Treaty of Paris, Great Britain ceded to the United States not only

"Times Are Altered with Us": American Indians from First Contact to the New Republic, First Edition. Roger M. Carpenter.

the territory occupied by the original 13 colonies, but also all of the lands in between the Appalachian Mountains and the Mississippi River. The Confederation Congress, the federal governing body that succeeded the Second Continental Congress and was the immediate predecessor to the United States Congress, argued that since more native groups sided with Great Britain – and had been on the losing side – their lands now belonged to the United States by right of conquest. Not surprisingly, Native Americans had a very different interpretation of the terms of the treaty, often arguing that it was true the United States defeated Great Britain, but that it was not true that the United States defeated any native peoples. Moreover, no group of native people had ever ceded its lands to the King; therefore, he could not in turn cede them to the Americans.

The Confederation Congress had several concerns regarding the formulation of an Indian policy. For one thing, the delegates to that body recognized the policy would require the United States to keep garrisons west of the Appalachians. Given the strained finances of the new Republic, this would be virtually impossible. The government also feared that some native peoples would move farther west, thereby granting them *de facto* control of the westernmost reaches of the new nation. It also realized that it had to exercise caution in its treatment of native people. While the Treaty of Paris specified that the British would leave American soil, English troops still occupied posts in the Northwest Territory (present-day Wisconsin, Michigan, Illinois, Indiana, and Ohio). The English responded to Congress' demands that they vacate the posts by pointing out that the Americans had not yet fulfilled all of their obligations under the treaty, most notably the promise to repay prewar debts to British merchants. As long as the British remained in the Northwest Territory, they competed with American traders, and exploited their advantages in being able to provide native people with manufactured goods, and at better prices. British officials and Indian agents also encouraged native people to resist the Americans, while surreptitiously supplying them with powder, shot, and other provisions.

The Confederation Congress soon discovered that it had another problem when it came to conducting diplomacy with native peoples. The individual colonies-turned-states, despite the provisions and the Articles of Confederation that gave the central government the exclusive authority to deal with American Indian nations, sent their own representatives to treaty councils. These state representatives, as in the case of the Treaty of Fort Stanwix in 1784, and the Treaty of Hopewell signed with the Cherokee in 1785, sometimes interfered with negotiations, or conducted their own dealings with native people without the knowledge of the central government. In the Treaty of Hopewell, the United States promised to punish non-Indians who settled to the south or west of the line of settlement agreed to in the pact. As the Cherokee and other native people would discover over the course of the next century, there was always a wide gulf between what the United States promised Indians and what they could or would actually do for them. Like the British after the issuance of the Proclamation of 1763 two decades earlier, the new United States government lacked the wherewithal to control all of its citizens, especially those on or moving onto the frontier. Despite having two regiments stationed in North America after the conclusion of the Great War for Empire, the British army could not effectively police the boundary line between the colonists and the Indian reserve. The nascent United States, with an army that totaled only 120 men, had even fewer resources on which to draw.

Alliances with Europeans

Well aware that the American settlers intended to expand westward, and take their lands in the process, native peoples sought alliances with European powers whom they hoped could continue to supply their material needs. In the Northwest Territory, native people of course turned to the British.

In the Southeast, native leaders such as Chief Alexander McGillivray of the Creek turned to the Spanish. During the Revolution, the Spanish were not allied to the Americans. They did, however, have an alliance with the French (who were allied to the Americans). The Spanish were not a party to the Treaty of Paris (of 1783) that ended the American Revolution. During the war, the Spanish had fought British troops in the Gulf Coast region, and regained control of the Florida Peninsula. After the Revolution, the Spanish signed a separate treaty with the British that granted them Florida and the Gulf Coast. The boundaries of that treaty, however, overlapped the territory that England ceded to the United States, setting up a conflict between the new Republic and Spain. It is possible that the British did this intentionally in order to sow discord.

The offspring of a Scottish father who had been an Indian trader in the Southeast, and a Creek-French mother, Alexander McGillivray had risen to prominence in Creek society during the Revolution by serving with the British army. In the wake of the American victory, the Creeks and other tribes in the Southeast found themselves pressured by the states of Georgia and South Carolina to surrender their lands. The Creek, like other Native Americans, still needed European trade goods but did not wish to trade with the Georgians or the Carolinians. In 1784, McGillivray led a Creek delegation to Pensacola, where they signed a treaty with the Spanish. In exchange for the weapons, powder, and shot that they would need to resist Americans on the frontier, the Creek agreed to become Spanish subordinates. This agreement obviously had benefits for the Spanish as well since it allowed them to employ the Creek as military proxies who would serve as a counterweight to Americans encroaching upon Spanish Florida from the north, as well as in the territory the two powers disputed.

The Confederation Congress did not remain entirely oblivious to the problems Native Americans posed in the South. As early as August 1787, Congress received a report that, to some degree, misstated the difficulties the United States faced along its southern border. Congress learned of the trade that native people in western Georgia and the Carolinas carried on with the Spanish and the British, rather than with American traders. Congress also learned that Spanish and British goods and prices were somehow more competitive than those of American traders. While the report specifically mentioned the mistreatment native people endured at the hands of American land-jobbers and traders, Congress seems to have missed this as a probable cause of Native American discontent.

The Northwest Confederacy

At the same time in the Old Northwest, encouraged and supplied by the British, native peoples also pushed back against American assertions that they had lost their lands through conquest. After a series of treaties at Fort Stanwix, Fort McIntosh, and Fort Finney, in which native representatives had been browbeaten into granting the excessive land claims of the Americans, the Iroquois and nine other tribes convened in a large meeting at Detroit late in 1786 with the purpose of forming a united front to counter the Americans. Their message to the Confederation Congress emphasized that they wanted peaceful relations with the new Republic, and asked that the Americans meet them halfway. But they also pointed out that if violence broke out between native people and the Americans, they would defend themselves. The Northwest Confederacy (or Confederated Tribes) repudiated the treaties that had been negotiated at Stanwix, McIntosh, and Finney on the grounds that one tribe could not sell land. The Northwest Confederacy argued that land cessions would require its member nations to meet in council to consider the sale of land to the United States. If a decision was reached to allow the ceding of territory to the new Republic, it would require the consent of all of the tribes.

From the end of the American Revolution to 1790, the Northwest Confederacy backed their stance by attacking American settlers they discovered living on what they considered to be their side of the Ohio River. Approximately 1,500 settlers perished at the hands of Indian warriors in the Ohio country over this period. In the meantime, the American government, first under the Articles of Confederation and later under the United States Constitution, continued their attempts to craft an Indian policy.

In 1786, the Confederation Congress drafted an ordinance to govern Indian affairs that very much followed the British model. Like the British, the American drafters of the confederation ordinance envisioned two Indian departments divided into two districts, one northern and one southern. Each would have their own superintendent. Unlike the British system, however, the superintendent would be permitted to hold his post for only two years. The ordinance also specified that American traders in Indian country must be licensed, and to avoid a conflict of interest, forbade Indian superintendents from engaging in trade themselves. The ordinance had little time to be put into effect – the Articles of Confederation would shortly be replaced by the Constitution – but some parts of it could be found in later American Indian policy.

The most significant piece of legislation the Confederation Congress passed regarding native people was the Northwest Ordinance of 1787. It specified how land would be surveyed and distributed by the United States, and how it would be settled by Americans. It also forbade slavery in the lands north of the Ohio River, creating for the first time in American history a section of the nation where the peculiar institution would be expressly forbidden. But it also had something to say about Native Americans:

> The utmost good faith shall always be observed towards the Indians, their lands and property shall never be taken from them without their consent; and in their property, rights and liberty, they never shall be invaded or disturbed, unless in just and lawful wars authorised by Congress; but laws founded in justice and humanity shall from time to time be made, for preventing wrongs being done to them, and for preserving peace and friendship with them.

Given the subsequent history of strife between native people and the United States, it is easy to doubt the sincerity of this pronouncement.

The End of the Conquest Policy

Some American officials did, however, realize that much of the friction between native peoples and settlers on the frontier could not be blamed entirely on the Indians. In 1788, Secretary of War Henry Knox (who would also hold the same position in the Washington Administration after the Constitution was ratified in 1789) reported that the inability of the United States to maintain peace with native peoples on its frontiers could be traced to the actions of American citizens, particularly in the South. Knox feared that if the United States did not act to remove or restrain its own citizens "the powerful tribes of the Creeks, Choctaws and Chickesaws will be able to keep the frontiers of the southern states constantly embroiled with hostilities." Nearly a year later, in another report that dealt with the difficulties the United States faced with Indian nations, this time in the Old Northwest, Knox expressed concern that dishonest dealings with native people by the government and American citizens would affect the international reputation of the United States. Echoing the language of the Northwest Ordinance, Knox noted that Indians "possess the right of soil. It cannot be taken from them unless by their free consent, or by right of conquest in case of a just war. To dispossess them on any other principle, would be a gross violation of the fundamental laws of nature, and of the distributive justice which is the glory of a nation."

Knox also raised concerns about the cost and feasibility of the United States fighting a conflict against native people in the Old

Northwest, noting that it appeared that along the Wabash River (which runs mostly through present-day north central Indiana), the Shawnee, Wayandot, Lenni-Lenape, Miami, and Kickapoo could place anywhere between 1,500 to 2,000 warriors in the field. If the United States decided to use military force against them, Knox estimated, it would require a force of at least 2,500 men. Knox noted that the entire US Army consisted of only 600 men, only 400 of whom were stationed on the frontier. To raise, equip, and provision a force adequate to fight the northwest Indians for a period of six months would cost over $200,000, far more than the United States in 1789 could afford.

Harmer's Defeat

Unfortunately for Knox, within a year the United States would be engaged in the very type of war in the Old Northwest that he had hoped to avoid. Ably led by the Shawnee Blue Jacket and the Miami Little Turtle, and supplied and encouraged by the British, the Northwest Confederacy continued their attacks on American settlers west and north of the Ohio River. Forced to act, President Washington requested that Kentucky, Virginia, and Pennsylvania provide 1,200 militiamen to augment the 300 regulars already stationed there, who would be placed under the command of General Josiah Harmar, a veteran of the Revolution.

Harmer assembled his force at Fort Washington (present-day Cincinnati, Ohio) in September of 1790. Marching northward to the Maumee River (in northern Ohio), the Americans burned several Indian villages. Harmer's force, however, kept shrinking as the undisciplined militiamen often straggled away from the army's line of march, and in many cases simply left of their own accord. What Harmer did not know was that the Indians were withdrawing, consolidating their forces, and watching his force gradually dwindle. On October 19 and 22, 1790, a large Indian force, consisting mainly of Miami, Shawnee, and Kickapoo warriors, ambushed Harmer's army near the present-day site of Fort Wayne, Indiana. Approximately 200 American militiamen were killed, while the remainder, most of them discarding their weapons and equipment so they could run faster, fled for their lives to Fort Washington.

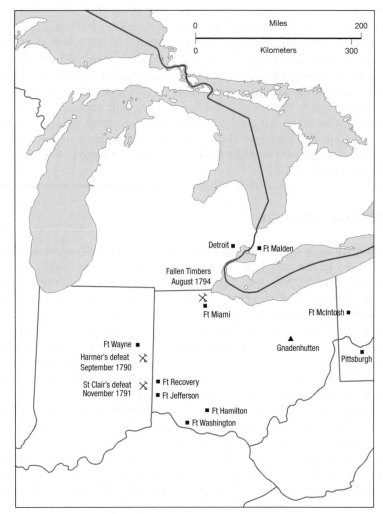

Map 12.1 Wars in the Ohio Country, 1791–1794

St Clair's Defeat

The disaster on the Maumee led President Washington to order another expedition, this time commanded by the governor of the Northwest Territory, Arthur St Clair. Like Harmer, St Clair had also served in the Revolution. Secretary of War Henry Knox determined

266

that now 3,000 men, twice the number of Harmer's expedition, would be needed to subdue the Indians in the Northwest Territory. Despite receiving his orders in March 1791, St Clair faced a number of delays in raising troops and securing equipment for the expedition. Most of the troops that he did receive came from the East, had little experience in the forest, and had enlisted in the army for only a six-month term.

Lacking adequate time to train his troops, St Clair led his army – inexplicably accompanied by 200 camp followers, the vast majority of them women – out of Fort Washington in early September. For nearly two months the Indians led by Little Turtle and Blue Jacket shadowed the army, occasionally sniping at the troops. But for the most part, the Indians largely avoided contact with the St Clair's forces.

On November 4, 1791, St Clair established a poorly prepared and loosely guarded perimeter around his camp on the Wabash River (in what is now east central Indiana). Near dawn, Little Turtle and Blue Jacket led an attack that quickly overran the American defenses. The Indians first targeted the militia, most of whom threw away their weapons and fled. Little Turtle and Blue Jacket made it a point to strike at the gun crews of St Clair's artillery early in the battle, ensuring that the army could not use cannon against the Indians. At first, many of the regulars held fast, forming ranks and firing volleys that forced the Indians back. But Little Turtle and Blue Jacket responded by flanking the American ranks. Several times during the three-hour melee St Clair ordered bayonet charges against the Indian positions. Each time, the Indians gave way, reforming themselves in a half-moon formation that allowed them to place the American units in a crossfire, and cut them to pieces. At around nine o'clock in the morning, nearly surrounded, St Clair led a last desperate charge in which he managed to extricate himself and the surviving members of his army. More than 600 American soldiers lay dead on the battlefield, with approximately 300 wounded. In addition, at least 30 of the camp followers perished in the battle. St Clair reported that his army had lost all of their horses and artillery, and that his forces had dissolved into a headlong flight for Fort Jefferson, 29 miles away.

St Clair had presided over the worst defeat Native Americans ever inflicted on the US Army, but it is easy to forget this fact. Most Americans tend to believe that Custer's defeat at the Little Bighorn more than 80 years later was the worst loss that the US Army ever suffered at the hands of Native Americans. Several factors account for why Americans regard the two battles differently. For one thing, many Americans have never heard of St Clair or his epic defeat. The Battle of Little Bighorn, on the other hand, has been the subject of innumerable books, films, and an untold number of dramatic reenactments. St Clair's defeat had been inflicted on the bulk of the US Army at the time. Custer's defeat represented only a small portion of the US Army in 1876. In 1791, the United States was not among the great military powers of the earth. In 1876, the United States was a rapidly industrializing nation that would soon be ranked among the great powers of the world. Another difference could be the shock that Americans felt upon hearing of the two defeats. In St Clair's case, the army had suffered a humiliating defeat in the previous year; that it could be defeated again, while disheartening, may not have been all that surprising to many Americans. In the case of Custer, most Americans learned what transpired at the Little Bighorn in the first week of July 1876, just as the nation prepared to celebrate the one-hundredth anniversary of its independence. And, finally, it must be considered that the American public of 1876, thanks to more extensive and sophisticated press coverage, was probably more familiar with Custer than Americans were with St Clair in 1791.

It has been said that upon learning of St Clair's defeat, President Washington let a few profanities escape from his lips – something that by all accounts was a rarity. In the wake of the debacle on the Wabash, the United States adopted a two-pronged approach to solve its difficulties with the Indians in the Northwest Territory. One part of the plan called for negotiations, mainly as a device to buy time. This part of the American strategy got off to a very bad start, as President Washington's two agents to the Confederated Tribes were murdered. Washington still pursued negotiations, authorizing the Seneca leader Red Jacket and Hendrick Aupaumut, a Stockbridge veteran of the Revolution who reached the rank of captain, to serve as emissaries in the United States' negotiations with the Indians. During the Revolution, Red Jacket performed diplomatic missions for the Iroquois, representing their interests to the British. After the war, he participated in treaty negotiations between the Iroquois and the United States. The second part of the American strategy for dealing with the Confederated Tribes called for raising a new military force. This time – although the government could ill afford it – Congress appropriated $1 million and authorized an army of

5,000 men to be placed under the command of yet another veteran of the Revolution, "Mad" Anthony Wayne.

British Interference

The greatest stumbling block in reaching a diplomatic settlement with Miami, Shawnee, and other peoples of the Northwest Territory, was that they felt no need to negotiate; after all, they had defeated two American armies. Egged on by the British, the Confederated Tribes rejected a proposal presented by Red Jacket and Aupaumut that would have established the Muskingum River as the boundary between the United States and native people in the Northwest. When the Confederated Tribes sent Red Jacket and Aupaumut away in September, the Shawnee and Miami leaders declared they would recognize no boundary except the Ohio River. Red Jacket, Aupaumut, and other Indian observers friendly to the Americans noted a distinct change in the conduct of the meetings. Instead of the civic chiefs taking the lead, Shawnee and Miami war chiefs did most of the talking and were clearly in charge.

Besides the interference of British Indian agents, there were other reasons why diplomatic initiatives failed, some of which could be traced to the growing distrust of the Iroquois among native people. Red Jacket, a Seneca, represented the westernmost of the Iroquois Six Nations. At the same time, although he was not present for the negotiations, Joseph Brant also encouraged the Confederated Tribes to negotiate, reasoning that they would be doing so from a position of strength, having twice defeated the Americans. But many of the Delaware and Shawnee people who lived in the Ohio country knew of the problematic history they shared with the Six Nations. After all, the Iroquois had performed the bidding of Pennsylvania in enforcing the terms of the Walking Purchase nearly 50 years earlier. A quarter century later at Fort Stanwix the Iroquois sold much of present-day Tennessee and Kentucky out from under the feet of the Shawnee and other peoples who actually lived there.

The presence of British Indian agents such as Matthew Elliot and Alexander McKee also stiffened native resolve not to negotiate with the Americans. Simon Girty also served as an intermediary between the British and native people. Captured with two of his brothers when he was young, Girty grew up among native people and learned their language and customs. During the Revolution, Girty at first sided with the Americans. However, his commanders at Fort Pitt accused him of insubordination, and later brought the far more serious charge of treason against him. Acquitted of treason, Girty left the Americans and went to Detroit to offer his services to the British. He served as an interpreter for the English and also led Indian assaults against American outposts. The three British Indian agents, Elliot, McKee, and Girty, as well as other British officials, encouraged native resistance toward the Americans by assuring them they would receive supplies of powder, shot, and muskets. They also dropped hints that at some point in the near future, the United States and England would be at war, and they could count on the King to send troops to aid them.

The Confederated Tribes were further encouraged when the British made the bold move of constructing Fort Miamis, which they completed in July 1794, near the site of present-day Toledo, Ohio. Like other British officials, the fort's commander, Major William Campbell, also encouraged native people to resist the Americans, leading them to believe that if the United States made another incursion into the Ohio country, he would provide them with both supplies and sanctuary at Fort Miamis if needed.

Still needing to buy time for General Wayne to raise and equip his army for the coming fight in the Ohio country, Washington made another attempt at diplomacy, dispatching Benjamin Lincoln (another veteran of the Revolution), diplomat Timothy Pickering, and former Virginia governor Beverly Randolph to the lower Sandusky in the spring of 1793. Throughout the negotiations, Elliott, McKee, and Girty always lurked nearby, secretly advising the Confederated Indians. The Indians pointed out to the Americans that the British had no right to cede their land to the United States in the first place since the King had never obtained it from them. The Indians at one point suggested that the Americans should take the money they offered for their lands and distribute it among the settlers in the Ohio country, who would then be displaced but have the funds to start over elsewhere. They also pointed out that the United States would save a great deal of money by not sending military expeditions against them. It became clear to the Americans that the Indians were not going to negotiate – after all, they felt they had no need to do so – and it became equally clear to the Indians that the Americans were stalling for time.

The Indian representatives at the lower Sandusky had read their American counterparts correctly. During the negotiations, Anthony

Wayne had not been idle. Having raised a force of 2,000 regular troops, he proceeded to train and drill them into an excellent fighting force. A strict disciplinarian, Wayne had little patience with soldiers who deserted or who drank and slept while on duty, and harshly punished those who did. In 1793, Wayne led his army north from Fort Washington to the site of St Clair's defeat two years earlier, where he erected two strongpoints, Forts Greenville and Recovery, which would serve as supply depots for the upcoming campaign. Wayne continued to drill and train his men, and in the summer of 1794, he made preparations to move north to attack the Indian villages near Fort Miamis.

Division in the Northwest Confederacy

Just as Wayne made his preparations for battle, the Northwest Confederacy began to weaken. Divisions began to appear among the members of the confederacy for number of reasons. Just as native people had experienced during Pontiac's Rebellion, the warriors of the confederacy had scattered to their homes the previous autumn. They had to hunt in order to provide food for their families, and not all of them had returned to Ohio come the spring.

If it is possible to point to a date when the confederacy began to disintegrate, one could posit June 30, 1794. Learning from an informant that the Americans would be moving 300 horses from Fort Recovery to another post, a force consisting of Lenni-Lenape, Shawnee, Ottawa, Potawatomi, and Ojibwa warriors gathered and lay in wait. The Lenni-Lenape and Shawnee warriors attacked the detail moving the horses almost as soon as it left the fort. The Ottawa, Potawatomi, and Ojibwa elected to assault the fort itself, and quickly discovered that it was well defended when they came under intense artillery fire and had to pull back. In the aftermath of the failed attack, the Ottawa, Potawatomi, and Ojibwa quarreled with the Lenni-Lenape and Shawnee, accusing them of being more interested in obtaining horses than in fighting the Americans. Disgusted with what they saw as a lack of support, many of the Ottawa, Potawatomi, and Ojibwa warriors simply left and returned to their homes in Michigan. In some respects, it may seem strange that the leaders of the Northwest Confederacy allowed them to leave. But it must be kept in mind that Native American leaders did not exercise the same amount of control over their followers as did, say, an officer in the US Army over his troops. Native leaders could not simply issue orders and expect them to be obeyed. The departure of the Ottawa, Potawatomi, and Ojibwa was a serious blow to the confederacy, since they represented almost half of the manpower that the Indians could put in the field.

At the same time, a crisis erupted among the leadership of the confederacy. Little Turtle of the Miami, who had been instrumental in helping guide the Indians to two victories over the Americans, now maintained that instead of fighting Wayne and his army, the time had come to negotiate. Little Turtle's views may have changed because he received reports from scouts who had observed Wayne's army, and recognized that the Confederated Tribes would now face a very different force from the ones fielded by Harmer and St Clair. Rather than a largely undisciplined militia, they now faced a well-trained and well-equipped force, which was also much larger than the two previous armies the Indians had defeated. Little Turtle also began to have his doubts about the sincerity of the British. His suspicions regarding British support would prove to be correct. When Little Turtle suggested negotiation, other leaders of the confederacy, including Blue Jacket, opposed him. Little Turtle opted to step down, and Blue Jacket replaced him as the military leader of the confederacy.

Fallen Timbers

Nearly a month after the failed attack on Fort Recovery on July 28, General Wayne led his army out of Fort Greenville. Wayne not only had 2,000 regulars, but he also led 1,500 volunteers from Kentucky. The departure of the Ottawa, Potawatomi, and Ojibwa reduced the number of warriors that Blue Jacket could field. Despite being augmented by small numbers of Detroit and Canadian militia, he could only assemble approximately 1,300 warriors, who took up positions among a cluster of trees that had been felled by a recent tornado near the site of present-day Toledo, Ohio. Blue Jacket chose the battleground because it seemed probable that the dense tangle of trees and brush would neutralize the American advantages in artillery, and impede the effectiveness of their dragoons (cavalry). The battlefield also had the advantage of being only three miles from the British post of Fort Miamis. Should the battle go badly for the Indians, they could seek safety in the fort; it may even be possible that the British would openly come to their aid.

On August 18, General Wayne halted his army four miles from Fallen Timbers. Meanwhile, Blue Jacket's warriors fasted in order to purify themselves for the coming battle. Thanks to Wayne's delay, the warriors became hungry and many of them left the battlefield and went to Fort Miamis seeking provisions. With many of Blue Jacket's men still away in search of food, Wayne finally struck on August 20, and the battle did not go as Blue Jacket had envisioned. While the fallen trees may have impeded Wayne's dragoons, they provided little protection from American artillery. The Indians fled the battlefield as the disciplined American infantry forced them back in a series of bayonet charges. But at this point, the Indians had still not lost heart as they retreated toward Fort Miamis, certain that their British allies would give them shelter or openly aid them.

Major Campbell, as it turned out, offered them neither sanctuary nor aid. Seeing the Indians fleeing in the direction of his fort, with the American army in pursuit, Campbell realized that if he allowed the Indians into his post, there was a possibility that Wayne's troops may follow them. The situation had all the makings of a major international incident; Major Campbell evidently decided that he did not want to have to answer to British authorities if he should inadvertently start a war with the United States. The Indians were demoralized when, on Campbell's orders, the gates of the post were shut in their faces. The Indians would soon have more reason to be disgusted with the British, and Campbell in particular. While General Wayne and Major Campbell exchanged insulting notes with one another for several days after the battle, native people looked on as Wayne put his men to work burning the Indian villages and cornfields within sight of the British post.

Many native people never forgave the British for this treachery. Even two decades later, when the famed Shawnee leader Tecumseh – who fought at Fallen Timbers – became a British ally during the war of 1812, he did not hesitate to remind them of the time they sorely betrayed the Indians.

The Treaty of Greenville

In the spring of 1795, the United States and England signed the Jay Treaty, which tied up many of the loose ends left over from the American Revolution. One of the consequences of the treaty was that the British would soon turn over the forts in the Northwest Territory to the United States. Having lost – for good reason – their faith in British promises, and since they would soon be deprived of their support, many of the Indian nations that made up the Confederated Tribes signed separate peace agreements with the Americans. In August 1795, American and native representatives met at Fort Greenville. The resulting Greenville Treaty saw native peoples cede much of eastern and southern Ohio to the Americans. It also allowed the Americans free, unimpeded passage on the roads and waterways that linked their posts throughout the Northwest Territory. In return, the Americans agreed to relinquish their claims to lands north of the Cuyahoga River and westward to the Mississippi. The Indians received $20,000 in goods, mainly consisting of blankets, tools, and livestock. The United States also guaranteed them an annual payment of $9,500 in goods. One of the pact's clauses stated that the Indians could retain the lands the treaty permitted them to keep for as long as they wanted. However, it also emphasized that native people who wished to dispose of their lands could sell them to only one entity: the United States. The treaty was important in some respects in that it asserted American dominance of the Northwest Territory and brought peace to the frontier, for the time being. But, like many treaties the United States would go on to sign with native people over the next seven decades, not all of its provisions would be honored, and it would not be long before American settlers violated the boundary that the Treaty of Greenville established.

The "Blessings of Civilization"

In his 1791 message to Congress, President Washington expressed his desire to bring the "blessings of civilization" to Native Americans. Native people, of course, already considered themselves civilized. In 1793, when Congress passed the second of the Intercourse Acts, designed to regulate trade with Native Americans, it also established an initial fund of $20,000 that would be used to purchase livestock, plows, spinning wheels, and farming equipment that would be used "to promote civilization among the friendly Indian tribes." President Washington also appointed Indian agents, and saw to it that the government hired farmers to teach the Indians European agricultural techniques, and blacksmiths to repair their tools. The government also set up mills to grind grain, and also promoted education. Missionaries from various denominations also contributed to the civilization effort.

The effects of the civilization program varied from tribe to tribe, and region to region. Generally speaking, it seemed to be more successful among the peoples of the Southeast than among those of the Northwest Territory. There were exceptions, of course, such as the Shawnee under Black Hoof, who accepted the American civilization program and the presence of Indian agents and missionaries as well. However, this appears to have been an exception in the Northwest Territory. Many of the United States' recent foes in the Northwest Indian wars preferred their traditional way of life.

The story in the Southeast is a bit more complex. In this region there had been more intermarriage between European traders and native women, particularly among the Cherokee, Creek, Choctaw, and Chickasaw. Many of the English and Scottish traders did well financially, and made it a point to send their male offspring to American schools so that they would learn to read and write, and be prepared to participate in the emerging American economy. The offspring of these mixed marriages competed for leadership with full-blooded members of their native communities in the Southeast.

Generally speaking, mixed-blood (also known as Metis) leaders encouraged their communities to cooperate with the United States and promoted the emergence of a sort of hybrid culture. Many of these leaders acquired large tracts of land, and began raising cash crops and livestock. In the early portion of the next century, many of them would start to acquire African American slaves. In some respects, there would be little to differentiate them from their white neighbors.

At the same time, full-blooded native leaders attempted to hold on to tradition and the old ways of life. This created tensions, which sometimes turned into open conflict, as among the Creek in the early nineteenth century. But for the most part, the traditionalists were losing to those who advocated assimilation. Assimilating held out the promise of economic prosperity, and perhaps most important for native people of the Southeast, the possibility – which would be bitterly thwarted in the 1830s – of keeping their lands.

As the nineteenth century dawned, native people in the new Republic found themselves under assault on several fronts. Militarily, they had been bested in the Northwest and forced to cede lands to the United States. In the Southeast, in particular, they now saw divisions within their own societies as to which path to pursue in the future: would they follow the traditional route, or would they allow themselves to become more like white Americans? Would taking the latter path permit them to keep their lands? They also found themselves under assault spiritually, as the old ways had, in some respects, failed them and they were beset by Christian missionaries from various denominations. Many of these missionaries were sincere in their desire to help the native people, but they often wanted to help only on their own terms.

Spiritual Renewal

Yet, in the realm of spirituality, there lay a glimmer of hope. In June 1799, Handsome Lake, a Seneca relative of the diplomat Red Jacket and the war chief Cornplanter, experienced a vision after an alcoholic binge. In his vision, Handsome Lake learned that the Creator wished for him to preach a message that would tell other Iroquois how things should be on earth. If he refused, he would be buried in a hot, smoky place. The Creator also ordered Handsome Lake to tell people to stop drinking whiskey and to cease practicing witchcraft and other forms of magic. Those who had done wrong must admit it and never again sin. When Handsome Lake recovered from his stupor, he immediately ceased drinking and began preaching the message that the Creator had given him. He had subsequent visions, including one in which he met Jesus Christ and George Washington. Handsome Lake's teachings included some Christian elements. For example, he forbade wife-beating and sexual promiscuity. But he also advocated a shift in the Iroquois kinship structure away from matrilineal clans, to smaller male-dominated families, much like those of the Americans. Handsome Lake encouraged other Iroquois to send their children to school, and to move away from communal agriculture in which women did the bulk of the labor, to the type of private agriculture in which men did most of the work, also like the Americans. Handsome Lake's vision had staying power, coalescing into the Church of Longhouse, which can still be found in Iroquois communities today.

Handsome Lake's spiritual movement did not represent the only attempt of native people to cope with the new realities that they faced. Other native prophets would soon appear and preach messages that in many respects differed significantly from Handsome Lake's.

With the dawn of a new century, native people in the Southeast were divided as to what road into the future they should follow. Within many of the major Native American nations of the Southeast – the

Cherokee, Creek, Choctaw, and Chickasaw – there was a great deal of disagreement between full bloods, who largely preferred traditional ways, and mixed bloods, many of whom favored assimilation and adhered to the US government's civilization program. The Creek would even experience an internal civil war over this question. Among the other native peoples, however, assimilation gradually won out. But in the end, assimilation did not help these people keep their lands.

There was less division in the Northwest, but there was bitterness not only at the defeat the native people sustained at the hands of the United States, but also at the betrayal that the British had inflicted on them at Fallen Timbers. Tecumseh, who would become one of the most famous Native American leaders, had begun to envision the formation of a new confederacy that could resist American westward expansion. What he could not know, as the new century began, was that his brother, Tenskwatawa, would also be known as the Shawnee Prophet, one who would provide the metaphorical glue that would allow him to formulate his alliance. Tenskwatawa had been largely a no-account, an alcoholic, and a braggart who in some ways exemplified the worst effects of European civilization on native people. But he would have a religious experience, which would, for a time, transform him and give the peoples of the Ohio country hope as Native Americans faced a new and challenging century.

Bibliographical Essay

Beginning in 1960s, scholars began to realize that Native Americans were central rather than peripheral to the story of early America. Over the last four decades, the amount of scholarship dealing with the first three centuries of contact between native people and Europeans is truly astonishing. The following is organized by chapter and attempts to address the important points in each.

Chapter 1: 1492 and Before

Two articles that provide an excellent starting point for examining initial native-European contacts are Neal Salisbury, "The Indians' Old World: Native Americans and the Coming of Europeans," which appeared in the *William and Mary Quarterly* 3rd Ser., LIII (July 1996), 435–458. *America in 1492: The World of the Indian Peoples before the Arrival of Columbus* (New York, 1993), edited by the late Alvin M. Josephy, Jr., contains essays by a number of scholars that offer a good introduction to the pre-contact world of native people. It is also worthwhile to take a look at James Axtell's "Colonial America without the Indians: Counterfactual reflections," *The Journal of American History* Vol. 173, No. 4 (March 1987), 981–996. Charles C. Mann's *1491: New Revelations of the Americas before Columbus* (New York, 2005) is an interesting read

"Times Are Altered with Us": American Indians from First Contact to the New Republic, First Edition. Roger M. Carpenter.
© 2015 John Wiley & Sons, Inc. Published 2015 by John Wiley & Sons, Inc.

and provides a continent-wide overview. An excellent synopsis of the invasions of America can be found in Daniel K. Richter's *Facing East from Indian Country: A Native History of Early America* (Cambridge, MA, 2001), which examines the invasions of America by Europeans. A good overview of European invasions in Eastern North America can be found in Ian K. Steele, *Warpaths: Invasions of North America* (New York, 1994). For the Bering Strait theory, see Alfred Crosby, *Ecological Imperialism: The Biological Expansion of Europe, 900–1900* (New York, 1986). For Native American stories as to their origins, see Alice Marriott and Carol K. Rachlin, *American Indian Mythology* (New York, 1968) and Fred B. Kniffen, Hiram F. Gregory, and George A. Stokes, *The Historic Indian Tribes of Louisiana: From 1542 to the Present* (Baton Rouge, 1987). George Lankford has edited a collection, *Native American Legends: Southeastern Legend: Tales from the Natchez, Caddo, Biloxi, Chickasaw, and Other Nations.* (Little Rock, 1987). For Southwest native cultures prior to contact, see Linda S. Cordell, *Ancient Pueblo Peoples* (Washington, 1994). For more on Mississippian cultures, consult *The Forgotten Centuries: Indians and Europeans in the American South, 1521–1704* (Athens, GA, 1994), edited by Charles Hudson and Carmen Chaves Tesser. *A more recent work is Robbie Ethridge's From Chicaza to Chickasaw: The European Invasion and Transformation of the Mississippian World, 1540–1715* (Chapel Hill, 2010). An excellent discussion of Cahokia and the problems that modern archaeologists face can be found in Timothy R. Pauketat, *Cahokia: Ancient America's Great City on the Mississippi* (New York, 2009). The classic work about the Columbian Exchange is the aptly titled *The Columbian Exchange: Biological and Cultural Consequences of 1492* (Westport, CT, 1972) by Alfred W. Crosby, Jr. For more on how European pathogens affected Native Americans, see David Noble Cook, *Born to Die: Disease and New World Conquest, 1492–1650* (New York, 1998). Examples of the pre-contact population debate can be found in Russell Thornton, *American Indian Holocaust and Survival: A Population History since 1492* (Norman, OK, 1987), and David Henige, *Numbers from Nowhere: The American Indian Contact Population Debate* (Norman, OK, 1998).

Chapter 2: Encountering the Spanish

An excellent overview of Spanish exploration and encounters with native people in North America can be found in David J. Weber, *The Spanish Frontier in North America* (New Haven, 1992). A very readable recent treatment of Cabeza de Vaca's wanderings in North America is Andrés Reséndez, *A Land So Strange. The Epic Journey of Cabeza de Vaca: The Extraordinary Tale of a Shipwrecked Spaniard Who Walked Across America in the Sixteenth Century* (New York, 2009). Also consult David A. Howard, *Conquistador in Chains: Cabeza de Vaca and the Indians of the Americas* (Tuscaloosa, 1997). There have been several books that examine the De Soto expedition. One of the best is Charles Hudson, *Knights of Spain, Warriors of the Sun: Hernando de Soto and the South's Ancient Chiefdoms* (Athens, GA, 1997). Patricia Galloway edited a fine set of essays about the De Soto expedition, which can be found in *The Hernando de Soto Expedition: History, Historiography, and "Discovery" in the Southeast* (Lincoln, NE, 1997). For the Coronado expedition, consult Jack D. Forbes, *Apache, Navaho, and Spaniard* (Norman, OK, 1994). Also see Ramón A. Gutiérrez, *When Jesus Came, the Corn Mothers Went Away: Marriage, Sexuality, and Power in New Mexico, 1500–1846* (Palo Alto, 1991). Also consult Richard Flint, *No Settlement, No Conquest: A History of the Coronado Entrada* (Albuquerque, 2008). For discussion of Spanish conversion efforts among the Pueblo, consult Carroll L. Riley, *The Kachina and the Cross: Indians and Spaniards in the Early Southwest* (Salt Lake City, 1999). For the Pueblo Revolt, see Andrew Knaut, *The Pueblo Revolt of 1680: Conquest and Resistance in Seventeenth-Century New Mexico* (Norman, OK, 1995).

Chapter 3: Encounters with the French

A good overview of the explorations of Verrazanno and Cartier can be found in J.H. Parry, *The Age of Reconnaissance* (New York, 1963) and Samuel Eliot Morison, *The European Discovery of America: The Northern Voyages, A.D. 500–1600* (New York, 1971). For Champlain, see David Hackett Fischer's *Champlain's Dream* (New York, 2008). For the fur trade and the Jesuits, consult James Axtell, *The Invasion Within: The Contest of Cultures in Colonial North America* (New York, 1985). For more on Jesuit missionary efforts in Canada, see Carole Blackburn, *Harvest of Souls: The Jesuit Missions and Colonialism in North America, 1632–1650* (Montreal, 2000). Also see John Webster Grant, *The Moon of Wintertime: Missionaries and the Indians of Canada in Encounter since 1534* (Toronto, 1984). For an interesting look at interactions between Jesuits and their converts, see Allan Greer, *Mohawk Saint: Catherine Tekakwitha and the*

Jesuits (New York, 2005). For a treatment of the French in Louisiana, consult Daniel H. Usner, *Indians, Settlers, and Slaves in a Frontier Exchange Economy: The Lower Mississippi Valley before 1783* (Chapel Hill, 1992).

Chapter 4: English and Native People in the Southeast

A classic work that offers an excellent overview of the settling of Virginia, and includes native people as part of the narrative, is Edmund S. Morgan's *American Slavery, American Freedom* (New York, 1975). Because of the mystery associated with the colony, there has never been (and probably never will be) a shortage of books about the Roanoke colony. One of the best recent works is James Horn's *A Kingdom Strange: The Brief and Tragic History of the Lost Colony of Roanoke* (New York, 2010). Another recent work, which emphasizes the relationship between Roanoke's natives and the colonists, is Michael Leroy Oberg's *The Head in Edward Nugent's Hand: Roanoke's Forgotten Indians* (Philadelphia, 2008). As the title indicates, relations were sometimes a little grim. Helen C. Rountree has written several books about the Powhatan people of Virginia. *Among her works are Pocahontas's People: The Powhatan Indians of Virginia Through Four Centuries* (Norman, 1990) and the more recent *Pocahontas, Powhatan, Opechancanough: Three Indian Lives Changed by Jamestown* (Charlottesville, 2008). Because of the popularity over time of the story in which Pocahontas comes to the rescue of John Smith, there has never been a shortage of biographies about her. They vary considerably in quality, but Camilla Townsend's *Pocahontas and the Powhatan Dilemma* (New York, 2004) looks at her life in the context of the challenges the arrival of the English brought to the Powhatan people. Nathaniel Bacon's rebellion ranks as one of the most confusing events of the colonial period. It began as an Indian war, morphed into a civil war between the colonists, and then morphed once again, back into an Indian war. James D. Rice's *Tales from a Revolution: Bacon's Rebellion and the Transformation of Early America* (New York, 2012) offers some much needed clarity. Until recent years, there were very few works that dealt with the Indian slave trade. That changed with the publication of Alan Gallay's *The Indian Slave Trade: The Rise of the English Empire in the American South, 1670–1717* (New Haven, 2002). William L. Ramsey's *The Yamasee War: A Study of*

Culture, Economy, and Conflict in the Colonial South (Lincoln, 2010) is a fine study of that conflict.

Chapter 5: Native Americans in New England

For a discussion about Native American manipulation of New England landscape see William Cronon, *Changes in the Land: Indians, Colonists, and the Ecology of New England* (New York, 1983). For early native-European contacts in the region, consult Neal Salisbury, *Manitou and Providence: Indians, Europeans, and the Making of New England, 1500– 1643* (*New York*, 1982). Alfred A. Cave's *The Pequot War* (Amherst, 1996) is a brisk study of that conflict. Michael Leroy Oberg's *Uncas: First of the Mohegans*, (Ithaca, 2003) is the only biography of this Native American leader. This study examines how Uncas carved out a place for his people in a rapidly changing New England and discusses his rivalry with the Wampanoag leader Miantonomi. Francis Jennings's classic *The Invasion of America: Indians, Colonialism, and the Cant of Conquest* (New York, 1975) may seem a bit dated in some respects, but it was one of the first academic works to examine European intru-sions into the New World in the context of conquest. It also has a good section on the Pequot War and Metacom's Rebellion. For the Praying Towns, James Axtell discusses them extensively in *The Invasion Within*. Jean M. O'Brien discusses the first Praying Town, Natick, in her *Dispossession by Degrees: Indian Land and Identity in Natick, Massachusetts, 1650–1790*. Russell Bourne's *Gods of War, Gods of Peace: How the Meeting of Native and Colonial Religions Shaped Early America* (*New York*, 2002) also has a discussion of the Praying Towns. Metacom's Rebellion is the topic of James D. Drake's *King Philip's War: Civil War in New England, 1675–1676* (Amherst, 1999). Jill Lepore's elegant *The Name of War: King Philip's War and the Origins of American Identity* (New York, 1998) not only deals with Metacom's Rebellion, but also examines how the war was remembered and how those memories changed over time.

Chapter 6: The Five Nations, the Dutch, and the Iroquois Wars

Dutch relations with native people are addressed in Allen W. Trelease's *Indian Affairs in Colonial New York: The Seventeenth Century*

(1960; reprinted, Lincoln, 1997). Matthew Dennis addresses native relations with both the Dutch and the French in his *Cultivating a Landscape of Peace: Iroquois-European Encounters in Seventeenth-Century America* (Ithaca, 1993). Bruce Trigger's magnum opus *The Children of Aataentsic: A History of the Huron People to 1660* (Kingston, 1976) includes Huron participation in the Beaver Wars. The Beaver Wars are also addressed in George T. Hunt's *The Wars of the Iroquois: A Study in Intertribal Trade Relations* (Madison, 1940), although some of his interpretations may seem a bit dated. Jon Parmenter's *The Edge of the Woods: Iroquoia, 1534–1701* (East Lansing, 2010), Daniel K. Richter's *The Ordeal of the Longhouse: The Peoples of the Iroquois League in the Era of European Colonization* (Chapel Hill, 1992), and Roger Carpenter's *The Renewed, the Destroyed, and the Remade: The Three Thought Worlds of the Iroquois and the Huron, 1609–1650* (East Lansing, 2004) examine the Beaver Wars. Gilles Havard's *The Great Peace of Montreal of 1701: French-Native Diplomacy in the Seventeenth Century* (Montreal, 2001) is an interesting study about the agreements that brought the Beaver Wars to an end.

Chapter 7: Seeking a Middle Ground

James H. Merrell's *Into the American Woods: Negotiators on the Pennsylvania Frontier* (New York, 1999) looks at relations between the Quaker colony and native people, as does Eric Hinderaker's *Elusive Empires: Constructing Colonialism in the Ohio Valley, 1673–1800* (New York, 1997). *Promised Land: Penn's Holy Experiment, the Walking Purchase, and the Dispossession of Delawares, 1600–1763* (Bethlehem, PA, 2006), by Stephen Craig Harper, examines the Walking Purchase and the deterioration of relations between the Pennsylvania colony and the Delaware people. A recent history of the Delaware is Amy C. Schutt's *Peoples of the River Valleys: The Odyssey of the Delaware Indians* (Philadelphia, 2007). For the Iroquois as enforcers for Pennsylvania, consult Francis Jennings, *The Ambiguous Iroquois Empire: The Covenant Chain Confederation of Indian Tribes with English Colonies from its Beginnings to the Lancaster Treaty of 1744* (New York, 1984). Also see Timothy J. Shannon, *Iroquois Diplomacy on the Early American Frontier* (New York, 2008). For the middle ground, see the work of the same name, Richard White's *The Middle Ground: Indians, Empires, and Republics in the Great Lakes Region, 1650–1815* (New York, 1991). For native people as military proxies in the South, see Daniel H. Usner,

Indians, Settlers, and Slaves in a Frontier Exchange Economy: The Lower Mississippi Valley before 1783 (Chapel Hill, 1992) and Allan Gallay's *The Indian Slave Trade: The Rise of the English Empire in the American South, 1670–1717.*

Chapter 8: The Imperial Wars

For an overview of the Imperial Wars and native involvement, consult Ian K. Steele, *Warpaths: Invasions of North America.* For the Iroquois League, consult Daniel K. Richter, *The Ordeal of the Longhouse: The Peoples of the Iroquois League in the Era of European Colonization* and Jon Parmenter, *The Edge of the Woods: Iroquoia, 1534–1701.* Howard H. Peckham *offers a good overview of the four conflicts in his The Colonial Wars, 1989–1762* (Chicago, 1964), while Fred Anderson's *Crucible of War: The Seven Years' War and the Fate of Empire in British North America, 1754–1766* (New York, 2000) is a dense, detailed yet wonderfully readable account of the great war for empire. Tom Hatley discusses the Cherokee war in his *The Dividing Paths: Cherokees and South Carolinians through the Revolutionary Era* (New York, 1995).

Chapter 9: Pontiac's Rebellion

Gregory Evans Dowd's *A Spirited Resistance: The North American Indian Struggle for Unity, 1745–1815* (Baltimore, 1992) and his *War under Heaven: Pontiac, the Indian Nations, and the British Empire* (Baltimore, 2002) examine the influence of Native American prophets on resistance movements. The second book, of course, offers a fairly detailed look at Pontiac's Rebellion. The Paxton Boys are one of the topics of Kevin Kenny's *Peaceable Kingdom Lost: The Paxton Boys and the Destruction of William Penn's Holy Experiment* (New York, 2009).

Chapter 10: The Great Plains and the Far West

Colin G. Calloway's *One Vast Winter Count: The Native American West before Lewis and Clark* (Lincoln, 2003) provides an excellent overview of the West prior to the nineteenth century, and provides a thorough discussion of the arrival of the horse. Juliana Barr's *Peace Came in the Form of a Woman: Indians and Spaniards in the Texas Borderlands*

(Chapel Hill, 2007) discusses Native Americans in the Texas and Louisiana borderlands claimed by Spain and France. Pekka Hämäläinen's *The Comanche Empire* (New Haven, 2008) demonstrates how the horse helped make the Comanche into a major power on the southern plains. Andrew C. Isenberg's *The Destruction of the Bison* (New York, 2000) is a very good natural history. The continent-wide smallpox pandemic is mentioned throughout the book, but I have again noted its importance in this chapter about the West. The best work regarding this epidemic is Elizabeth A. Fenn, *Pox Americana: The Great Smallpox Epidemic of 1775–82* (New York, 2001). For Russian encounters with native people, see Glynn Barratt, *Russia in Pacific Waters, 1715–1825* (Vancouver, 1981). For California's Native Americans, see Albert L. Hurtado, *Indian Survival on the California Frontier* (New Haven, 1988). For Spanish missions in California, see Steven W. Hackel, *Children of Coyote, Missionaries of Saint Francis: Indian-Spanish Relations in Colonial California, 1769–1850* (Chapel Hill, 2005).

Chapter 11: Native Americans and the American Revolution

The standard work that examines the role of Native Americans during the Revolution is Colin G. Calloway's *The American Revolution in Indian Country: Crisis and Diversity in Native American Communities* (New York, 1995). For the Iroquois during the American Revolution, see Barbara Graymont, *The Iroquois in the American Revolution* (Syracuse, 1972). For the Shawnee during the Revolution, see Calloway, *The Shawnees and the War for America* (New York, 2007). For the Stockbridge Indians, see David J. Silverman, *Red Brethren: The Brothertown and Stockbridge Indians and the Problem of Race in Early America* (Ithaca, 2010). For the northern frontier during the Revolution, see Alan Taylor, *The Divided Ground: Indians, Settlers, and the Northern Borderland of the American Revolution* (New York, 2006).

Chapter 12: Coping with the New Republic

Among the works that examine early US Indian policy are Francis Paul Prucha, *American Indian Policy in the Formative Years: The Indian Trade and Intercourse Acts, 1790–1834* (Lincoln, 1962) and

Reginald Horsman, *Expansion and American Indian Policy, 1783–1812* (1967; reprinted, Norman, 1992). For the conflict in the Old Northwest, see Richard White, *The Middle Ground*. Also consult Timothy D. Willig, *Restoring the Chain of Friendship: British Policy and the Indians of the Great Lakes, 1783–1815* (Lincoln, 2008). For the actions of the US Army against native people, see Barbara Alice Mann, *George Washington's War on Native America* (Westport, CT, 2005) and Wiley Sword, *President Washington's Indian War* (Norman, 1985).

Index

"Times Are Altered with Us": *American Indians from First Contact to the New Republic*, First Edition. Roger M. Carpenter.
© 2015 John Wiley & Sons, Inc. Published 2015 by John Wiley & Sons, Inc.